FROM BATTLEFIELDS RISING

RANDALL FULLER

FROM BATTLEFIELDS RISING

How the Civil War Transformed
American Literature

OXFORD
UNIVERSITY PRESS
2011

OXFORD
UNIVERSITY PRESS

Oxford University Press, Inc., publishes works that further
Oxford University's objective of excellence
in research, scholarship, and education.

Oxford   New York
Auckland   Cape Town   Dar es Salaam   Hong Kong   Karachi
Kuala Lumpur   Madrid   Melbourne   Mexico City   Nairobi
New Delhi   Shanghai   Taipei   Toronto

With offices in
Argentina   Austria   Brazil   Chile   Czech Republic   France   Greece
Guatemala   Hungary   Italy   Japan   Poland   Portugal   Singapore
South Korea   Switzerland   Thailand   Turkey   Ukraine   Vietnam

Copyright © 2011 by Oxford University Press, Inc.

Published by Oxford University Press, Inc.
198 Madison Avenue, New York, New York 10016

www.oup.com

Oxford is a registered trademark of Oxford University Press

Library of Congress Cataloging-in-Publication Data
Fuller, Randall, 1963–
From battlefields rising : how the Civil War transformed
American literature / Randall Fuller.
p. cm.
Includes bibliographical references and index.
ISBN 978-0-19-534230-7 (cloth : alk. paper)   1. American literature—
19th century—History and criticism.   2. United States—History—Civil War,
1861–1865—Literature and the war.   3. War and literature—
Southern States—History—19th century.   4. Nationalism in literature.
5. United States—In literature.   I. Title.
PS217.C58F85 2010
810.9'358—dc22   2010011752

1 3 5 7 9 8 6 4 2

Printed in the United States of America
on acid-free paper

FOR MY MOTHER AND FATHER

Contents

Introduction   Emerson's Dream   1

Chapter 1   Beat! Beat! Drums!   11

Chapter 2   Concord   34

Chapter 3   Shiloh   52

Chapter 4   Telling It Slant   74

Chapter 5   Port Royal   93

Chapter 6   Fathers and Sons   116

Chapter 7   Phantom Limbs   136

Chapter 8   The Man without a Country   160

Chapter 9   In a Gloomy Wood   182

Chapter 10   Heaven   207

Notes   225

Index   245

Acknowledgments

THIS BOOK COULD not have been written without the work of three eminent precursors: Edmund Wilson, Daniel Aaron, and George M. Frederickson. Their investigations of Civil War era culture and literature (*Patriotic Gore: Studies in the Literature of the American Civil War*, *The Unwritten War: American Writers and the Civil War*, and *The Inner Civil War: Northern Intellectuals and the Crisis of the Union*, respectively) remain standards in the field. My debt to scholars of nineteenth-century American literature is too large to delineate here, but I would like to make special mention of Alice Fahs, Timothy Sweet, and John Dawes, who have each explored language and the Civil War.

Many people and institutions helped to bring this book to fruition. I am hugely grateful to the National Endowment for the Humanities for a fellowship that enabled me to devote a year to writing. Two workshops at the National Humanities Center—one on Melville, led by Andrew Delbanco, and the other on Dickinson, led by Sharon Cameron—came at just the right time to inform my thinking about those authors. For kind permission to quote from manuscripts in their collections, I am grateful to Houghton Library at Harvard University and the Missouri Historical Society. And my thanks go also to the various museums and university collections that granted permission to reproduce the images found throughout the book.

As usual, Bob Milder provided penetrating comments on much of *From Battlefields Rising*. Daniel T. O'Hara and Ken Egan did yeomen's service by reading and helping me to rethink my manuscript. Shannon McLachlan was an enthusiastic supporter of this book from its inception, and her vision and able editing have made it much better. Bruce Callen and Peter Meidlinger, founding members of the Scramblers Club, forced me to formulate my ideas more clearly. Without Jay Karr, I would not have seen the parade grounds and battle sites where Thomas Wentworth Higginson led his history-making unit of African-American soldiers. Bill Garvin and Katherine Bohnenkamp were tremendously helpful in locating arcane material, and Cassy Cochran, student extraordinaire, made my life far less stressful by formatting the book's images.

Finally, as always, this book would have been unimaginable without Julie. To her, I offer love and gratitude for the extended honeymoon we call our life.

FROM BATTLEFIELDS RISING

Introduction: Emerson's Dream

O N A CRISP autumn night in 1861, Ralph Waldo Emerson, one-time radical turned respected man of letters, awoke in his bedroom in the village of Concord, Massachusetts, startled by a troubling dream. He had been reading "a discourse somewhere to an assembly" when suddenly he "rallied in the course of it to find I had nearly or quite fallen asleep."[1]

Rousing himself in the dream, Emerson stood and hesitated, somewhat confused. He then wandered "into what seemed a new house, the inside wall of which had many shelves let into the wall, on which great & costly Vases of Etruscan & other richly adorned pottery stood." These walls, on closer inspection, were marred by "great clefts, intended to be filled with mortar or brickwork, but not yet filled, & the wall which held all these costly vases, [was] threatening to fall." He then noticed "in the centre shelf or alcove of the wall a man asleep, whom I understood to be the architect of the house. I called to my brother William, who was near me, & pointed to this sleeper as the architect, when the man turned, & partly arose, & muttered something about a plot to expose him."[2]

Emerson was fifty-eight at the time of the dream. He was tall and slim-shouldered, his face eagle-like in appearance. His thick, dark hair and kindly blue eyes endowed him with a boyish quality, and his slight build made his resonant baritone all the more surprising (see figure 1). As a young minister, he had suffered crippling shyness toward his parishioners, but literary success had changed all that. He now stood at ease before audiences, conversed fluently with artists and heads of

FIGURE 1 Ralph Waldo Emerson (ca. 1857).

state, carried himself with the confidence and élan of one who had accomplished more than he had ever imagined.

His was a generation that had grown up in the shadow of the founding fathers, a restive, energetic generation that sought to establish a cultural and intellectual home for itself in much the same way as it busily hacked towns and villages, railroads and stagecoach trails from the vast swaths of untrammeled wilderness west of the Appalachians. "Our age is retrospective," he had brashly asserted in his first work, *Nature*, published in 1836. "It builds the sepulchres of the fathers. The foregoing generations beheld God and nature face to face; we, through their eyes. Why should not we also enjoy an original relation to the universe?"[3]

Two years after uttering this call for an expansive new life, Emerson had been banned from Harvard for preaching the heresy that God resided within every human being and that individual conscience and moral intuition were therefore more significant than the hidebound laws of society. He called his trust in the unfettered soul "self-reliance," and this American twist on Romantic philosophy would resonate throughout the young nation like an "intellectual declaration of independence," as one contemporary referred to it.[4] Over the intervening years, Emerson had become America's preeminent intellectual figure and its first literary superstar. He lectured throughout the United States and Europe, spreading transcendental philosophy and New England high-mindedness wherever he went.

Audiences prized his Yankee shrewdness, his otherworldly abstraction, his ability to compress lofty ideas into memorable aphorisms. Most of all, they prized his difficulty. Americans had long suffered from a cultural inferiority complex that rendered them acutely aware that their country had so far produced no great artists or thinkers. Emerson's complexity and convolutions, his transcendental obscurity, were what distinguished him in the eyes of many contemporaries as an intellectual heavyweight. In 1857, he spoke before an Amherst audience that likely included an alert, birdlike young woman named Emily Dickinson, whose brother hosted a reception for the distinguished visitor afterward. The lecture met with a surprisingly tepid response. "Ralph Waldo Emerson's lecture greatly disappointed all who listened," reported the local paper. "It was in the English language instead of the Emersonese in which he usually clothes his thoughts, and the thoughts themselves were such as any plain commonsense person could understand and appreciate." In the spring of 1861, his oldest daughter, Ellen, attended one of his lectures and afterward wrote to her sister: "I understood the whole lecture, and really I don't like to understand them, because I'm afraid they may be a lighter kind of lecture than the others used to be, and I couldn't bear to have Father come down at all from his pinnacle."[5]

Emerson's dream, like many of his best lectures and essays, is rich and allusive, dense with associations, and deeply engaged with the topics of the day. The "new house" in which his dream-self awoke echoed an image made popular throughout the nation by Abraham Lincoln in his famous "House Divided" speech. Lincoln had delivered the address three years earlier, at the close of the Republican state convention in Illinois. "I believe this government cannot endure, permanently half *slave* and half *free*," he announced to a gallery packed with women in hoopskirts and men in frock coats, each anxious to hear the latest riposte in the national debate over slavery. The tall, shambling senator, whose folksy manner concealed a bottomless capacity for reflection, admitted that while he did not "expect the Union to be *dissolved*," he did "expect it [would] cease to be divided."[6] And he expressed his profound hope that the hardening positions over slavery might still be resolved before a cataclysm tore the nation asunder.

Initially skeptical of the rawboned, uncouth president, Emerson nevertheless shared with Lincoln the belief that the United States represented a remarkable step in the upward march of humanity. The audacious vision upon which the nation had been founded—the vision that a free people might govern themselves and determine their own destiny—seemed to him the only solution for escaping the chains of oppression. In a young nation dedicated to liberty to a greater extent than any known to history, human beings were "costly vases," brimming with the spark of innate divinity, precious for their individuality.

Yet by September 1861, the month of Emerson's dream, the national house had divided and crumbled as spectacularly as Edgar Allan Poe's doomed House of Usher. The "great cleft" of slavery, a social fact so deep and pervasive that it had spawned cracks and fissures throughout the nation's very foundation, had split America in two. Lincoln's surprising election to the presidency and the southern secession that swiftly followed had disrupted the grand experiment of creating a more perfect union. As if in the final, ineluctable act of a Greek tragedy, the structure gave way entirely in April 1862, producing a war whose costs and carnage no one could yet anticipate.

This war appeared in Emerson's dream by way of a somewhat less obvious image: the volcano. Emerson had long been fascinated by volcanoes. "We always look at volcanoes with great respect," he wrote in

1833 when, as a young man touring Europe, he had hiked up Mount Vesuvius to marvel at how "the soil was warm and smoking all around and above us" and the "sulphur smoking furiously beneath us." Imagining the tremendous forces unleashed by volcanic eruption, he marveled at the trembling of the earth, the explosive surge of molten lava. When he returned from Europe to Concord, he hung in the entranceway of his home a bright print of Vesuvius spewing lava and belching forth clouds of cinders. To a friend, he candidly confessed, "Tis a fearful place."[7]

In 1833, he had been particularly captivated by the buried Roman city of Pompeii, still in the process of excavation some "1700 years after it had been hid under a mountain of ashes." Once inhabited by Etruscans and Greeks—the ancient peoples whose precious artifacts appeared in his dream almost thirty years later—the city was now an eerie mausoleum that suggested to intrepid visitors just how quickly and unequivocally a culture might be extinguished. Walking through the depopulated neighborhoods, Emerson had "read the inscriptions, & scribblings on the walls, & examined the frescoes, as if in houses not twenty years vacant." He lamented that the statues and valuable pottery once adorning niches in these homes "have all been carried away to the Museums of Naples & Sicily."[8]

Despite the destructive power of the volcano, Emerson considered it a model for his creative process. The earth-shattering volcano, he noted in 1842, was "the most affecting symbol…of what man should be." Artists were not merely seismometers of their society, sensitively registering the tremors of change. They *were* that change, that molten force on the brink of bursting forth. A "mass of fire reaching from earth upward into heaven," Emerson continued, "this is the sign of the robust, united, burning, radiant soul." In 1849, the *Boston Evening Transcript* reviewed one of Emerson's public lectures and noted that he "smokes, he sparkles, he improvises, he shouts, he sings—HE EXPLODES LIKE A BUNDLE OF CRACKERS—he goes off in fiery eruptions like a volcano, but he does not *lecture*."[9]

Emerson's fascination with volcanoes was by no means a personal idiosyncrasy. Throughout the first half of the nineteenth century, artists, authors, scientists, and theologians were obsessed with volcanic activity, many of them making regular visits to the geological curiosities. The volcano was a central and defining metaphor for these men, appearing so prevalently and pervasively in their paintings, sermons, and magazine articles that one quickly begins to suspect there was more at stake than geology.

FIGURE 2 J. M. W. Turner's *Eruption of Vesuvius* (ca. 1817–1820).
Courtesy Yale Center for British Art, Paul Mellon Collection.

To Europeans of the late eighteenth century, the volcano reflected the turbulent energies of revolution. Edmund Burke, England's arch-conservative during the Enlightenment, roundly condemned the "volcanic revolution" across the channel and warned that hasty political transformations had the capacity to produce violent eruptions, such as the Reign of Terror in neighboring France.[10] Romantic authors soon rejected this version of the volcano and discovered in it an image of themselves: explosive, protean, creative. To make the world anew through poetry or art required the destruction of a fallen, corrupt world. It required the volatile re-creation of that world through the molten imagination. European Romantics such as Goethe and Victor Hugo reverently trekked to Vesuvius and peered into its simmering caldera as if peering into a mirror; their prose is peppered with references to the natural wonder. J. M. W. Turner's enormous painting *Eruption of Vesuvius* has an almost autobiographical intensity. Awash in tumultuous color, a titanium-white plume of painterly lava illuminates a seascape in which a host of tiny figures gather in awe below (see figure 2).

In the United States, the fascination with volcanoes took on an indigenous character, the sublimity of nature combining with a sense of national purpose to form what Emerson termed a "renaissance" of

FIGURE 3 *Cotopaxi* (1862), by Frederic Edwin Church. Courtesy Detroit Institute of the Arts.

artistic creativity during the 1850s. "Give me a condor's quill!" exclaims Ishmael, the rambunctious narrator in Herman Melville's *Moby-Dick:* "Give me Vesuvius' crater for an inkstand!" Melville's artistic ambition and New World confidence were echoed in the work of his friend and Hudson River School painter Frederic Edwin Church, who created vast, operatic canvases devoted to the Ecuadoran volcano Cotopaxi (see figure 3). Henry David Thoreau quite likely had one of these canvases in mind when he wrote to a friend that the Bhagavad Gita, the Hindu scripture in which he was then immersed, was "that which dimmed the brightness of the day, like the apex of Cotopaxi's cone, seen against the disk of the sun by the voyager of the South American coast."[11]

Melville's explosive imagination and Thoreau's mind-expanding vision of Cotopaxi notwithstanding, the American author who identified herself most closely with the volcano was Emily Dickinson. "I have never seen 'Volcanoes'—," she confessed, then promptly launched upon a convincing description of their capacity for pain and destruction. Throughout her life, Dickinson compared her poetry to a "still— Volcano—Life—": quiet on the exterior, combustible within. Like "The reticent volcano" she so admired, her poetry cultivated the capacity to "populate / With awe." "Volcanoes be in Sicily / And South America," she admitted before smugly suggesting that her poetry provided a "Volcano nearer here." Elsewhere, she claimed that her imagination was so powerful that she could "climb / A Crater [that] I may contemplate / Vesuvius at Home." Characteristic of her time and place, Dickinson was particularly attracted to the volcano's unfettered force, its power to remake the world through time-shattering self-liberation:

> The soul has moments of escape—
> When bursting all the doors—
> She dances like a Bomb, abroad,
> And swings opon the Hours.[12]

Not all of the era's references to the volcano were so personal or so poetic. Antebellum America's most intractable social problem—the bitter fact of slavery, which had distracted political and social life since the nation's inception—was also figured as a volcano. In 1845, the New England abolitionist Nathaniel Peabody Rogers bluntly announced in the *Herald of Freedom*, "Slavery is a *moral* evil." The fallacy of enslaving human beings on the basis of skin color prompted him to ask, "Would not the news that white Irishmen were sold at auction, in New Orleans, set all New England in a blaze? And not the glare of the conflagration strike down that gloomy man-market, and make the dark waters surround it as ruddy as with the light of a volcano?" Three years later, the escaped slave Frederick Douglass more ominously warned, "The slaveholders are sleeping on slumbering volcanoes, if they did but know it." Melville lifted the phrase for his great novella about slave revolt, *Benito Cereno*, in which the bland, naive ship captain, Amasa Delano, wonders whether the Spanish ship *San Dominick* (so named by Melville to recall the slave rebellion in Saint-Domingue, or Haiti, at the end of the eighteenth century) might not, "like a slumbering volcano, suddenly let loose energies now hid?"[13]

This book is about the great volcano of civil war that erupted in the middle of the American nineteenth century. It is also about the way a remarkable group of writers experienced that civil war, the bloodiest conflict in American history. Among the authors included in this account are Ralph Waldo Emerson, the serene transcendentalist whose flirtation with volcanoes led him to glorify war and then to the brink of despair; Walt Whitman, who sought to redeem himself and his nation through a Christ-like ministering to the wounded; Emily Dickinson, whose reclusive imagination captured the anguish of war in pared-down and pitiless verse; Louisa May Alcott, whose experiences in a Washington hospital became the foundation for her literary fame; Frederick Douglass, the most perspicacious African-American intellectual of the era; Nathaniel Hawthorne, who found himself incapable of writing romances on account of the war; and Herman Melville, who attempted to resurrect a literary career he had destroyed a decade earlier and who believed that the horrors of modern warfare might enable him to do it.

Together, these writers had helped to create a literary culture that would play a significant role in the escalation of hostilities. When Abraham Lincoln met Harriet Beecher Stowe at a White House reception and grandly announced that *Uncle Tom's Cabin* was "the book that started this Great War," he was pointing to an important truth: sectional and political animosities had been inflamed by a new national literature. Among the complex and interwoven causes of the U.S. Civil War—slavery, political strife, sectional distrust, and even religious revivalism—was an indigenous and influential literature that demanded moral transformation from society. The writings of Emerson and his contemporaries, as we shall see, helped to propel the country into war.

But if this extraordinary group of men and women fanned the flames of national division, they were also wracked by a pained ambivalence about the ensuing war. Like Emerson, they had longed for the volcanic destruction of a corrupt society and the molten renewal of human potential. Like him, they were haunted by doubt and guilt when that devastation at last arrived. The core of Emerson's dream is not so much about the volcano of war or the fractured nation; it is about the *architect* of the house divided. The "man asleep, whom I understood to be the architect of the house," was none other than Emerson himself. It was Emerson who had "nearly or quite fallen asleep" at the beginning of the dream, who awoke to the nightmare of national dissolution, and who accused himself at his dream's conclusion when he "pointed to this sleeper as the architect."

This, then, is a story of America's greatest writers as they struggled to make sense of the Civil War in old and new literary forms and to uphold their highest ideals, whether for the preservation of the Union or for the emancipation of the slaves or for the simple dignity of human life. It is a story about how these writers came to realize, as would their culture, that upholding their beliefs had come at an enormously high price and that their faith in liberty and human rights had resulted in unprecedented death and misery. It is a story, ultimately, about how the war tested their deepest commitments.

Shortly after recording his dream, Emerson began a new journal, on the cover of which he neatly inscribed a blunt, if descriptive, title: "WAR." The journal was devoted to a national cataclysm that shook and exploded an old order, an engulfing fire that blazed and raged until

FIGURE 4 The volcano of war erupts at Fort Sumter. Cover of *Harper's Weekly*, May 4, 1861.

it seemed as if all the hope and promise and optimism of the American experiment must be consumed. Emerson remained convinced of the moral justice of the war, and he consoled himself as best he could in the face of the carnage and loss of life that threatened to destroy the nation. On the inside cover of his journal, he neatly copied a passage from the German philosopher Johann Paul Friedrich Richter: "Vesuvius stands in this pastoral poem of Nature, & exalts everything, as War does the Age."[14] (See figure 4.)

CHAPTER I

Beat! Beat! Drums!

N o one expected the war to last very long.
Certainly not Walt Whitman, poet, flaneur, self-styled
rough, and the genial owner of an outsized self-regard.
Strolling along Broadway one pleasant April evening (he had just
attended an opera by Verdi and was still in raptures), Whitman heard
the shrieks and panicked cries of newspaper boys announcing the bombardment of Fort Sumter. He bought a paper and carried it quickly to
the broad circle of light emanating from the Metropolitan Hotel, but
instead of reading the news himself, he listened in stunned silence—
listened as so many others would listen during the next four years—
while a stranger read the bulletin to the hushed crowd.

A single shell from a ten-inch mortar, arcing high over the harbor
in Charleston, South Carolina, threatened the very existence of the
United States of America. The mortar's burning fuse had lit the cool
night, leaving a shimmering, ruddy reflection in the water below.
Moments later, its explosive boom rattled window sashes and rippled
palmetto fronds. To the thousands of spectators, mostly women, gathered on rooftops and balconies and along the battery, the shell seemed
to pause a moment over Fort Sumter before bursting in a brilliant star
pattern. Like a volcano rumbling to life, the besieged federal fort smol-
dered, shook, and erupted in flame.

Whitman's immediate impression was that the world had gone mad,
had lost its bearings—that the American ship of state, once so buoyant
and promising, was foundering in a storm unleashed by its own contra-
dictions. In the preliminary draft for a poem he never finished or
published, he portrayed the sudden outbreak of hostilities between

North and South in language that drew upon the storm scene in *King Lear*. In Whitman's poem, the war was a crashing fury that threatened to whelm the fragile nation:

Blow mad winds!
Rage, boil, vex, yawn-wide, yeasty waves
Crash away—
Tug at the planks—make them groan—fall around, black clouds—
Clouds of death
Come now we shall see what stuff you are made of Ship of Libertad.[1]

The core image here was by no means original (see figure 1.1). A generation earlier, Oliver Wendell Holmes had imagined America's fledgling democracy as a venerable, war-ravaged vessel in his popular "Old Ironsides." More recently Henry Wadsworth Longfellow had employed the same image in "O Ship of State," where the impending storm of civil war "'Tis but the flapping of the sail, / And not a rent made by the gale!" But Whitman added a twist to these assertions of national endurance by evoking the tragic, mad Lear. It was not just the nation that resembled Shakespeare's vain and overweening old man. It was also the poetic speaker, alone and grief-maddened, his booming voice the result of impotent rage. Exiled amid the storm, he no longer had a nation to rule.

Yet the faintest flicker of hope—a candle in a lighthouse—feebly illumined the last line. Exuding a gruff confidence, Whitman claimed to see that the ship of liberty would survive the storm of sectional fury. The turbulent squall of war would sweep clean the skies, purify the air, restore to wholesome balance the Union he had revered as a secular religion. "Come now we shall see what stuff you are made of Ship of Libertad."

The lines are pure Whitman. They are also fraught with uncertainty and denial.

A year earlier, in the spring of 1860, a gentleman named Thomas Wentworth Higginson had stopped by the Washington Street offices of Boston publishers Thayer and Eldridge and "saw before me, sitting on the counter, a handsome, burly man, heavily built."[2] It was Whitman, as ever flouting convention by refusing to sit in a chair, basking in the huge physicality he celebrated, scandalously and unabashedly, in poem after poem in his self-published book *Leaves of Grass*. At age forty, with an ailing mother and several indigent siblings who depended upon him for support, he still enjoyed escaping from his Brooklyn household as

With one exulting, joyous bound,
She leaps into the ocean's arms.

FIGURE 1.1 Longfellow's *O Ship of State*.

often as possible to bathe in the brisk waters of Long Island Sound. Naked and joyous, spray clinging to his prematurely gray beard, he strode up and down the deserted beach declaiming lines of Shakespeare at the top of his lungs.

Whitman loved Brooklyn and New York. He relished strolling amid the bustle of Broadway, immersing himself in the cacophony of tram drivers and dockyard workers, and delighting in the tinny pianos that filled the hot, crowded streets with popular tunes. He never tired of the peacock display of fashionable men and women promenading along the battery in their woolen pinks and browns, the brilliant white sails of a regatta snapping and furling in the wind of the East River, the beer joints and opera houses and gaudy theaters crammed cheek-to-jowl along the Bowery, one of his favorite haunts. He was fascinated by the revolutionary history that still clung to Brooklyn Heights and Fort Greene, especially as these pertained to his hero, George Washington, and when he left the city for the occasional weekend, he explored the coastal fishing villages dotting Long Island, walking vast stretches of shoreline, scribbling in his notebook, studying the flora and fauna that would appear in many of his poems.

So it was no typical day that found him in a publisher's office in the provincial, buttoned-up city of Boston. Tempting him to travel north had been an unsolicited letter written by one William Thayer, who together with Charles Eldridge had recently formed a publishing firm that specialized in all things radical. In its brief history as a commercial enterprise, Thayer and Eldridge had published James Redpath's *Echoes of Harper's Ferry* and *The Public Life of Capt. John Brown*, both passionate vindications of the recently martyred abolitionist, and it had just signed a contract to publish Harriet Jacobs's *Incidents in the Life of a Slave Girl*, a pseudonymous autobiography that would one day shock northern readers with its account of the author's repeated sexual abuse by her master. The letter to Whitman, written with the boisterous and giddy enthusiasm of young men in their twenties, implored the poet to allow them to publish the next edition of *Leaves of Grass*.

He was flattered, to say the least. After years of itinerant journalism, carpentry, teaching, and general loafing about, Whitman had celebrated his artistic awakening in the sprawling first poem in *Leaves of Grass*, published at his own expense in 1855. "Song of Myself" would change poetry forever. Its lines lurched and sprawled to the margins of the page, threatening to burst all boundaries. Crammed to the rafters with catalogs of persons and places, the poem was propelled by loose-jointed and incantatory rhythms. And it introduced subject matter previously considered offensive to the sensibilities of mid-Victorian America. Whitman wrote about prostitutes and alcoholics. He described murderous rage, shameful dishonesty, sexual longing. He also celebrated the body, the soul, and love. It was as if he were trying to fit everything he had ever known, seen, or thought into a single rambunctious work, as if he were attempting to compel the vulgar energies of the young nation into a visionary poem. He did all this by assuming the persona of a democratic, working-class Everyman—"one of the roughs," as he called himself.

Part of the poem's radical nature was its author's refusal to sound like a poet. Whitman didn't even *look* like a poet (see figure 1.2). On the frontispiece of the first *Leaves of Grass*, he had printed a portrait of

FIGURE 1.2 Frontispiece portrait of Walt Whitman (1855).

himself that was distinctly at odds with the public conception of the rarefied man of letters. Instead of the stiff black frock coat and silk cravat found in the austere engravings that graced the books of the Fireside Poets, the brazen "poet of the body" stood gazing at the reader in an open blouse and workmen's trousers, a dark slouch hat cocked to one side. His right hand was placed insouciantly on his hip, and his expression resembled anything but the ethereal gaze of a poet. It was, in fact, mildly confrontational. The man gazing from the page looked as though he had just been interrupted in a heated discussion among bricklayers and hod carriers and was mildly annoyed to be thrust into the realm of polite readership. His eyes stared directly at the reader, as if asking: Are you one of us?

Leaves of Grass gained instant notoriety among northern literati for its frank descriptions and unconventional style. When asked whether she had read anything by Whitman, Emily Dickinson tartly replied, "I never read his Book—but was told it was disgraceful." Emerson was more receptive. Reading the volume soon after it was published, he thought it "the most extraordinary piece of wit and wisdom that America has yet contributed," and bestowed upon Whitman the following famous blurb: "I greet you at the beginning of a great career." Whitman was so delighted with this statement that he had it embossed in gilt on the green spine of the next edition, which came out the following year. (Characteristically, he neglected to secure Emerson's permission, a sore point in the two men's relationship.)[3]

Emerson was responding to Whitman's promise to democratize poetry, to make it representative of the nation. "America is a poem in our eyes," Emerson had asserted a decade earlier in "The Poet"; "its ample geography dazzles the imagination, and it will not wait long for metres." Because of the formless immensity and boundless aspirations of the new nation, the American poet could ignore formal restrictions, such as how to structure a sonnet. But Emerson also stressed that the American poet was filled and guided by the divine poet, whose prodigious creativity surpassed old forms. Poets were "thus liberating gods," "children of the fire, made of it, and only the same divinity transmuted." As a result, it was "not metres, but a metre-making argument, that makes a poem."[4]

Whitman had pored over Emerson's essay as if it were an instruction manual for his life. "I was simmering, simmering, simmering," he later acknowledged. "Emerson brought me to a boil." The explosive result first appeared in the preface to *Leaves of Grass*, an artistic manifesto that answered Emerson's ideas in "The Poet" note for note. "The

Americans of all nations at any time upon the earth have probably the fullest poetical nature," he boasted. "Here are the roughs and beards and space and ruggedness and nonchalance that the soul loves." Because the nation acted on "the best authority...namely from its own soul," it would one day produce a poet who knew that soul and who did not moralize but rather focused on common men and women. That poet, Whitman implied, was himself—but he required a reciprocal effort on the part of his audience. "The proof of a poet," he wrote, "is that his country absorbs him as affectionately as he has absorbed it."[5]

Therein lay the problem. Whitman had earnestly absorbed his country and had translated it into poetry. The country had been decidedly slower in absorbing its self-proclaimed poet. Despite Emerson's praise, the first edition of *Leaves of Grass* sold only a few hundred copies, much to its author's disappointment. This poor reception initiated a pattern of national neglect that continued with the next edition a year later. As the 1850s drew to a close, Whitman found himself adopting that time-honored pursuit of Manhattan's misunderstood geniuses. He began to frequent a bar, in this case a bohemian tavern in lower Manhattan populated by a seedy group of journalists, playwrights, poets, and revolutionaries. At Charles Pfaff's beer cellar, Whitman talked art and politics, argued over free soil and free love, drank beer and struggled not to feel neglected.

The letter from Thayer, arriving in early 1860, promised a change in fortune. His new publishers were "a couple of young Yankees," Whitman reported to friends back home, adding that, unlike most of the other publishers he had spoken with, these two were open to his ideas for the new edition of *Leaves of Grass*, which would be "very finely printed, good paper, and new, rather large-sized type." They had agreed to print the book in a variety of colored bindings, to use different fonts to indicate new sections of the book, and to illustrate specific poems with line drawings of butterflies and cloudbursts.[6]

And they introduced him to Boston—at the time, the literary capital of America. It was in Boston that a small group of New England poets and authors had assumed broad moral and cultural leadership. Writers like Emerson and poets like Oliver Wendell Holmes, John Greenleaf Whittier, James Russell Lowell, and the tremendously popular Henry Wadsworth Longfellow all lived in or near the tree-shaded city, where they had fused a Puritan sense of moral purpose with a young nation's desire for an indigenous culture. The result had been a nascent literary tradition that distinguished itself from "the courtly muses of Europe," as Emerson dismissively described belles lettres on the other side of the Atlantic, by being loftier, freer, and more activist. Literature, as these authors conceived it, demanded of its readers nothing less than a complete revolution of the moral imagination.

Strolling with delight along the narrow, twisting streets of the New England city, Whitman was certain he had at last arrived. He was introduced to Longfellow, a genial man with elegant clothes and refined manners, who was sufficiently polite, if not disingenuous, to express interest in Whitman's poems. He renewed his acquaintance with the homely, rough-hewn Henry David Thoreau, with whom he immediately felt a bond of spiritual kinship. Wherever he went, he made an "immense sensation." The town had never seen anyone quite like him, he boasted. "Every body here is so like everybody else—and I am Walt Whitman!"[7]

So successful was his tour of Boston that Whitman even managed to place several poems in the *Atlantic Monthly*, the nation's premier journal, which had been founded several years earlier as "a magazine of literature, art, and politics." The eminent poet, Harvard professor, and staunch abolitionist James Russell Lowell was the editor of this bastion of good taste and moral fastidiousness. Lowell had dramatized his disgust with slavery in his poetry, especially his popular *Biglow Papers*, but it was as the *Atlantic*'s editor that he most successfully combined the growing popularity of New England literature with the politics of radical abolitionism. In the process, he created a journal that stood less for a particular literary style than for a progressive cultural politics (see figure 1.3).

The first issue of the *Atlantic* had featured poetry by Emerson, an installment of Oliver Wendell Holmes's *The Autocrat of the Breakfast-Table*, and essays on Florentine mosaics. The second contained a scathing article on slavery entitled "Where Will It End?" According to the anonymous author, the "northern half of the great American continent" had "been kept back by Nature as a *tabula rasa*, a clean blackboard, on which the great problem of civil government might be worked out." That grand and noble experiment was increasingly threatened by the "baleful influence thus ever shed by Slavery on our national history." There would come a time, the article warned, "when the millions of the North and of the South shall rise upon this puny mastership [of slaveholders], and snatch from its hands the control of their own affairs."[8]

It seems rather mild now, but publishing the article in 1857 was an incendiary act. Events in "bloody Kansas," where pro- and antislavery factions contended for the soul of the new state, had recently revealed

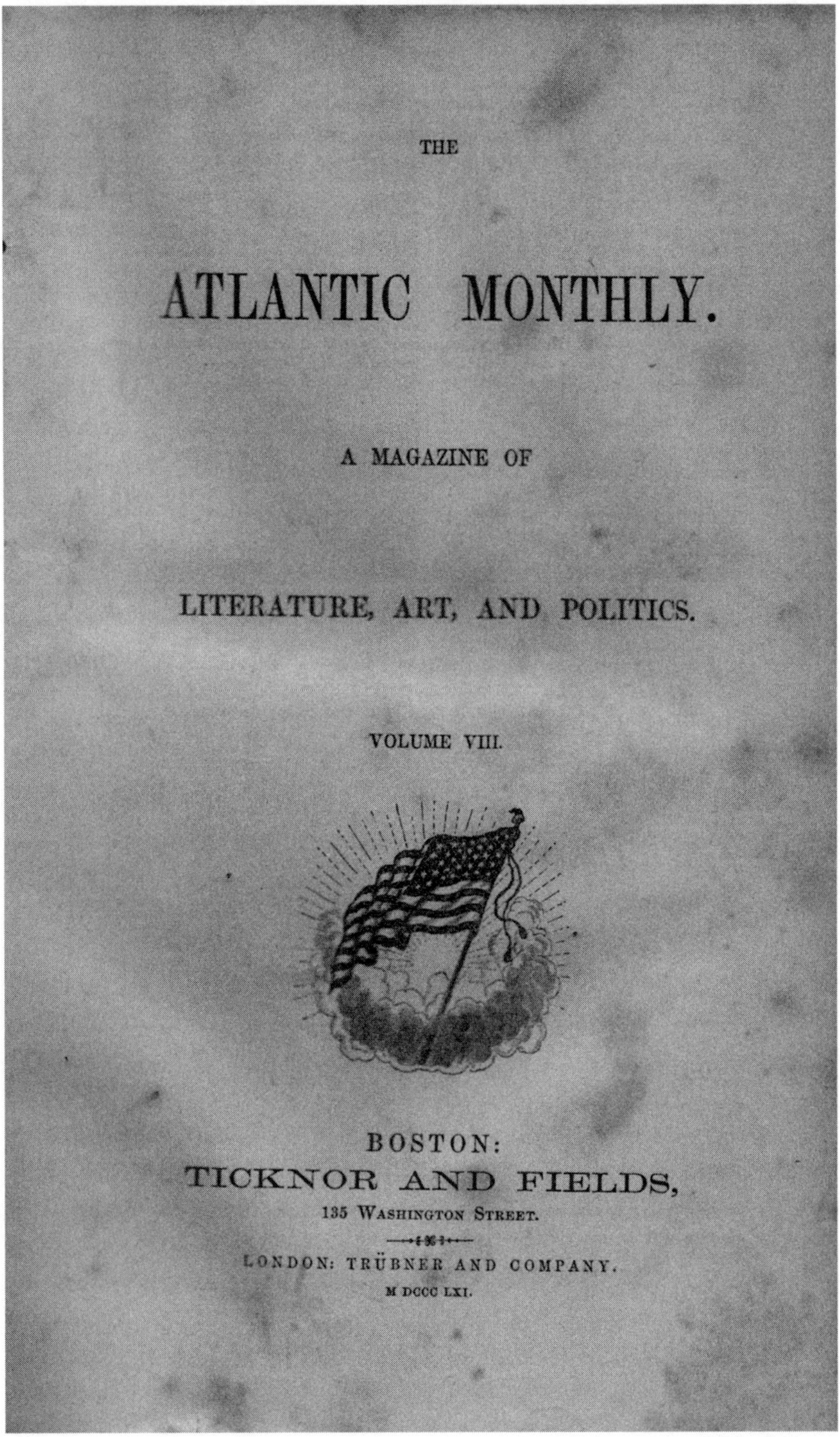

THE

ATLANTIC MONTHLY.

A MAGAZINE OF

LITERATURE, ART, AND POLITICS.

VOLUME VIII.

BOSTON:
TICKNOR AND FIELDS,
135 WASHINGTON STREET.

LONDON: TRÜBNER AND COMPANY.
M DCCC LXI.

FIGURE 1.3 Cover of *Atlantic Monthly*, vol. 8, 1861; the flag appeared soon after the start of the war.

just how violent the antagonism between the sides could be. Kansans and outsiders divided by the issue had butchered one another, executing entire families, burning homes and villages. To publish "Where Will It End?" at the peak of this violence was to push readers into ever more extreme positions. Lowell later described these tense days as a "war of tongue and pen," a cultural crusade in which authors "Learn[ed] with what deadly purpose [they were] fraught."[9]

Apparently the South saw it that way, too. Citing the *Atlantic's* condemnation of "the coarse and solid oligarchy (the slave States)," the editor of the *Southern Literary Messenger* drew attention to the potent mixture of politics and literary culture encouraged by Lowell and pointed out the dangers of mixing such volatile ingredients: "Libels like these carry with them greater power for mischief in a periodical which charms the ear with the strains of tuneful poetry, and warms the heart with passages of eloquent description." In words that would prove prophetic, the Richmond-based journal proclaimed that the sole aim of this "new literary and anti-slavery magazine"— the *Atlantic Monthly*—was nothing less than "to wage war upon Southern society."[10]

Whitman's appearance in the *Atlantic* would turn out to be provocative as well, but for completely different reasons. He confided to a friend that Thayer and Eldridge had refrained from inquiring "at all what I am going to put into the book." This meant that the *Atlantic* would publish an author who would soon be notorious for breaking even more taboos in the third edition of his book than he had in the previous two. Among the 146 new poems Whitman added to the new edition (which he privately had begun to refer to as *"The Great Construction* of the *New Bible"*) were several dozen that dealt with sexuality more frankly and explicitly than any American poetry had before.

The first batch of poems, appearing in a section entitled "Enfans d'Adam," focused on sexual love between men and women: what Whitman called the "pent-up aching rivers" of desire. These erotic verses would provoke a heated disagreement with Emerson, who endeavored one spring afternoon in Boston Commons to persuade Whitman to omit the salacious material. Recalling the episode decades later, an unrepentant Whitman maintained that "the sexual passion in itself, while normal and unperverted, is inherently legitimate, creditable, not necessarily an improper theme for the poet." And he added, "*That* is what I felt in my inmost brain and heart, when I only answer'd Emerson's vehement arguments with silence, under the old elms of Boston Commons."[11]

The grouping of poems under the heading of "Calamus" described an even more forbidden topic. Whereas "Enfans d'Adam" celebrated procreative sex and loving physicality between men and women, the "Calamus" poems portrayed "adhesiveness," or love between men, in terms that were as much political as they were sexual. At a time when the Union and democracy seemed terribly imperiled, Whitman claimed, male companionship was the basis for both. "I will make the continent indissoluble," Whitman prophesied in "For You O Democracy," one of the "Calamus" poems, "I will make inseparable cities with their arms about each other's necks, / By the love of comrades, / By the manly love of comrades."[12]

The third edition of *Leaves of Grass* was published in May 1860. By July, Thayer and Eldridge announced that a second printing of 1,000 copies was certain to sell out, and they proposed a third printing, to be divided into a cheap paperback edition and a deluxe hardbound version. Whitman could scarcely contain himself. Finally, Americans were beginning to see themselves reflected in the poetic summing up he offered in *Leaves*. "I am more pleased with Boston than I anticipated," he wrote, hinting at the success promised by Thayer and Eldridge. "I am very glad I [have] come, if only to rub out of me the deficient notions I had of New England character." So confident in the future was he that he planned a new work to be called *The Banner at Day-Break*, which Thayer and Eldridge advertised in November. This book would attempt nothing less than the healing of a nation driven increasingly to disunion by sectional tension and the disagreement over slavery. In Whitman's grandiose scheme, the book would save America from itself.[13]

And then, in December, Thayer and Eldridge suddenly declared bankruptcy. The publishers had overextended themselves financially, a problem that might have been fixed over time but for the growing expectation of hostilities between the North and South, which had dried up investment capital. Whitman learned of the disappointing news back at home as winter descended on Manhattan.

While the bankruptcy of Thayer and Eldridge delivered a serious blow to his ambitions, the attack on Fort Sumter completed the destruction. The North quickly rallied around the Union and the streets swelled with fresh-faced recruits after President Lincoln's call for 75,000 volunteers to protect the capital, but the future of the nation—the *United States of America*—remained in stark and solemn doubt.

In such heady, urgent times, writing suddenly seemed frivolous. From his book-lined study in Cambridge, Henry Wadsworth Longfellow confessed to his journal, "When the times have such a gunpowder flavor, all literature loses its taste. Newspapers are the only reading. They are at once the record and the romance of the day." In Concord, Nathaniel Hawthorne irritably admitted to his publisher, William D. Ticknor, "The war continues to interrupt my literary industry, and I am afraid it will be long before Romances are in request again." George William Curtis, the urbane editor of *Harper's Monthly* and one of the founders of the Republican Party, noted that the nation's preoccupation with "The beat of the drum, the bugle-call, the shrill, passionate shock of martial music" had profoundly affected literary culture. Even "the bookshops," he claimed, "have only placards of books of tactics and the drill."[14]

As a result, publishers suffered a recession at the outbreak of hostilities. Ticknor and Fields, the Boston publisher of Emerson and Hawthorne and the owner of the *Atlantic*, lost money in 1861 for the only time in its fabled existence. Periodicals and newspapers, on the other hand, experienced an immediate surge in demand. Oliver Wendell Holmes, the diminutive physician and author whose son had volunteered in the first wave of recruits and who was among the literary establishment's earliest and most vocal war boosters, described an acquaintance in Boston who habitually traveled the "side streets on his way for the noon *extra*,—he is so afraid somebody will meet him and *tell* the news he wishes to *read*, first on the bulletin-board, and then in the great capitals and leaded type of the newspaper."[15]

The rabid desire for war news soon opened doors for literary treatments of the conflict, however. Louisa May Alcott, daughter of Emerson's close friend Bronson Alcott and an aspiring author when the war began, found the literary marketplace transformed. Try as she might, she could not persuade James T. Fields, the *Atlantic*'s new editor, to accept her fledgling stories about domestic life. He "has Mss. enough on hand for a dozen numbers & has to choose war stories if he can, to suit the times," she explained, adding, "I will write 'great guns' Hail Columbia & Concord fight, if he'll only take it."[16]

An audience for patriotic writing formed overnight as northern readers came together, "united…en masse," as one observer put it, at "the outrageous conduct of the South in the attack on Fort Sumter. There is a degree of unanimity in the non-slaveholding states, which has *never* existed before." Longfellow concurred, marveling at the "sudden uprising of a whole people," while the Quaker poet John Greenleaf Whittier announced, "The old fires of Liberty are rekindled, and there is a spirit of sublime self-sacrifice pervading all classes. It is more than I had ever dared hope for."[17] (See figure 1.4.)

FIGURE 1.4 "Uprising of the North." *Harper's Weekly*, April 19, 1862.

Amid this spontaneous accord, Walt Whitman found himself strangely at sea. Like a castaway on the tides of public opinion, he strolled the crowded sidewalks of Brooklyn and surveyed a battalion of newly enlisted troops as it marched in dress parade, headed south to protect the nation's capital. The recruits had been provided with a piece of rope, he recalled some years later, "conspicuously tied to their musket-barrels, with which to bring back each man a prisoner from the audacious south, to be led in a noose, on our men's early and triumphant return!"[18] Whitman watched with mixed feelings, excited by the display but mourning the Union he had so fervently summoned in verse.

Closer to home, his brother George, a cabinetmaker who lived in Brooklyn with the rest of the family, enlisted with the Thirteenth New York State Militia. Walt applauded his younger brother's decision as an act of courage and patriotic duty. He discerned in it something even grander: an example of the "national uprising and volunteering" that had spontaneously erupted in response to national division. "The volcanic upheaval of the nation, after that *firing* on the flag at Charleston," he later wrote, years after the war, "proved for certain something which had been previously in great doubt, and at once substantially settled the question of disunion."[19]

But in the tumultuous weeks that followed the attack on Fort Sumter, Whitman wavered in his response. Should he join his brother and enlist with the great democratic mass of recruits? Should Walt Whitman, "one of the roughs," sign up in the most socially representative army in U.S. history, a vast collection of laborers and skilled and white-collar workers from New England, the middle states, and as far west as California? A day after Lincoln's call for volunteers, Whitman made the following declaration: "I have this hour, this day, resolved to inaugurate for myself a pure, perfect, sweet, cleanblooded robust body by ignoring all drinks but water and pure milk—and all fat meats, late suppers—a great body—a purged, cleansed, spiritualized, invigorated body."[20] Was he preparing himself for the stoic life of an enlisted man?

If so, he soon changed his mind. Depressed by current events, he launched into a series of nostalgic pieces about Brooklyn for a local newspaper, recalling his boyhood in the outer borough when its muddy streets and clapboard buildings had seemed a bucolic kingdom. As troops massed in and around Washington, he escaped to Long Island, pacing the shore, bathing in the choppy surf, identifying with the solitary songbirds that called forlornly in the night. He quickly abandoned his resolve to drink nothing but "water and pure milk" and returned to Pfaff's beer cellar, where he spent hours with the bohemian set, arguing about the latest actions taken by the South. Afterward, he strolled the avenues of Manhattan, hands in pockets, eyes hungry for some clue about the future.

He was forty-one—certainly not too old to enlist in an army that accepted recruits at age sixty or even higher. He was inordinately proud of his physique, frequently boasting of his weight (200 pounds) and strength. Thomas Wentworth Higginson, the abolitionist author who befriended Emily Dickinson and commanded the first African-American troops for the Union, recalled "thinking of Whitman" during this time "with hope and satisfaction." Regiments "were to be raised for the war," he explained, and Whitman's habitat, the Bowery, seemed to Higginson "the very place to enlist them." He was soon disappointed in his expectations, however. "[I]f all men, South and North, had taken the same view of their duty that Whitman held," he remarked, "there would have been no occasion for hospitals on either side."[21]

One of Whitman's drinking buddies at Pfaff's would become the war's first literary celebrity. Theodore Winthrop was a thin, wiry, earnestly shy young man with auburn muttonchops and an impeccable New England pedigree. He was a descendant of the Puritan leader John

Winthrop and the eighteenth-century divine Jonathan Edwards. Restless, moody, impetuous, and inquisitive, he followed in his industrialist father's footsteps by graduating from Yale, and then departed from family expectations by venturing to Europe, Panama, and the Far West in search of adventure. He tried and then quickly abandoned business and law, at last determining to become a novelist like his literary hero, Nathaniel Hawthorne. This new occupation led him to Whitman's motley circle of artists and social rebels (see figure 1.5).

Winthrop wrote in his family's capacious house on the northern shore of Staten Island, where the northeastern window of his room was shaded by an enormous elm. His neighbors included William Emerson, the older brother Emerson had called to in his dream; the influential editor at *Harper's Monthly*, George William Curtis; and the wealthy, close-knit family of Francis Shaw. All of these neighbors were fervent abolitionists; all worshipped at the altar of transcendentalism. All became fierce Unionists the moment war was declared.

A month before the attack on Fort Sumter, the thirty-three-year-old Winthrop received a letter from James T. Fields, the new editor at the *Atlantic Monthly*, who wished to congratulate him on the acceptance of a short story. Before the story could be published, however, Winthrop had joined a New York regiment. Seizing on the opportunity, Fields promptly hired the young man as a war correspondent and agreed to publish his monthly accounts of soldiering.

Winthrop's first article, "Our March to Washington," reveals just how thoroughly his understanding of war had been shaped by antebellum literary culture. It displays little interest in military strategy or the contentious political issues that had caused the crisis, focusing instead on the perspective of an individual soldier guided by patriotic enthusiasm. "It was worth a life, that march,"[22] he proclaimed, referring to a regimental dress parade down Broadway much like the one Whitman had witnessed.

Winthrop's "Washington as a Camp," published a month later in the July 1861 issue of the *Atlantic*, was even less concerned with the tedium of military life. "Spring was at its freshest and fairest," he wrote. "Every day was more exquisite than its forerunner....Let the ivy-colored stem of the Big Oak of Camp Cameron take its place in literature!" Yet in at least one spot he came close to dropping his heroic tone and portraying camp life as it actually was for the new recruits. "It is monotonous, it is not monotonous," he confessed, "it is laborious, it is lazy, it is a bore, it is a lark, it is half war, half peace, and totally attractive, and not to be dispensed with from one's experience

Engraved by J.C.Buttre

FIGURE 1.5 Theodore Winthrop, from the frontispiece of Edmund C. Stedman and Ellen M. Hutchinson, *A Library of American Literature from the Earliest Settlement to the Present Time* (New York: Charles L. Webster, 1889) volume 9.

in the nineteenth century." The article concluded with his suggestion that the uneventful routine of military life was but preparation for the kind of heroism to be immortalized in future books. "Is my gentle reader tired of the short marches and frequent halts of the Seventh? Remember, gentle reader, that you must be schooled by such alphabetical exercises to spell bigger words—skirmish, battle, defeat, rout, massacre—by and by."[23]

Winthrop's literary celebrity was ultimately the result of his experience with these "bigger words"—more precisely, his death on June 10, 1861, at the Battle of Big Bethel, the first land battle of the war. On paper, the Union strategy for this Virginia skirmish had seemed apt; superior troops would launch a surprise attack on thinly held Confederate outposts at the Little and Big Bethel churches. But when a frightened Union detachment accidentally fired into its own soldiers and destroyed the element of surprise, Confederate forces fell back to well-fortified entrenchments, and in the ensuing confusion General Benjamin Butler, under whom Winthrop served, quickly signaled a retreat.

Winthrop ignored the signal. Whether he sought to change the battle's dynamic or simply to enact his own private version of the literary beau geste, he instead charged the enemy entrenchments, reportedly shouting, "One more charge and the day is ours!" Accounts vary as to whether he raised a rifle or a sword as he made this announcement. There was similar confusion about who or what killed him. Some contemporaneous sources claim a "drummer boy" fired the fatal shot, others a North Carolina sharpshooter.[24] Later accounts determined that the abolitionist author and the first Union officer to become a casualty in the Civil War was in fact killed by a slave named Sam Ashe. Little is known about Ashe, except that he had accompanied his southern master to the front and apparently knew how to handle a rifle.

Many of these details appeared in George William Curtis's elegiac profile in the August 1861 *Atlantic*, one of a dozen articles that contributed to Winthrop's spontaneous martyrdom in the North. According to Curtis, the slain author was a combination of the Renaissance soldier-poet Philip Sidney and the moody, courageous Byronic hero. Before the war, he wrote, Winthrop had been prone to a "reserve of sadness" that led to "verses in which his heart seems to exhale a sigh of sadness." The firing on Sumter shocked him out of his sensitive brooding, calling forth "the manly and poetic qualities" latent within him. Once "elegant and listless and aimless," Winthrop had been "a lovely possibility...until he went to the war." His death, Curtis wrote, was symbolic of the nation's aspirations:

For one moment that brave, inspiring form is plainly visible to his whole country, rapt and calm, standing upon the log nearest the enemy's battery, the mark of their sharpshooters, the admiration of their leaders, waving his sword, cheering his fellow-soldiers with his bugle voice of victory,—young, brave, beautiful, for one moment erect and glowing in the wild whirl of battle, the next falling forward toward the foe, dead, but triumphant.[25]

* * *

By the fall of 1861, Whitman had come to believe he needed to do *something* for the war effort. His first act was to contribute a patriotic broadside that appeared simultaneously in the *Boston Evening Transcript*, the *New York Leader*, and *Harper's Weekly*:

> Beat! beat! drums!—blow! bugles! blow!
> Through the windows—through doors—burst like a ruthless force,
> Into the solemn church, and scatter the congregation,
> Into the school where the scholar is studying;
> Leave not the bridegroom quiet—no happiness must he now have with his
>   bride,
> Nor the peaceful farmer any peace, ploughing his field or gathering his
>   grain,
> So fierce you whirr and pound you drums—so shrill you bugles blow.[26]

The poem is rich with hearty imperatives: *Sweep away schools, work, even weddings: war is at hand!* As with much patriotic verse of the era, Whitman's poem not only celebrates the drums and bugles of war but attempts to become those drums and bugles—to embody the martial music that would lead an army to victory.

Yet anxiety permeates every line of Whitman's first significant war poem. Behind the call to abolish daily life is a keen nostalgia for all that will soon be destroyed. The sound of war bursts "like a ruthless force, / Into the solemn church," but instead of uniting the worshippers, it merely "scatter[s] the congregation." The sacrifice of the bridegroom, enacted throughout the nation, erodes the most basic unit of social life: "no happiness must he now have with his bride." Faith and domesticity, Whitman suggested, are the first casualties of the war.

The source of this insight and the inspiration for the poem was Bull Run. On July 21, 1861, a month and a half after the disastrous skirmish at Big Bethel, hundreds of curiosity seekers and politicians from Washington had filled their picnic hampers and piled into carriages and veronicas for the twenty-mile ride to Manassas Junction. The day was insufferably hot and dusty, but the scalding Virginia summer did little to alter the atmosphere of general merriment. The crowd of spectators expected nothing less than to witness a heroic battle that would conclude, if God had any say in the matter, with the punctual reunification of the country.

What they saw instead was panic and confusion. Entire companies of men fled, some dazed and bloodstained, some screaming in pain. They ran from the battlefield as fast as they could, stunned by what they had just experienced in nearby fields and woods. The fear was contagious. Hearing hysterical soldiers shriek, "Turn back! Turn back! We are whipped!" the civilians fled in as hurried and disorganized a fashion as the disgraced Army of the Potomac.

At the time of the First Battle of Bull Run, John Newton Breed was twenty-three years old: a husband, father, and bugler in the Fifth Massachusetts Volunteer Infantry. In his manuscript reminiscence written more than thirty years later, Breed attempted to tell in clear and unemotional language what it felt like to hear bullets slap into the meat of the person beside him, to see bloody pieces of human beings scattered underfoot, and to march toward an enemy entrenched less than a hundred yards away. "As we crossed Bull Run at Sudley Ford," he recollected, "we saw for the first time the results of real war. It was a new sight probably to everyone in the regiment; the dead and wounded lying where they fell."

Made solemn by these scenes, Breed's battalion continued toward the field of action, where things only got worse. A mile from the Bull Run River, he saw "the killed and wounded…lying by the score, and rifle and cannon balls were flying thick and fast." He asked himself

whether I should go forward and do my duty, or slink out with the field music. I was frightened, and am not ashamed to own it. I thought it was sure death if I went on. I thought of my wife and helpless child, what a pity it was to leave them to the mercy of the world; while, on the other hand, I could not be a coward, for I was the descendant of revolutionary heroes, therefore I would go where duty called.

Later in the afternoon, something occurred that would haunt him for the rest of his life.

I had gone but twenty or thirty steps when a cannon-ball, passing a few feet from my head, struck a comrade who was walking nine or ten feet from us and severed his head from his body as clean as it could have been done by a guillotine. The headless trunk remained trembling, and still holding his gun in his hand—I stood gazing on the terrible object, unable to move hand or foot—I do not know that I breathed—how long I know not—it seemed hours, but it could not have been but minutes, it may have been but a few seconds—I can remember five other cannon-balls striking the road at my side and in front, and yet I could not stir, until at last the headless trunk swayed and fell, almost to my feet.[27]

Whitman later called Bull Run a "crucifixion," a defeat he included in the two days "of all the war...I can never forget." (The other was April 14, 1865, the day of Lincoln's assassination.) The defeat obsessed him for years, appearing again and again in his writings. Although he had been in Brooklyn at the time and had yet to see the war up close, he wrote about the battle as if he had been there, relying upon news-paper accounts to provide details of the chaotic retreat. "The Saturday and Sunday of the battle (20th, 21st) had been parch'd and hot to an extreme," he reported,

the dust, the grime and smoke, in layers, sweated in, follow'd by other layers again sweated in, absorb'd by those excited souls—their clothes all saturated with the clay-powder filling the air—stirr'd up every-where on the dry roads and trodden fields by the regiments, swarming wagons, artillery, &c.—all the men with this coating of murk and sweat and rain, now recoiling back, pouring over the Long Bridge—a horrible march of twenty miles, returning to Washington baffled, humiliated, panic-struck.[28]

There is something deeply personal about this description. Julia Ward Howe, soon to write "The Battle Hymn of the Republic," had commemorated the first wave of volunteers by comparing them to "new-fledged eagles" who met "unscared the dazzling front of day."[29] William Cullen Bryant and Oliver Wendell Holmes boasted of the heroic recruits in their own poems, "Our Country's Call" and "The Wide-Awake Man." But Whitman's description of these same men after Bull Run is stripped of patriotic ideology, of cheap glory or contrived heroics. His focus instead is on the fear and humiliation of the soldiers following a crushing defeat—a perspective made possible in part by his emotional identification with the men and their experience.

Like John Newton Breed, who had never seen war until he marched into its chaotic maw, Whitman would be changed forever by Bull Run. Never again would he boast so confidently about the future of America. "The dream of humanity, the vaunted Union we thought so strong, so impregnable," he wrote after the war, recalling the first summer of war, "lo! it seems already smash'd like a china plate." Implicitly criticizing the poetry of *Leaves of Grass*, with its confident assertions of national destiny and personal freedom, he asked of the young recruits, "Where are the vaunts, and the proud boasts with which you went forth? Where are your banners, and your bands of music, and your ropes to bring back prisoners? Well, there isn't a band playing—and there isn't a flag but clings ashamed and lank to its staff."[30]

It wasn't just young men who were wounded in the rout at Bull Run, Whitman asserted; it was the nation. "The fact is," he reported, that this "hour was one of the three or four of those crises we had then and afterward, during the fluctuations of four years, when human eyes appear'd at least just as likely to see the last breath of the Union as to see it continue." He described an incident in which one "of our returning colonels express'd in public that night...the opinion that it was useless to fight." No one in "that large crowd of officers and gentlemen" bothered to contradict him.[31]

The malaise and handwringing that inevitably followed Bull Run also prompted the writing of "Beat! Beat! Drums!" In it, Whitman tried to record as honestly as possible the social costs of the war while at the same time conveying the urgency of restoring the Union:

Make no parley—stop for no expostulation,
Mind not the timid—mind not the weeper or prayer,
Mind not the old man beseeching the young man,
Let not the child's voice be heard, nor the mother's entreaties,
Make even the trestles to shake the dead where they lie awaiting the
    hearses,
So strong you thump O terrible drums—so loud you bugles blow.[32]

Shrill and mildly panicked, "Beat! Beat! Drums!" is by no means a great Whitman poem. Yet it manages to express a sentiment that few of his poetic contemporaries were willing to articulate so early in the war: saving the Union would require the ugly realities of modern warfare. The nation would have to become acquainted with the stench of terror and the sorrows of bloodshed if it were to be reunified, and in the aftermath, celebrating America would become increasingly difficult.

A week or so before Bull Run, Whitman had rather blithely suggested in a chatty note to his brother George, "All of us here think the rebellion as good as broke—no matter if the war does continue some months yet."[33] In truth, George would spend the next four years in the Union army, marching thousands of miles, camping in swamps, riverbeds, and unprotected fields in the hottest of summer days and coldest

FIGURE 1.6 A soldier gazes at wooden grave markers at Bull Run
(ca. 1861). Photograph by George N. Barnard. Civil War Treasures,
New-York Historical Society (nhnycw/ad ad33008).

of winter nights, subsisting on hardtack and whatever game could
be shot, fighting in more than twenty battles, including Antietam,
Fredericksburg, and the Wilderness. Of the original 1,100 enlistees in
his regiment, George Whitman was among only 20 percent who survived. Referring to this fact, a comrade called him "just the luckiest
man in the American army." Rising from private to major, he was
finally captured toward the end of the war and placed in a rebel prison,
which he managed, improbably, to survive as well. Always more laconic

than his older brother, he would compress all the terror and hardship of those four years into a simple phrase scrawled in a hasty letter to his mother: "it was mighty trying to a fellows nerves, as the balls was flying around pretty thick."[34]

Even after the shock of Bull Run, the sequence of events George Whitman would experience seemed impossible to imagine in the fall of 1861. Almost as unlikely was the transformation of Whitman's poetry. Emerson's prediction that *Leaves of Grass* marked the "beginning of a great career" would prove to be correct. The gaudy emerald-green volume of poems first written in 1855 and revised during the next four decades would launch one of the most remarkable careers in American literary history. It would permanently alter what poetry could be, what it could look and sound like, what it could discuss and signify.

Endowing that poetry with meaning, however, was the Civil War. The war made a significant impact on Whitman's art in *Drum-Taps*, a collection of poems later absorbed into *Leaves of Grass*, and in the nonfiction prose of *Specimen Days* and *Memoranda during the War*, written a decade or so later. More important, it provided an experience bigger than Whitman, bigger than the nation, bigger than poetry itself. It did so, he observed years later, by revealing to him "Some pang of anguish—some tragedy, profounder than ever poet wrote."[35] (See figure 1.6.)

CHAPTER 2

Concord

IN JULY 1862, the erstwhile transcendentalist, author, and former Unitarian minister Moncure Daniel Conway opened the latest issue of the *Atlantic Monthly* to find an article entitled "Chiefly about War-Matters" by a pseudonymous Peaceable Man. At the time, Conway was residing in Concord, having migrated north years ago from that land of mental sloth and moral indolence, the South. He had left the Tidewater well before the war in order to be closer to Emerson, the man he claimed had changed his life when, as a young man bewildered by the course his future should take, he had stumbled upon a single sentence in one of the great man's *Essays*. (Conway was coy about *which* sentence; he never revealed it.)

Like everyone else in the elm-shaded village, he was still upset by the death in May of Henry David Thoreau, the town's irritant and self-proclaimed "chanticleer," who had brashly crowed the wrongs of the smug and complacent townspeople while gradually winning their begrudging affection. According to Bronson Alcott, the kindly, gabby, and famously improvident transcendentalist who lived nearby, Thoreau on his last day alive had been "lying patiently & cheerfully on the bed he would never leave again. He was very weak but suffered nothing & talked in his old pleasant way saying 'it took Nature a long time to do her work but he was most out of the world.'" The naturalist's last words were "Now comes good sailing," followed by two more stripped entirely of syntax: "moose" and "Indian."

Despite Thoreau's wishes, he had been buried in a church ceremony at the insistence of Emerson, whose "sorrow," he said, "was so great he wanted all the world to mourn with him." The mercurial and

FIGURE 2.0
Henry David
Thoreau (1861).
Photograph by
Edward S. Dunshee.
Courtesy Library of
Congress
(LC-USZ61-361).

undisciplined poet William Ellery Channing wrote stanzas to be sung, Alcott read selections from Thoreau's works, and Emerson gave an address that on the surface had little to do with the dead man except for its final stirring passage. "In the Tyrol," he concluded,

> there grows a flower on the most inaccessible peaks of the mountains called "Adelvezia" or "noble purity," it is so much loved by the maidens that their lovers risk their lives in seeking it & are often found dead at the foot of the precipices with the flower in their hands. I think our friend's life was a search for this rare flower, & I know that could we see him now we should find him adorned with profuse garlands of it for none could more fitly wear them.[1]

Concord had lost not only a brilliant prose stylist but also its moral conscience: a town crank who had railed against his fellow citizens'

materialism and had rung the church bells to announce an antislavery speech when both rector and deacon refused. Now, hard on the heels of this communal tragedy came an assault on the probity and rectitude of the village. The attack was upon the author of "Chiefly about War-Matters," whose cognomen, the Peaceable Man, as everyone knew, belonged to none other than Nathaniel Hawthorne, the reclusive genius who lived down the road in an old house he had purchased a decade earlier from Bronson Alcott and recently spent a small fortune refurbishing.

Moncure Conway was apparently the first person in town to read the new issue of the *Atlantic*, and he was deeply unsettled by what seemed to him a series of "terrible editorial comments" that appeared as footnotes to the article. Time and again, the Peaceable Man was scolded, censured, and rebutted for his unpatriotic sentiments by an intrusive and somewhat choleric editor. Although

Hawthorne was close friends with William Ticknor and James Fields, the publisher and editor of the magazine, these editorial intrusions permitted little latitude for interpretation. The point was abundantly clear: Hawthorne did not admit sufficiently of the Union's holy cause. His politics were suspect. He was, the footnotes suggested, a traitor.

Carrying the journal through the streets of town, walking rapidly until he reached Emerson's house, Conway stepped past the picture of exploding Vesuvius and entered Emerson's study, handing the offending matter to his mentor. There was a moment's silence. "Emerson read the censorious notes," Conway later reported, "and quietly said, 'Of course he wrote the footnotes himself.'"[2]

It was Hawthorne's great misfortune to have settled in Concord. Twenty years earlier, when he and Sophia Peabody were newlyweds and so poor that he dared not brush his coat for fear of wearing it out too soon, Hawthorne had set up house in the picturesque town over which Emerson presided, renting the Old Manse, a colonial era home built by Emerson's grandfather and owned by his uncle, dining on peas and squash planted as a house-warming gift by Thoreau, and enjoying an extended honeymoon that lasted until, in 1846, he was rewarded with the position at the Salem Custom House he so memorably described in the introduction to *The Scarlet Letter*. Memories of this happy period had prompted him to purchase the Wayside, a former pig farm on the main road through town, before leaving America in 1853 for a lucrative post as the consul of Liverpool. The position was a political reward for writing a campaign biography for his college friend Franklin Pierce, which had funded seven years abroad, including more than a year in Italy. Returning to New England a wealthy and famous author in 1860, he hoped to spend the rest of his life writing romances in the stillness of his parlor.

But Concord had changed. Even on his first night back in town, when Emerson opened his house and hosted a "strawberry party" to welcome back the illustrious author, Hawthorne could see that the sleepy village had become a hotbed of abolitionism. This wasn't particularly surprising. He had long ago noticed Concord's tendency to follow its famous citizens in such matters and had gently burlesqued the town for its trendy radicalism in the preface to *Mosses from an Old Manse*. "Never before was a poor little country village infested with such a variety of queer, strangely-dressed, oddly behaved mortals," he wrote in 1846, "most of whom took themselves to be important agents of the world's destiny yet were simply bores of a very intense water."[3]

As he had settled into the Wayside, he had realized just how extreme the positions of Emerson, Thoreau, and Alcott had become. Each man seemed to view the impending conflict between North and South as the consummation of millennial reform, the fulfillment of America's destiny to lead the world in moral perfection. Emerson in particular seemed to relish the possibility of war, which he believed would purge the nation of its blot upon the citizens' souls, the moral stain preventing it from achieving its promise as the New Canaan.

And Concord seemed to agree. To Hawthorne's dismay, the town had become the nation's chief exporter of extremism, political upheaval, and uncompromising militancy. No better example illustrated this transformation than the John Brown affair, which had occurred while Hawthorne and his family still resided in England. From afar, he had followed the repercussions of Brown's arrest in 1859. The wild-eyed abolitionist, along with his small but committed band of renegades, had attempted to provoke a slave insurrection by capturing the national

FIGURE 2.2
John Brown (ca. 1846). Smithsonian Institution, National Portrait Gallery.

armory at Harpers Ferry, Virginia. The trial that followed Brown's capture and his subsequent hanging galvanized the nation.

Most people on both sides of the Mason-Dixon line held Brown to be a fanatic, a traitor, a domestic terrorist. But Concord's transcendentalists viewed him as a throwback to militant Puritanism, a brave visionary who refused to compromise his principles. Even before his botched insurrection, Brown had become a potent symbol to Emerson and Thoreau, who believed that his homely utterances achieved an almost scriptural quality, especially his remark that "better a whole generation of men, women and children should pass away by violent death than that one word" of the Golden Rule or the Declaration of Independence "be violated in this country."[4] Henry David Thoreau would deliver an impassioned "Plea for John Brown" in late 1859, shortly before the prisoner was martyred by hanging.

From England, Hawthorne followed these proceedings with growing unease. Thoreau's address didn't rankle him nearly as much as a comment Emerson made during a lecture called "Courage" in Boston on November 7, 1859. The statement, apparently improvised, appeared in the *New York Daily Tribune*, where it created a furor, taking on a life of its own, repeated and revised in newspapers, lectures, and sermons throughout the nation. The comment summed up an attitude widely held by New England intellectuals and abolitionists who wished to draw a stark contrast between themselves and those who remained complicit with the slaveholders' interest. John Brown, proclaimed Emerson before his spellbound audience, was a "Saint, whose fate yet hangs in suspense, but whose martyrdom, if it shall be perfected, will make the gallows as glorious as the cross."[5]

Emerson, it turned out, had cadged these words from his friend and fellow abolitionist Theodore Parker, the preacher at Boston's Twenty-eighth Congregational Society. Parker was a member of the Secret Six, a group of radicals that had covertly funded Brown's misbegotten raid, as was the Concord schoolmaster, Franklin B. Sanborn, who would soon instruct Hawthorne's son. In February 1860, Sanborn arranged to bring Anne and Sarah Brown, two of the executed man's young children, to Concord, where they attended school with Julian Hawthorne and lodged with the Emerson family down the road. Around this time, Hawthorne learned of yet another distressing connection to Brown. Mary Mann, Hawthorne's sister-in-law and the widow of the educational reformer Horace Mann, had resided at the Wayside the previous year, preparing the house for the Hawthorne family's return. In the spring of 1860, when it was feared that Sanborn would be seized by federal

FIGURE 2.3 The Wayside, with appended tower; Nathaniel and Sophia Hawthorne stand in the foreground. Courtesy Concord Free Public Library.

authorities for his involvement in the Brown affair, she had found a hiding place for him in the attic.

All of this troubled Hawthorne more than he had expected. Brown's actions, he felt, begged questions of morality that were too easily obscured by the transcendentalists' lofty rhetoric. How could the man's admirable vision of slavery's wrongs ever justify his murderous actions? Didn't the deaths of soldiers, innocent bystanders, and his own men negate the righteous imperatives Brown felt he represented? And how could responsible thinkers so blithely excuse these consequences? "If Emerson chooses to plant John Brown's gallows on Mount Calvary," Hawthorne grumbled, "the moral and religious sense of mankind will insist on its being placed between the crosses of the two thieves, and not side by side with that of the Savior." Continuing in the same mood, he admitted, "I wish [Emerson] would not say such things, and deem him less excusable than other men; for his apophthegms (though they often have strange life to them) do not so burn and sting his mouth that he is compelled to drop them out of it."[6]

Hawthorne expressed his discomfort with Concord in another way, hiring two local carpenters to modify the house he had purchased a decade earlier from Bronson Alcott. As if to rise above the fractious disarray of American politics, he had the workers construct a "tower room," twenty feet square and modeled on the ancient tower of Villa

Montauto in Tuscany, where the Hawthorne family had vacationed for several memorable months in the summer of 1858. Reachable by a steep ladder and trapdoor, commanding a fine view of the woods and meadows surrounding Concord, the author's "sky-parlour," as he called it, was his escape from the issues of the day.[7] If, as often happened, he glimpsed Alcott or Emerson strolling up the turnpike toward the Wayside, he ascended at once, leaving a message to be imparted by someone else in the family. He was upstairs writing and not to be disturbed.

A week after the firing on Fort Sumter, Hawthorne watched a small company of Concord volunteers march out of town to join what would soon be known as the Army of the Potomac. Like most soldiers and civilians in the North, this group was confident it would return home victorious by autumn. Within months, it became apparent the war would be more violent, costly, and dispiriting than anyone, including the nation's literary class, had initially imagined. James Russell Lowell lost two nephews. Jim Lowell, the poet's namesake, had served with Oliver Wendell Holmes, son of the Boston author, who recalled catching Jim's eye before the start of the Seven Days Battle. The two friends saluted one another and then marched into the conflict. "When next I looked," recalled Holmes, a future Supreme Court justice, "he was gone." Holmes himself was wounded a year and a half after Sumter, shot through the base of his neck. Telegraphs and newspapers conveyed these casualties, prompting Hawthorne to quit reading them. If he was glad about anything, he wrote to a friend one month after the departure of the Concord volunteers, it was that his son "Julian [was] too young" to fight.[8]

The galling thing was that Hawthorne largely *agreed* with the abolitionists. "If we are fighting for the annihilation of slavery," he wrote to his friend Horatio Bridge when the war was but a month old, "it may be a wise object." He added, "The war, strange to say, has had a beneficial effect upon my spirits, which were flagging woefully before it broke out." What energized him was the chance "to share in the heroic sentiment of the time, and to feel I had a country—a consciousness which seemed to make me young again." To his friend the publisher of the *Atlantic*, William D. Ticknor, he more or less agreed with Emerson, who wished for a complete separation between New England and the South. "I spend two or three hours in my sky-parlour, and duly spread a quire of paper on my desk," he reported, promising to "have a new Romance ready by the time New-England becomes a separate nation—a consummation I rather hope for than otherwise."[9]

What Hawthorne found so confoundedly wrongheaded about the Concord abolitionists was their certainty, their self-righteousness, their fanaticism, and their scarcely concealed bloodlust. As a young writer studying Puritan history in order to one day transmute it into fiction, he had been made aware of the danger and mischief created by those who espoused unwavering conviction in their causes. The lesson was personal. Hawthorne's great-great-grandfather John Hathorne had played a prominent role in the Salem witch trials, helping to sentence nineteen innocent people accused of witchcraft to death on Gallows Hill. This ugly incident in New England history was made possible by a man whose moral fanaticism had combined with "the persecuting spirit," as Hawthorne noted in his introduction to *The Scarlet Letter*, to make him "so conspicuous in the martyrdom of the witches, that their blood may fairly be said to have left a stain upon him."[10]

The emphasis on sin and guilt that permeates Hawthorne's greatest tales and romances was the expression of an author who understood human nature as fallen, deeply flawed, in need of restraint. We are *all* young Goodman Brown, his fiction suggests: drawn inexorably to the moral wilderness of evil, fatally susceptible to the forbidden voices in the forest. Long suspicious of the American creed that human life was perfectible, Hawthorne grew increasingly frustrated with the tone of moral superiority he heard in Concord just before and after the start of the war. In his eyes, abolitionists, Republican partisans, and the transcendentalist literary culture in general could all stand to read the inscription his wife, Sophia, had scratched some two decades earlier on a window-pane of the Old Manse: "Man's accidents are God's purposes."

"[T]hough I approve of the war as any man," he confided in 1861, "I don't quite understand what we are fighting for, or what definite result can be expected. If we pummel the South ever so hard, they will love us none the better for it; and even if we subjugate them, our next step should be to cut them adrift." To an English friend, he expanded on this idea: "We are, as you know, at the beginning of a great war—a war, the issue of which no man can predicate." The problem, as Hawthorne saw it, was that

> we seem to have little, or, at least, a very misty idea of what we are fighting for. It depends upon the speaker, and that again, depends upon the section of the country in which his sympathies are enlisted. The Southern man will say, We fight for state rights, liberty, and independence. The middle and Western states-man will avow that he fights for the Union; whilst our Northern and Eastern man will swear that, from the beginning, his only idea was liberty to the Blacks, and the annihilation of slavery.[11]

The start of the war had been refreshing, Hawthorne admitted, but its realities soon grew wearisome. "I wish they would push the war a little more briskly," he feebly joked in late May 1861. The humiliating defeat at Bull Run provoked an even stronger reaction. To James Russell Lowell, he wrote that if the battle "puts all of us into the same grim and bloody humour that it does me, the South had better have suffered ten defeats than won this victory." The death of so many young men troubled him deeply, as did the partisan rhetoric used to justify the bloodshed. "What a terrible amount of trouble and expense," he wrote about the war, "and, after all, I am afraid we shall only variegate [the nation] with blood and dirt."[12]

A lifelong Democrat, Hawthorne complained to Ticknor that the *Atlantic Monthly* had been "getting too deep a black Republican tinge," referring to the term derogatively applied to radical abolitionists. The time was "pretty near at hand when you will be sorry for it. The politics of the Magazine suit Massachusetts tolerably well (and only tolerably) but it does not fairly represent the feeling of the country at large; and it seems to me that it would be good policy to be preparing to respond to another, and wiser, and truer mood of public sentiment."[13]

Offering to correct this misrepresentation, he set out in March 1862 for Washington, where he hoped to examine the war firsthand.

It was still winter when Hawthorne left Concord. A thin layer of ice covered Walden Pond, but as his train traveled south, "the long, dreary January of our Northern year" gave way to warmer weather. By the time he reached New Jersey, "the face of Nature" was "visible through the rents in her white shroud," and in Philadelphia, miraculously, "the air was mild and balmy." "We had met the Spring half-way, in her slow progress from the South," Hawthorne would later write, "and if we kept onward at the same pace, and could get through the Rebel lines, we should soon come to fresh grass, fruit-blossoms, green peas, strawberries, and all such delights of early summer."[14]

He was headed to Washington, the strategic center of the Union. At that time of the year, the city was raw and muddy, unpaved, crowded with lobbyists, overwhelmed by soldiers. "What a city!" wrote Union recruit Elijah Rhodes. "Mud, pigs, negroes, palaces, shanties everywhere." Earlier in the winter, Emerson had traveled to the rough-hewn capital, where he talked politics and military strategy with many of the nation's most powerful men. He had listened to congressional speeches and been introduced to Lincoln, who joked about a lecture he had heard the transcendentalist deliver years earlier. Impressed with the Union's leadership, Emerson nevertheless was dismayed by its philistinism. The congressional library contained "no copy of the 'Atlantic Monthly,'" he noted, "or of the 'Knickerbocker,' none of the 'Tribune,' or 'Times,' or any N.Y. Journal. There was no copy of the 'London Saturday Review' taken, or any other live journal, but the 'London Court Journal,' in a hundred volumes, duly bound."[15]

The city was limited in other ways that Emerson probably didn't notice. According to one reporter, Washingtonians clung to several core beliefs during the spring of 1862: "That McClellan was a heaven-born general, that the army of the Potomac must take Richmond, that the rebellion was nearly crushed, that the rebels were, one and all, villains of the deepest dye, that the North was wholly and altogether in the right, and the South was wholly and altogether in the wrong."[16] These axioms ignored the lamentable facts that, after a year of warfare, the Union had lost more battles than it had won and that Confederate troops, villains or not, seemed poised to overtake the capital.

Into this anxious atmosphere, Hawthorne debarked, settling into a noisy hotel and soon meeting President Lincoln. "I have shaken hands with Uncle Abe," he wrote to his oldest daughter, Una, adding with feigned annoyance that the city was "infested by people who want to exhibit me as a lion." In addition to Lincoln, he would meet the federal army's chief commander, General George B. McClellan, a proud, vain stickler for discipline who was convinced the Republican administration despised him and equally certain the Confederate army outnumbered him two to one. From McClellan's headquarters near the Potomac, Hawthorne traveled to Harpers Ferry, where he visited the arsenal John Brown had briefly occupied in his disastrous campaign three years earlier. At the invitation of Secretary of War William H. Seward, the New York abolitionist and Lincoln cabinet member who in 1850 had argued that there was a "higher law" than even that of the Constitution, he took a steamer to Fort Monroe, where Theodore Winthrop had served before the ill-fated attack at Big Bethel. Hawthorne explained in a letter to his son Julian that, while on board the steamer, he had passed "the frigate Congress, and the three masts of the Frigate Cumberland, sticking out of the water, with a tattered bit of the American flag fluttering from the top of one of them; for you know," he continued, "that she refused to surrender to the Merrimac, and went down with the old flags still flying, and firing her last gun at the enemy after her decks were partly under water. A braver thing was never done; and I only wish I could write a song about it."[17]

Instead of writing a patriotic song, however, Hawthorne was gathering material for one of the most scathing accounts ever written about the war. "Chiefly about War-Matters" began as a contribution to the emerging genre of literary war reportage popularized by Winthrop and others, but it quickly became a subversive critique of the righteous certainty that held sway in the northern press and at after-dinner conversations in Concord. The heart of the essay is a fictional dialogue between a narrator who styles himself a "peaceable man" and an anonymous, pro-war "editor." In footnotes scattered throughout the essay, this editor offers wry, opprobrious commentary on the Peaceable Man's descriptions of the war.

In the opening paragraph, the Peaceable Man confesses that the recent "heart-quake" of war has compelled him, "reluctantly, to suspend the contemplation of certain fantasies, to which, according to my harmless custom, I was endeavoring to give a sufficiently life-like aspect to admit of their figuring in a romance." The phrase *heart-quake* had first appeared in "The Custom-House" introduction to *The Scarlet Letter*, where Hawthorne described his writing as similar to sitting in a dark parlor at night when the soft moonlight poeticizes the familiar household objects. This kind of writing, he claimed, requires an imagined space between the real and ideal, a "neutral territory, somewhere between the real world and fairy-land, where the Actual and the Imaginary may meet, and each imbue itself with the nature of the other."[18]

"Chiefly about War-Matters" chronicles a historic moment when the silvery moonlight of romance has been destroyed by a new reality. Squalid and ugly, this diminished reality emerges in Hawthorne's descriptions of the devastation he saw from the window of his train to Washington, "the deserted houses, unfenced fields, and [the] general aspect of nakedness and ruin" where "the war [has] spoilt what was good." Passing a ragged encampment of men who loiter on the margins of what had formerly been a forest, the Peaceable Man recoils at "the unsightly stumps of well-grown trees, not smoothly felled by regular axe-men, but hacked, haggled, and unevenly amputated, as by a sword." "The carcasses of horses," he quietly notes, "were scattered along the way-side."[19]

These were certainly not the sights described by Theodore Winthrop a year earlier. Nor were they the kind of scenes expected from the most famous retailer of delicate romances and elaborate ambiguities in America. Oliver Wendell Holmes believed Hawthorne's works were known chiefly by "their atmospheric effects, by the blue of his distances, by the softening of every hard outline he touches, by the silvery mist in which he veils deformity and clothes what is common so that it changes to awe-inspiring mystery, by the clouds of gold and purple which are the drapery of his dreams."[20] Holmes's blurry, verbose impressionism managed to suggest just how difficult it was to arrive at meaning in Hawthorne's prose.

Yet there was nothing ambiguous about the prisoners of war Hawthorne described for the *Atlantic*'s readers. He encountered them in the engine house at Harpers Ferry, two dozen men, ragged, filthy, dejected, and detained in the same room where John Brown had been held after his capture in 1859. The coincidence prompts the Peaceable Man to muse on Brown, a "blood-stained fanatic" who had been done no favors by Emerson, "whose happy lips have uttered a hundred golden sentences" but who had gravely erred in celebrating the condemned man. Brown's actions and Emerson's plaudits, Hawthorne implies, had led to precisely this group of Confederate prisoners, "simple, bumpkin-like fellows, dressed in homespun clothes, with faces singularly vacant of meaning," who "had [not] the remotest conception of what they had been fighting for."[21]

The statement about the southern prisoners clearly annoys Hawthorne's fictitious editor. An imaginary descendant of those Puritans who had burned witches and flogged Quakers with gloomy satisfaction, this "editor" was created to emend and censor the Peaceable Man whenever he strayed from orthodox opinion. He first interjects himself after a description of Congress: "We omit several paragraphs here, in which the author speaks of some prominent Members of Congress with a freedom that seems to have been not unkindly meant, but might be liable to misconstruction." In a series of increasingly intrusive footnotes, he sourly questions the author's decorum in describing "the deportment of the President," claiming to omit a passage that "appears to have been written in a benign spirit, and perhaps conveys a not inaccurate impression" of President Lincoln, but that "lacks *reverence*, and it pains us to see a gentleman of ripe age, and who has spent years under the corrective influence of foreign institutions, falling into the characteristic and most ominous fault of Young America."[22]

A jostling match ensues. The Peaceable Man satirizes those who advocate the spiritual benefits of war, ironically asserting, "The atmosphere of the camp and the smoke of the battle-field are morally invigorating.... The enervating effects of centuries of civilization vanish at once, and leave [young soldiers] to enjoy a life of hardship, and the exhilarating sense of danger—to kill men blamelessly, or to be killed gloriously,—and to be happy following out their native instincts of destruction." A recent congressional report had claimed that Confederate soldiers used the skulls of slain northerners to drink from, prompting the Peaceable Man to muse on the Homeric implications of such behavior: "Heaven forgive me for seeming to jest upon such a subject!—only, it is so odd, when we measure our advances from barbarism, and find ourselves just here!"[23]

Here, the editor inserts himself in a comic, blood-curdling misinterpretation: "We hardly expected this outbreak in favor of war from the Peaceable Man; but the justice of our cause makes us all soldiers at heart, however quiet in our outward life. We have heard of twenty Quakers in a single company of a Pennsylvania regiment!"[24]

In addition to the dirty prisoners Hawthorne encountered on his travels, he also came across "a party of contrabands, escaping out of the mysterious depths of Secessia." *Contrabands* referred to slaves who had escaped from their masters and crossed Union lines. General Benjamin F. Butler coined the term in 1861 when a trio of slaves presented themselves for service after the seizure of Fort Monroe. He reasoned that, since slaves were the property of the enemy, they were subject to confiscation. And because they professed loyalty to the Union, they certainly deserved the protection of the government. The formulation was ingenious. It deprived the South of its workforce and, by utilizing contrabands for cooking and other noncombatant jobs, freed up more Union soldiers for fighting. In August 1861, Congress reinforced Butler's case by passing a confiscation act, and by the following spring thousands of slaves were escaping north and dramatically changing the dynamic of the war.

Hawthorne met the group of runaway slaves near Manassas, the railroad junction in northern Virginia where the debacle of Bull Run had occurred. Across the muddy thoroughfare they "trudged forward," every bit as ragged, confused, and frightened as the Confederate soldiers he had met earlier. Unlike those prisoners, however, these men until quite recently had been human livestock. They had been bought, sold, and bred for the sole purpose of engendering others' wealth, their legal status prohibiting them from learning to read and write, buying property, and in some cases even marrying. As the Peaceable Man notes, they walked northward, "rudely...attired,—as if their garb had grown upon them spontaneously," frightened, distrustful, curious about freedom, and perhaps a little in awe at the enormity of their decision to escape.[25]

FIGURE 2.4 Thomas Moran, *Slaves Escaping through the Swamp* (1862).
Courtesy Philbrook Museum of Art, Tulsa, Oklahoma.

FIGURE 2.5
Contrabands.
Courtesy Library of
Congress, Prints and
Photographs Division
(LC-B8171-2594
DLC).

The British journalist Edward Dicey would later claim that Hawthorne had aided these runaways, distributing "food and wine, some small sums of money," and ultimately helping them to find "a train going Northwards." None of this appears in "Chiefly about War-Matters." The Peaceable Man instead is concerned with imagining just how these new citizens, born into slavery and raised to expect no rights, might fit into the Union. "For the sake of the manhood which is latent in them, I would not have turned them back," he admits. But, he confesses, "I felt almost...reluctant, on their own account, to hasten them forward to the stranger's land." The weary group seems to him "not altogether human, but perhaps quite as good, and akin to the fauns and rustic deities of olden times."[26]

Troubling as this last sentence may sound to modern ears, its reference to "fauns and rustic deities" is designed to conjure up a character Hawthorne had introduced in his last romance, *The Marble Faun*. Donatello, the Italian rustic befriended by a coterie of American artists, is said to be the descendant of satyrs, a warm personality whose innocent human nature is a relic from a time before the fall into knowledge. Hawthorne is by no means suggesting that slavery is a form of prelapsarian paradise. His point, rather, is that the contrabands' escape into northern society will certainly result in unforeseeable problems—problems unimagined by the abolitionists, who tended to show little concern for actual black people once they were free. "I felt most kindly toward these poor fugitives," the Peaceable Man acknowledges, "but knew not precisely what to wish in their behalf, nor in the least how to help them."[27]

The encounter would cause Hawthorne (through his thinly disguised narrator) to muse upon slavery's bitter legacy. While a consul in England, he had heard a story he now shared with the *Atlantic*'s readers.

> There is an historical circumstance, known to few, that connects the children of the Puritans with these Africans of Virginia....They are our brethren, as being lineal descendants from the Mayflower, the fated womb of which, in her first voyage, sent forth a brood of Pilgrims upon Plymouth Rock, and, in a subsequent one, spawned slaves upon the Southern soil,—a monstrous birth, but with which we have an instinctive sense of kindred, and so are stirred by an irresistible impulse to attempt their rescue, even at the cost of blood and ruin.

Hawthorne admits that the "character of our sacred ship" might suffer from this revelation, "but we must let her white progeny offset her dark one,—and two such portents never sprang from an identical source before."[28]

There was no factual basis for the *Mayflower* anecdote. Slaves *had* been delivered to Virginia in a ship with that name, but it was not the same vessel that had carried the Pilgrims to the frigid shores of Massachusetts. But Hawthorne's point was that the New World, from its founding, had been linked inextricably to the institution of slavery. The "sacred ship" of America—its providential undertaking, its glorious destiny—was the product of a mixed and tragic history. As a result, the ship of state could redeem its mission and become truly sacred only if "we let her white progeny *offset* her dark one."

Offset is a peculiarly Hawthornean word, obscuring as much as it reveals. At first glance, the statement seems to affirm Hawthorne's Concord neighbors, who asserted that Anglo-American culture would "civilize" the freed slaves, acculturating them into a market economy that values the autonomous worker. But there is something darker, more sardonic, at work here. Hawthorne is hinting that to correct the "monstrous birth" of slavery, a bloodletting among the white population might be necessary. That bloodletting, he suggests, might be as widespread and as horrible as the one already experienced by their dark brethren.

The idea, paradoxically, echoes the prediction of the man he considered disproportionately responsible for the war. With grim and fanatical certitude, John Brown had claimed, "Without the shedding of blood, there is no remission of sins." On the day he was led to the gallows, he handed his guard a hastily scrawled note: "I John Brown am now quite *certain* that the crimes of this *guilty, land: will* never be purged *away;* but with Blood." His prediction would be fulfilled, of course, by the Civil War, something Abraham Lincoln acknowledged in his Second Inaugural Address when he confessed, eloquently and solemnly, his face etched and exhausted by the worries of a prolonged war, that if the Almighty so willed the conflict to "continue, until all the wealth piled by the bond-man's two hundred and fifty years of unrequited toil shall be sunk, and until every drop of blood drawn with the lash, shall be paid by another drawn with the sword,...so it still must be said 'The judgments of the Lord, are true and righteous altogether.'"[29]

That speech was a plea for magnanimity toward the war's close, made at a moment when it appeared increasingly certain the North would prevail. But it was also a theological statement, a recognition that the will of God was unknown and unknowable. The impending northern victory and the restoration of the Union, Lincoln suggested, would not be the final chapter in providential history. "I think my prevalent idea," Hawthorne wrote, bidding farewell to the contrabands, "was that, whoever may be benefited by the results of this war, it will not be the present generation of negroes, the childhood of whose race is now gone forever, and who must henceforth fight a hard battle with the world, on very unequal terms."[30]

Toward the end of "Chiefly about War-Matters," the Peaceable Man cautions his readers: "No human effort, on a grand scale, has ever yet resulted according to the purpose of its projectors." Hawthorne was here repeating the sentiment his wife, Sophia, had scratched into a window at the Old Manse twenty years earlier. Like Lincoln, he was warning his audience against the folly of pretending to understand the intent of an inscrutable divinity. But the essay's factitious editor curtly interjects: "The author seems to imagine that he has compressed a great deal of meaning into these hard, dry pellets of aphoristic wisdom. We disagree with him. The counsels of wise and good men are often coincident with the purposes of Providence: and the present war promises to illustrate our remark."[31]

Although the Peaceable Man concludes by arguing for the need to sympathize with southerners, the editor is given the final word: "We regret the innuendo....The war can never be allowed to terminate, except in the complete triumph of Northern principles.... We should be sorry to cast a doubt on the Peaceable Man's loyalty, but he will allow us to say that we consider him premature in his kindly feelings towards the traitors and sympathizers with treason."[32]

In the early spring of 1862, when Hawthorne traveled south to see the war, no one could yet imagine just how accurate John Brown's prophecy would be. No one could foresee the nation's fields and pastures sodden with blood, the hundreds of thousands of lives expended in an effort to preserve the Union and protect the South, to prove the sanctity of a cause. It is the *Peaceable* Man who anticipates these things, suggesting how the early stages of the war would soon metastasize into a devastating conflict that would require a shift in its moral justification if it were to be sustained.

Before returning to the peaceful, shady streets of Concord, Hawthorne wrote Sophia a note that contradicted the blithe optimism so prevalent in his hometown. "Things and men look better at a distance than close at hand," he confided. "I see no reason to think hopefully of the final result of this war."[33]

Shiloh

HAWTHORNE HAD BEEN in Concord less than two weeks after his trip when the first major battle of 1862 occurred near a tiny log church called Shiloh. The word *shiloh* means "resting place" or "peace"; its name, of unknown origins, is mentioned in the first book of Samuel in the Old Testament. To Scots-Irish settlers in rural southwestern Tennessee, the word presaged the peaceful home in eternity promised by their religion. It foretold the reward for a pious and diligent life that included hard work, uncertain weather, wasting illness, and stunning loss. After the battle, the word became synonymous with Armageddon: a place of desolation so total and overwhelming as to beggar the imagination.

The battle began on April 6—a Sunday—and lasted two days. Lilacs and daffodils were blooming; sparrows darted into fields, gathering material for their nests. The surrounding woods, recalled a private from Arkansas, "would have been a grand place for a picnic, and I thought it strange that a Sunday should have been chosen to disturb the holy calm of those woods." Another survivor commented on how "[b]eautifully clear and calm the Sabbath morning dawned,... the sky was so blue and cloudless, the air so still, and all nature lay smiling so serene and fair in the glad sunshine." Such a day, he added, was like "that whereon the Creator...looked upon the newborn earth, and 'saw everything that He had made, and, behold, it was very good;' a day as if chosen from all its fellows and consecrated to a hallowed quiet, the blessedness of prayer and thanksgiving, praise and worship."[1]

The silence was broken soon after dawn. A morning attack by the Confederates surprised practically everyone in the Union's western army, including Ulysses S. Grant, who had recently been promoted to major general after his victory at Fort Donelson. Grant had sprained his ankle the night before when his horse slipped in the mud and fell on his leg. Having commandeered a fine house overlooking the bluff of the Tennessee River, he was sitting over his Sunday breakfast when the distant jar and shudder of rebel artillery disturbed his eating. Rising from the table with difficulty, he hobbled down a path on crutches and boarded a steamer that waited by the mansion's wharf.

He would become famous during the war for his implacable calm, for that air of preternatural tranquility that remained untouched and inviolate during the fiercest battle. Yet a faint tremor of panic now cracked his outward serenity. Thousands of Union soldiers had already fled the scene of battle. They huddled in terror along the embankment of the Tennessee River, where their escape had been blocked. Most of these men, Grant later wrote, "would have been shot where they lay, without resistance, before they would have taken muskets and marched to the front to protect themselves." In a terse letter, the major general ordered an officer whose troops remained on the wrong side of the Tennessee: "If you will get upon the field, leaving all your baggage on the east bank of the river, it will be a move to our advantage, and possibly save the day for us. The rebel force is estimated at over 100,000 men."[2]

As Grant scribbled this order, his frightened infantry fought as best they could. Unable to see more than a few feet through the heavy pall of smoke, some fired upon their own men. A federal regiment lined up to face the rebels, although it had not been issued ammunition. Within the epic battle were countless personal tragedies. A member of the Second Iowa, his arm torn from his shoulder by exploding artillery, jumped up from where he had been knocked back and yelled, "Here, boys! here!" before fainting.[3] Closer to the fighting was a dense thicket, a copse of trees matted with underbrush, where the wounded were carried and told to wait until they could be transported to the field hospital. Trees and foliage, briar and brush caught fire from the artillery, and more than a hundred men were incinerated (see figure 3.1).

In one day, the battle at Shiloh rendered those of Big Bethel and Bull Run quaint and obsolete. It prefigured battles to come in the next three years of civil war as well as in the bloody century that followed. Improvised military maneuvers and mechanized killing made the battle seem modern, but mainly it was the sheer scale and size that were new. Americans had been appalled by the combined death toll of 900 at Bull Run, sickened by the thousands of casualties at Wilson's Creek. But the

FIGURE 3.1 Chromolithograph of *Battle of Shiloh* (1888), by Thure de Thulstrup.

statistics that emerged from Shiloh, the casualties whose names soon appeared in newspapers surrounded by heavy black borders, were of another magnitude altogether. Roughly 100,000 soldiers fought in the battle, with one in four killed, wounded, or taken prisoner. More young men were killed in that single day than had been killed in the previous year combined.

In his *Memoirs*, Grant bluntly admitted that Shiloh forced him to give "up all idea of saving the Union except by complete conquest." Until that battle, he had "believed that the rebellion against the Government would collapse suddenly and soon, if a decisive victory could be gained over any of its armies." His particular genius as a military strategist was to realize that the troops he sent into combat were expendable, interchangeable, like the parts of a factory-made rifle. Although sensitive and humane, he had nevertheless discovered a new reality: company after company of soldiers might be sent to face enemy artillery, their bodies falling in windrows ("like grass before the scythe," according to a Union captain), in order to secure victory. When an officer, sickened by the day's casualties, asked Grant about his plans for a retreat at the end of the first day, the general replied, "Retreat? No! I propose to attack at daylight and whip them."[4]

Even William Tecumseh Sherman, who served under Grant and shared his willingness to use all resources necessary to defeat the foe, seemed chastened by the outcome of Shiloh. "The sights of that battlefield ought to cure anybody of war," he recalled years later, clinically describing them in order to prove his point: "Wounded men with mangled legs and arms and heads half shot off," "surgeons saw[ing] off legs and arms on outdoor tables."[5]

By the end of the first day at Shiloh, the battlefield was so thick with the dead, so carpeted with torn and discolored bodies that swelled and turned black in the heat, that in some places it was impossible to walk without stepping on a corpse. Bodies were sprawled in every conceivable position, arms and legs flung awkwardly, jackets and shirts clawed open as dying soldiers looked to see where they had been shot. A strange stillness had settled on their faces. Many looked upward, eyes still open, as if wishing to confront the afterlife as directly and frankly as possible. An hour or so after twilight, a torrential rain began to fall.

On April 10, three days after the Battle of Shiloh, Abraham Lincoln issued his second national proclamation. The first had followed the defeat at Bull Run and had called for a "day of national humiliation and prayer." Shocked by the catastrophe, Lincoln had emphasized the need to "acknowledge and revere the Supreme Government of God; to bow in humble submission to his chastisements; to confess and deplore their sins and transgressions in the full conviction that the fear of the Lord is the beginning of wisdom." The second proclamation delivered an entirely different message. It proposed a day of thanksgiving following the "signal victories" at Shiloh and Forts Henry and Donelson, each of which had been crucial to "suppressing an internal rebellion." Like the Puritan leaders of old, Lincoln exhorted the "People of the United States" "at their next weekly assemblages in their accustomed places of public worship" to "especially acknowledge and render thanks to our Heavenly Father for these inestimable blessings."[6]

One of those who complied was Ralph Waldo Emerson, who agreed to give a lecture titled "Moral Forces...Read on a Fast Day, Appointed by the President of the United States" exactly one week after the Battle of Shiloh. The address was delivered before a packed audience at the Twenty-eighth Congregational Society at Boston's Music Hall, a spacious building with vaulted ceilings, two levels of balconies, and a capacity of well over 1,000 people. During the 1850s, the notorious abolitionist preacher Theodore Parker had made the Music Hall famous with his fiery sermons attacking the sins of chattel slavery.

Anticipating Emerson's talk after Shiloh, he had said of "the moral universe" that "from what I see I am sure it bends toward justice."[7]

During the second spring of the Civil War, the Music Hall was in the process of consolidating Boston's history of political radicalism with its growing sense of cultural superiority. The largest organ ever built in the United States, a 5,474-pipe instrument commissioned in Germany and "covered with carved statues, busts, masks, and figures in the boldest relief," was in the process of installation.[8] When it was played, the earth trembled. Emerson stood before this ornate instrument as he began to speak, hoping to effect a moral earthquake in his listeners.

He had not come quickly or easily to the abolitionist cause. In his most famous essay, "Self-Reliance," published in 1841, he had fulminated against social activists who wore their causes on their sleeves and ignored the less glamorous forms of charity closer to home:

> If an angry bigot assumes this bountiful cause of Abolition, and comes to me with his last news from Barbadoes, why should I not say to him, "Go love thy infant; love thy woodchopper: be good-natured and modest: have that grace; and never varnish your hard, uncharitable ambition with this incredible tenderness for black folk a thousand miles off. Thy love afar is spite at home." Rough and graceless would be such greeting, but truth is handsomer than the affectation of love. Your goodness must have some edge to it—else is none.[9]

Behind this bristling condemnation of the abolitionist cause rested Emerson's belief that the moral regeneration of the individual was a precondition for social improvement. One simply could not hope to reform the world before reforming oneself. His conviction stemmed from personal experience. Emerson believed that we live in a mundane world, filled with the quotidian and marked by the calendar. Borrowing his terminology from Coleridge, he called this stultifying condition of everydayness the Understanding. He knew, however, that on occasions we are privy to an unpredictable but intense spiritual existence, an ecstatic, light-filled state that he termed the Reason.

Emerson described these moments of exultant being as the highest aspiration imaginable—the sole rationale for our existence. Reason, he wrote in his journal, catapulted us to "the top of our being," so that "we are pervaded, yea, dissolved by the Mind." Compared to this soul-ravishing experience, the cause of abolition appeared to Emerson, at least in the early 1840s, as partial and fragmentary. To protest slavery was a laudable pursuit, but one that mistook causes for effects and was therefore doomed to failure unless it was preceded by the moral regeneration of the individual.[10]

History radicalized him. A series of disastrous political concessions and legal decisions during the 1850s revealed all too clearly that the liberation of the soul would arrive less quickly than he had hoped. The Fugitive Slave Law, mandating the return of runaway slaves who had escaped to free states, particularly shocked his sense of justice. Hard on the heels of this execrable law came the infamous Kansas-Nebraska Bill of 1854, which allowed all new territories north of 36 degrees 30 minutes to choose to become slave states. In rapid succession came the beating of Massachusetts senator Charles Sumner by the southern congressman Preston Brooks, the eruption of violence in Kansas between pro- and antislavery settlers, the *Dred Scott* decision, John Brown's attack on Harpers Ferry and his subsequent hanging, and the secession of the South following Abraham Lincoln's election. As the nation spun out of control in this dizzying flurry of events, Emerson increasingly directed his focus to tangible political action, aligning himself especially with radical abolitionists.

His journals throughout the 1850s are interspersed with expressions of outrage. Sickened by the "filthy enactment" of the Fugitive Slave Law—a law he found hard to believe had been "made in the 19th Century, by people who could read and write"—he defiantly announced, "I will not obey it, by God." As political tensions escalated, he urged the dismantling of the Union in order to protect the freedom valued by the North. Slavery was a communicable disease, a contagion: "We intend to set & to keep a *cordon sanitaire* all around the infected district," he wrote, "& by no means suffer the pestilence to spread." In more dire moods, he believed it was too late: the virus had already contaminated the body politic. To Oliver Wendell Holmes, whose wit and verbal facility he admired but whose conservative politics he labored to change, he argued, "And for the Union with Slavery no manly person will suffer a day to go by without discrediting disintegrating & finally exploding it. The 'union' they talk of is dead & rotten, the real union, that is, the will to keep & renew union, is like the will to keep & renew life, & this alone gives any tension to the dead letter."[11]

Publicly, he was no less adamant in his condemnation of slavery. "I do not see how a barbarous community and a civilized community can constitute one state," he announced to audiences throughout the North. His conclusion was similar to Lincoln's in the "House Divided" speech: "I think we must get rid of slavery, or we must get rid of freedom." In martial tones that recalled the brisk energy of his inspired early essays, Emerson portrayed the recent history of political compromise as morally repugnant and contrary to logic. "We have attempted to hold together two states of civilization: a higher state, where labor and the tenure of land and the right of suffrage are democratical; and a lower state, in which the old military tenure of prisoners[,] of slaves, and of power and land in a few hands, makes an oligarchy; we have attempted to hold these two states of society under one law." The nation had split between Reason and Understanding; the cause of emancipation was now a transcendental cause.[12]

When southern forces fired on Fort Sumter, Emerson responded as though the slumbering volcano had at last awakened. Proclaiming the war "a great Revolution," he viewed the outburst of violence as a cosmic battle between good and evil, a clash over the soul of America, "enacting the sentiment of the Puritans, and the dreams of young people 30 years ago." The spirit of national purpose that followed Sumter's fall seemed the fulfillment of a long-dormant spiritual militancy, the awakening into a new era. "The times are dark," he admitted in his journal, "but heroic. The war uplifts us into generous sentiments. We do not often have a moment of grandeur in these hurried, slipshod times."[13]

His mood was ferocious and bittersweet. "Though practically nothing is so improbable or perhaps impossible a contingency for me," he remarked in 1862, when almost sixty years age, "yet I do not wish to abdicate so extreme a privilege as the use of the sword or bullet." In "Fortune of the Republic," an address delivered a year later, he declared with scarcely concealed envy, "It is the young men of the land, who must save it. It is they to whom this wonderful hour, after so many weary ages, dawns: the second Declaration of Independence, the proclaiming of liberty, land, justice, and a career for all men, and honest dealings with other nations."[14]

For Emerson, the conflict was holy. "'Tis vain to say that the war was avoidable by us, or, that both sides are in the wrong," he instructed audiences. "The difference between the parties is eternal,—it is the difference between moral and immoral truth." To one of his earliest biographers, James Elliot Cabot, he expressed his belief that "we shall redeem America for all its sinful years since the century began." Convinced the war was a fundamental contest between right and wrong, Emerson asserted that there could be "no durable peace, no sound Constitution, until we have fought the battle & the rights of man are vindicated."[15]

Despite this apparent certitude, the winter of 1862 had been difficult. The initial enthusiasm for war, followed by a renewed commitment to defeat the rebels after Bull Run, had begun to sour as the weather grew colder. To make matters worse, guerrilla warfare had become a feature of the age. Rebel sharpshooters targeted officers. A man might be in the process of drinking his morning cup of coffee or shaving before a shard of mirror when a bullet would abruptly conclude his action. "I don't know any other way to subdue [southern sympathizers]," wrote an Indiana sergeant late in December, except "to shoot them or hang them up and confiscate their property." An anonymous soldier in the Sixth Iowa Infantry agreed: "the only way to get the country rid of these sneaking devils," he wrote in December 1861, "is to...shoot them down where ever we find them."[16]

Emerson never entirely lost faith in the ultimate correctness of the Union cause, but he did believe the war was being mismanaged. The visit to Washington in January had done little to change his mind. There, he had lectured at the austere, crenellated Smithsonian Institution to some success, urging the immediate emancipation of the slaves as the surest way to turn around the war. But the trip did little to assuage his doubts about the Union's military leadership, especially the overly cautious Democratic general George B. McClellan, who refused to attack the entrenched Confederates near Richmond throughout the war's first year for fear of having too few men. McClellan's timidity would soon provoke a coaxing, cajoling, pleading letter from Lincoln that was a masterpiece of restrained impatience: "I beg to assure you," wrote the exasperated president, "that I have never written you, or spoken to you, in greater kindness of feeling than now, nor with a fuller purpose to sustain you, so far as in my most anxious judgment, I consistently can. *But you must act.*"[17]

Emerson's efforts to keep up his spirits had been made more difficult by the deteriorating health of Henry David Thoreau, his disciple and friend. Always more at home in the woods than the parlor, Thoreau was bedridden that winter. He spat blood and, when feeling up to it, wrote in his journal. To cheer him, Emerson journeyed each day to Walden Pond, where he passed the tiny cabin where the iconoclastic Thoreau had spent two years as an experiment in transcendental self-reliance, and returned with a report on the condition of the ice. A week before the battle at Shiloh, he had walked across the pond and "fancied it was late in the season to do thus; but Mr. Thoreau told me, this afternoon, that he had known the ice to hold to the 18th of April." The date had special resonance for both men; it commemorated the Concord battle that began the Revolutionary War, and it marked the departure of Concord's contingent of Union recruits a year earlier. A week later,

Emerson glumly recorded that "the cold days have again arrested the melting of the ice, & yesterday I walked again across the middle of Walden, from one side to the other."[18]

He was experiencing that scourge of New England: spring fever. Much of the important writing of antebellum America—Emerson's *Nature* and *Essays: First Series*, Thoreau's *Walden*, and Whitman's *Leaves of Grass*—was infused with a burgeoning sense of new growth, a rebirth of possibility. "[T]he coming in of spring," Thoreau marveled toward the end of *Walden*, "is like the creation of Cosmos out of Chaos and the realization of the Golden Age." The springtime exuberance of American Romanticism came in part from its contact with German and British Romanticism. It burgeoned as American authors translated religious fervor into a national literature. But it was also and ultimately a very human response to the hard, bitter, and protracted winters of New England.[19]

Upset by Thoreau's final illness and discouraged by the excruciating pace of the war, Emerson longed for warmer weather and disparaged himself for lacking the patience to wait for spring. In an April journal entry, he attempted to transform the dreary New England weather into an emblem of northern superiority:

> Spring. Why complain of the cold slow spring? [T]he bluebirds don't complain, the blackbirds make the maples ring with social cheer & jubilee, the robins know the snow must go & sparrows with prophetic eyes that these bare osiers yet will hide their future nests in the pride of their foliage. And you alone with all your six feet of experience are the fool of the cold of the present moment, & cannot see the southing of the sun. Besides the snowflake is freedom's star.[20]

He stressed these sentiments in the lecture commemorating Lincoln's proclamation of thanksgiving. Emerson was speaking the coded language of emancipation when he extolled the "blackbird" who could "make the maples ring with...jubilee." It was the North's duty, he would soon assert, to provide the necessary climate for freedom's joyous hymning.

Shiloh was never directly referred to in "Moral Forces." In his haste to produce the lecture, Emerson borrowed heavily from other addresses he was then giving.[21] But the battle was obliquely referenced when he asked his audience to "take thankful remembrance of the late public events," including "the deliverance of the Country from formidable domestic danger." This was a rosy assessment; Shiloh had not represented "deliverance" in any way. But Emerson's message was less concerned with specific victories or losses than with the idea that triumphs and defeats were part of larger forces, a grand, purposeful narrative that tended inexorably toward progress, liberty, and the realization of the self. Only as part of this larger story did Emerson propose "to see how the laws of the universe are justified in what we call our prosperity."[22]

A crucial subplot in this account was slavery. Theodore Parker had died two years earlier in Florence from tuberculosis, but his Twenty-eighth Congregational Society remained radically abolitionist in its sympathies. Julia Ward Howe and William Lloyd Garrison, two of the movement's most prominent spokespersons and activists, sat in the audience with rapt attention as Emerson spoke. "Things point the right way," he announced to his receptive listeners, noting with evident pleasure the recent congressional bill that would destroy "servitude in the District of Columbia" and that "only waits the signature of the President." Other developments were equally heartening. "An army of slaves is already escaped" from the South, and these "contraband" fugitives had proved enormously helpful in providing the Union army with information about Confederate troop placements and numbers, sometimes even serving as scouts through the unfamiliar swamps and wilderness of the South.[23]

These events pointed to a larger power, Emerson asserted, a power that could best be discerned when a person stepped away from the present moment, retreated from daily concerns, and surveyed the larger pattern of actions from a critical distance. Viewed through this cosmic perspective, personal triumphs evaporated into comparative insignificance. Even pain contributed something important to the progress of the universe. Southern secession had made all this abundantly clear: "At last," Emerson explained, "the slaveholder puts his own hand to the work" of emancipation, "declares war on the free states, and, in a moment, crowns the work which had languished so long...and breaks to pieces, once [and] for all, the doleful nuisance which had cursed this quarter of the globe."[24]

In many ways, it was the private quarrel about winter all over again, only this time applied to politics and morality. Those too anxious for the regenerative warmth of spring, too eager for a quick and decisive victory, had viewed affairs from too narrow a perspective: the "six feet of experience" displayed a fundamental distrust of the large yet benevolent forces inexorably at work in the cosmos. Those forces *were* at work, silent and invisible, always tending toward good. How else, Emerson asked, could one explain the "crystalliz[ation of] the North into a unit" following Sumter? How else could one make sense of the deterioration of slavery, evident in the thousands of slaves fleeing northward? "[M]y point," Emerson explained, "is that the movement of the whole machine, the motive force of life, and of every particular of life, is moral; that the world stands on thoughts, and not iron, or cotton; and the iron of iron, the fire of fire, the ether and source of all elements, is, moral forces."[25]

The world, Emerson continued, was profoundly divided between prosaic "facts" and a rarefied realm of "the Necessary, the True, the Good, or, what we call absolute truth." It followed that the goal for individuals was a conversion experience that would free them from the shackles of "facts" and irradiate their consciousness with the True and Good. "Even in war, which is the organization of brute force," Emerson explained, "moral force is immensely the stronger of the two." It was a sublime weapon, a "good cause" that "commanded the hands" and "fire[d] our soul[s] into service." War's slaughter actually provided an example of selfless action that ultimately ennobled society. "[T]he coldest of us must believe that the poetry of war, the picture, before the regiments engaged, of the general brandishing his sword, is too much for prudence, or reasoning, or terror: down goes discretion and arithmetic, and the youth who was lately fresh from a school makes a leap into the thick of bayonets."[26]

The question of human suffering did not come up in Emerson's address. He made no reference to the wounds caused by artillery designed to explode overhead and rain jagged shrapnel upon defenseless men, nor did he mention the wounded, immobile men at Shiloh who had called for help as the trees around them burst into flames. Confederate soldiers were "sure to cry out when they are hurt, and to find sympathy," Emerson conceded. But this was but a "friction which cannot be avoided," an unavoidable "fact" that could never thwart "the order of things in nature, which evermore brings out the right."[27]

These words, like the rest of his lecture, were greeted warmly by Emerson's audience. They would serve as an inoculation against the horrors to come, a defense against war's grim calculus. "I delight in tracing these wonderful powers,—the electricity and gravity of the human world," Emerson exclaimed toward the end of his address, his baritone filling the hall, his hands clasped before him, his eyes blazing. The "power of persistence, of enduring defeat, and of gaining victory by defeats," he said, "is one of these forces, which never loses its charm."[28]

He carried with him the thunderous applause, held it like a precious gem as he returned by train to Concord and to the close and stuffy sickroom of Thoreau, who would die in less than a month. A note in his journal indicated his mood: "Heard the purple finch this morning, for the first time this season." Spring had arrived, as it was bound to—just in time, he hoped, for the northern victories that would emancipate the slaves. Three days after his talk, however, he observed with some disappointment, "The ice not broken up on the pond this very warm day." He then switched topics. A Concord resident "tells me," he noted contentedly, "that the expenditure of gunpowder in war does not compare to the amount in peace."[29]

About 150 miles away from Concord, in a bright, yellow Berkshires farmhouse that would soon be sold so that its occupants could join the crowded streets and dinning populace of New York City, Herman Melville was preoccupied with the meaning of a war that had grown in scope and lethality with the arrival of spring vegetables and warmer weather. Aiding him in this project was a heated but private argument with Emerson, whose collections of essays he had recently purchased in a binge of book buying and was now in the process of rereading with a characteristic mixture of respect and indignation as he sat in an old rocking chair on the piazza he had built a decade earlier (see figure 3.2).

His response to Emerson had always been complex. It dated back to the late 1840s, when Melville had first burst upon America's nascent cultural scene as the bestselling author of two books about his travels to Polynesia. The young Melville, born of prominent New York families that had fallen on hard times, impulsively had signed up as a mate on the whaler *Acushet*, bound for the Pacific Ocean, when he was twenty-one years old. A year and a half later, in July 1842, he jumped ship in the Marquesas Islands and lived for three weeks with a group of natives called the Typees, providing himself with enough material to spin out several book-length "memoirs" when he returned. Melville was handsome, humorous, intense. Like a cloud flitting past the sun, he could change from buoyant spirits to bitter melancholy in the space of a minute. He had an insatiable hunger to read and learn and, most of all, write. "Lord, when shall we be done growing?" he once asked Hawthorne. "As long as we have anything more to do, we have done nothing." This insatiable curiosity, no doubt, prompted him to attend Emerson's lecture in New York in 1849. "Say what they will," he asserted the next day to Evert A. Duyckinck, his friend and literary mentor, after hearing the discourse "Mind and Manners in the Nineteenth

FIGURE 3.2 Herman Melville (1861).

Century," "he's a great man." Duyckinck apparently expressed some reservations about this estimate, because Melville defended Emerson with even greater energy in his next letter: "frankly, for the sake of argument, let us call him a fool;—then had I rather be a fool than a wise man."[30]

As with the extravagant praise he lavished several years later in "Hawthorne and His Mosses," Melville's appreciation of Emerson was enhanced by his ability to see a glimmer of himself in the other writer. "I love all men who dive," he said about Emerson in 1849. "Any fish can swim near the surface, but it takes a great whale to go down stairs five miles or more." Like the inscrutable leviathan Melville would soon immortalize (though without *Moby-Dick*'s menace), Emerson plumbed unfathomable depths. He belonged to history's "corps of thought-divers"—though his optimism, Melville added, also made him one of those "cracked right across the brow."[31]

It was Emerson's unwavering optimism that eventually caused Melville to modify his estimate. On closer inspection, Emerson didn't distinguish or discriminate. His cheerful vision of the world applied equally to providential intention, the natural world, and to human nature itself—and about these last two, Melville had experienced enough to know better. Within a year, his opinion of Emerson took an abrupt, almost savage turn. In 1851, with the publication of *Moby-Dick*, Melville leveled one of the most penetrating critiques of Emersonian self-reliance ever written in his portrait of the monomaniacal, quest-obsessed Ahab. Emerson's crack-browed optimism was even more mercilessly burlesqued six years later in the comic character of Mark Winsome, who appears in Melville's last full-length novel, *The Confidence Man.*

What prompted Herman Melville, age forty-two and in the prime of his intellectual life, to purchase and reread Emerson's *Essays* around the time of the Battle of Shiloh is one of the more poignant episodes in American literary history. Melville had been chastened, if not humbled, by the commercial and critical failure of his last three novels, especially the vitriolic reviews that accompanied *Moby-Dick*, the book he was certain would herald his entry into the pantheon of eternal writers, such as Shakespeare and Dante. "The calm, the coolness, the silent grass-growing mood in which a man *ought* always to compose," he complained to Hawthorne in 1851, "that, I fear, can seldom be mine. Dollars damn me.... What I feel most moved to write, that is banned,—it will not pay. Yet, altogether, write the *other* way I cannot. So the product is a final hash, and all my books are botches."[32]

By 1862, the once-exuberant young man, intoxicated by language and a sense of his own possibilities, had settled into that most trite of characters: the middle-aged disappointment. Harried by financial troubles and afflicted by what some contemporaries considered a fit of insanity, he now embarked on the excruciating project of reinventing himself. Which meant, in his case, becoming a poet.

Melville's turn to poetry has been portrayed as a retreat into a smaller and less demanding form. It was in fact an example of a Promethean literary ambition once more asserting itself. Poetry was accorded enormous cultural prestige in mid-nineteenth-century America; as one literary historian notes, "Of the three major fictive genres, poetry alone was held in anything like high regard" during the period immediately preceding the Civil War. Moreover, the voracious public appetite for war writing provided unprecedented opportunities for a talented (if now eclipsed) author who hoped to reestablish himself in the literary arena. Melville's efforts to become the poet laureate of the war was his final bid to achieve enduring stature in the American republic of letters, to reclaim the cultural significance he had once enjoyed with the bestselling books *Typee* and *Omoo* in the 1840s, and to secure for himself a legacy as the American Shakespeare as he had prophesied in "Hawthorne and His Mosses."[33]

Which is why, in the spring of 1862, he was educating himself by reading the most famous discussion of poetic theory ever written by an American, Emerson's essay "The Poet," the same work Whitman had used as a blueprint for his own career almost a decade earlier. The essay is less a call for the emergence of a national poet (as it is often described) than a quirky hybrid of aesthetic theory and metaphysical speculation. Emerson is particularly concerned to discover the habits, moods, and qualities of insight that lead to enduring poetry. In the famous "transparent eye-ball" passage of *Nature*, he had described a rarefied form of artistic experience when he proclaimed, "I am nothing; I see all." This experience of pure, exultant vision was explored more searchingly in "The Poet," where it was identified as the high point of literary creation. In Emerson's anatomy of the poetic process, insight and expression merged, became one and the same thing, so that the poet's "intellect [becomes] where and what it sees."[34]

This fusion occurred, Emerson suggested, because the beneficent laws of the universe flowed through poet and matter alike, expressing themselves in language and in nature. As Emerson had put it in the earlier essay "Art," the artist "should know that the landscape has beauty for his eye because it expresses a thought which to him is good, and this because the same power which sees through his eyes is seen in that spectacle."[35] The God in man viewed the God in nature; godlike, Emerson claimed, man then translated that vision into poetry.

The battle at Shiloh would do nothing to challenge these assumptions directly. It was too far away, too remote and unimaginable for those sitting in their comfortable studies on a brisk New England spring morning. But Shiloh would begin the slow and gradual process of raising troublesome questions that could no longer be answered by transcendentalist theory. What happened to poetic vision, for instance, when nature became a charnel house? Emerson's essay, written nearly two decades earlier, offered little guidance. If "[r]eaders of poetry see the factory-village, and the railway, and fancy that the poetry of the landscape is broken up by these," he remarked, "the poet sees them fall within the great Order." The visionary artist was capable of harmonizing ugly scenes because he saw them as part of a larger divine purpose—as precisely those "moral forces" Emerson had extolled in his speech before the Twenty-eighth Congregational Society. Whether gazing at railroad depots or sublime wilderness, factory villages or the ice-encrusted Walden Pond, poets organized all "within the great Order" because they were imbued with a "sense that the evils of the world are such only to the evil eye."[36]

The statement is a landmark in the history of vision. Serenely confident, it proclaims evil as a simple problem of perspective, a moral astigmatism. Reading this passage in 1862 elicited an angry outburst from Melville. In the margin of his newly acquired copy of the *Essays*, he wrote, "What does the man mean? If Mr. Emerson traveling in Egypt should find the plague-spot come out on him—would he consider that an evil sight or not? And if evil, would his eye be evil because it seemed evil to his eyes, or rather to his sense using the eye for instrument?"[37]

At stake here was the venerable question about the nature of evil—a question extensively explored by Melville and ignored, he believed, by Emerson. What made the quarrel urgent in the spring of 1862 was news of the bloodiest battle in U.S. history. Was evil immanent in natural phenomena? Did it manifest itself, for instance, in the "plague-spot" of war? Or was it an illusion, the "friction" Emerson described in "Moral Forces," that resided in the unenlightened mind? Could it be, as Emerson suggested, simply a form of blindness?

Melville's outburst pointed to another conundrum. Nature's raw power, its flagrant disregard for human interests and aspirations, made it an especially awkward guarantor of meaning. Seen from afar, the crevasses of Maine or the torrents of Niagara Falls hinted at America's glorious expectations. Up close, however, they bespoke frostbite, drowning: powerful forces of disintegration instead of harmony. In "The Poet," Emerson assured his readers that the true artist "names the thing because he sees it, or comes one step nearer to it than any other." Melville momentarily ceded ground. "This is admirable," he scrawled in the margin, "as many other thoughts of Mr. Emerson's are." Then, as if reconsidering, he continued: "His gross and astonishing errors & illusions spring from a self-conceit so intensely intellectual and calm that at first one hesitates to call it by its right name. Another species of Mr. Emerson's errors, or rather blindness, proceeds from a defect in the region of the heart."[38]

A year into the Civil War, then, Melville believed that Emerson's long-standing faith in moral forces posed a dangerous threat to the nation. It allowed Americans to understand the slaughter of young men as a mere footnote to the higher law. His quarrel with the transcendentalist, which he shared with Hawthorne, was not so much about whether God inscribed his will in nature but how that will was to be interpreted. It was a quarrel less over what kind of God allowed events like Shiloh to happen than about the damage caused by individuals certain about their reading of divine intention.

Melville would convey these concerns in the best poem ever written about the battle—"Shiloh. A Requiem (April, 1862)"—an elegy to the young men who died there, a funeral hymn for an entire culture in the habit of seeing itself through nature:

> Skimming lightly, wheeling still,
>   The swallows fly low
> Over the field in clouded days,
>   The forest-field of Shiloh—
> Over the field where April rain
> Solaced the parched ones stretched in pain
> Through the pause of night
> That followed the Sunday fight
>   Around the church of Shiloh—
> The church so lone, the log-built one,
> That echoed to many a parting groan
>   And natural prayer
>   Of dying foemen mingled there—
> Foemen at morn, but friends at eve—
>   Fame or country least their care:
> (What like a bullet can undeceive!)
>   But now they lie low,
>   While over them the swallows skim,
>   And all is hushed at Shiloh.[39]

There is a stunned, dreamlike quality to Melville's poem. The quiet is sustained by its seemingly endless sentence and the repetitive silence of the central image, the swallows. Recalling a different battle in Tennessee, a Union soldier recalled how, amid the clatter of artillery, flocks of sparrows from a nearby thicket of cedars "fluttered and circled above the field in a state of utter bewilderment."[40] Here, the birds are more reminiscent of a calm, static landscape painting; their tranquil flight intensifies the eerie aftermath of battle. Melville almost certainly had in mind the lines of solace from the Gospel of Luke, in which Christ asks, "Are not five sparrows sold for two farthings, and not one of them is forgotten before God?...Fear not therefore: ye are of more value than many sparrows." And Melville may have been thinking of the manner in which swallows appear in Renaissance paintings of the incarnation and the resurrection.[41] The poem conveys the hope of a redemptive afterlife for those who were sacrificed for their country.

Yet if these wheeling swallows guide our thoughts upward, they also divert our gaze from the bodies below, "parched ones stretched in pain." A script for the mind's eye, "Shiloh" subtly directs our focus on the sky, away from the battle. By doing so, the poem ensures that the war remains an abstraction, an idea. This strategy of abstraction emerges from Melville's understanding about the difficulty—the near-impossibility—of presenting modern combat through the conventional medium of mid-nineteenth-century poetry. The Battle of Shiloh doesn't fit his culture's expectation of appropriate poetic subject matter. The lone church and sodden pasture, transformed into killing fields and an impromptu crematorium, raised silent questions about the capacity of conventional poetry to grapple with senseless carnage.

How to describe this emerging form of warfare eventually became a central preoccupation for many writers. Whitman's comment that "the real war will never get into books" expresses his recognition that existing literary forms, even his own capacious and seemingly inexhaustible free verse, were not up to the task of conveying the suffering and bloodshed. In an 1862 issue of the *Atlantic Monthly*, the second-generation transcendentalist John Weiss worried whether "wars stimulate, [or] depress the intellectual life of nations." He suggested that "intellectual life begins while the pen is becoming tempered in the fires of a great national controversy...long before the blood-red aurora stains suddenly the midnight sky....Sometimes a people says all that it has in its mind to say, during that comfortless period while the storm is in the air and has not yet precipitated its cutting crystals." The poet and editor Richard Grant White agreed. "It is generally true that great events do not inspire great poems," he wrote. An anonymous writer for the *Atlantic Monthly* lamented that war seemed "to inspire the same rhetoric in every age, and to reproduce the same set of conventional war-images."[42]

Years after the conflict, Melville wondered how best "to speak of the hurricane unchained" that had been the war. For him, the Battle of Shiloh had rendered transcendental philosophy instantly and irrevocably obsolete. It suggested that the brittle veneer of society had begun to crack and flake away. The poem's single, parenthetical reference to the war's violence—"(What like a bullet can undeceive!)"—is precisely *like* a bullet, puncturing the stillness of the scene, awakening the complacent spectator to reconsider the skimming swallows, which represent a special and new form of sorrow: a recognition of the irremediable wilderness inside human beings.[43]

As usual, Melville was a rara avis, an outlier in the literary culture of his time. The Battle of Shiloh produced comparatively little imaginative writing. Later battles produced verses, songs, and even essays that placed readers in the environs of the conflict or that celebrated victory and commemorated the loss of soldiers. But aside from several brief articles and a Confederate song that became famous later in the war and continued in the folk repertoire well into the twentieth century, Shiloh seemed to stun and silence the literary imagination.

John Greenleaf Whittier's "The Watchers" took its cue from the battle, but was characteristically mute about its details. Written in 1862 and appearing a year later in Whittier's *In War Time*, the poem began, like Melville's "Shiloh," with the aftermath of a momentous clash of forces:

> Beside a stricken field I stood;
> On the torn turf, on grass and wood,
> Hung heavily the dew of blood.
>
> Still in their fresh mounds lay the slain,
> But all the air was quick with pain
> And gusty sighs and tearful rain.

Upon this scene of desolation descend "Two angels, each with drooping head / And folded wings," who gaze upon the scene as if it were a grim diorama. The angels epitomize Peace and Freedom, and their ensuing dialogue suggests the opposition of these two concepts. Invoking the name of Theodore Winthrop, Peace laments the fallen soldiers who have sacrificed their lives for an abstract cause. He is coldly rebuffed by Freedom, who is unyielding in his affirmation of the war's justice: "I shun/No strife nor pang beneath the sun,/When human rights are staked and won."[44]

The dialogue neatly encapsulated the conflicting emotions many Americans felt in the spring and summer of 1862, as the rising death toll provoked sorrow for the war's casualties and renewed confidence in the cause for which they had died. Whittier's Freedom articulates an Emersonian faith in a universe governed by moral forces. His Peace speaks to the melancholy consequences of that faith. Whittier, a pacifistic Quaker and stern abolitionist, was less interested in resolving these competing visions than in honoring them. Toward the end of the poem, Peace begs to postpone further killing until the issue of emancipation can be resolved, but Freedom blurts out, "Too late!" " 'Too late!' its mournful echo sighed." Like two startled birds, the angels abruptly ascend, "A rustling as of wings in flight" the only sound. The poem's speaker suddenly hears a voice "round me, like a silver bell":

> "Still hope and trust," it sang; "the rod
> Must fall, the wine-press must be trod,
> But all is possible with God!"[45]

*   *   *

Nearly twenty years would elapse before the Battle of Shiloh was described in a literary work that did not attribute deeper significance or higher causes to the carnage. Ambrose Bierce's classic essay "What I Saw of Shiloh" is still the most chilling description of the mundane horror and relentless indignity of nineteenth-century warfare.

Bierce was not yet twenty when he fought in Tennessee; he had enlisted as a private at the start of the war and was quickly promoted, becoming a first lieutenant by the spring of 1862. His essay doesn't begin with the spare, sardonic irony for which he would later become famous but rather with a confession of the high hopes and idealism he experienced in "those years of youth when I was soldiering!" Remembering the bugle call to battle on that fateful Sunday, Bierce tells us the sound went to his "heart as wine and stir[red] the blood like the kisses of a beautiful woman."[46] (See figure 3.3.)

This high-spirited reminiscence quickly dissolves into bewilderment and revulsion as the wounded are borne on litters past the narrator throughout the night that followed the first day of battle. Nearby, the dead are lined up in rows with their faces covered. Marching in the dark through a swamplike field, Bierce repeatedly trips over men too injured to move out of the way. Despite the torrential rain that drenches them, they beg for water. Dawn brings a new kind of landscape:

FIGURE 3.3 Ambrose Bierce.

"Knapsacks, canteens, haversacks distended with soaked and swollen biscuits, gaping to disgorge, blankets beaten into the soil by rain, rifles with bent barrels or splintered stocks, waist-belts, hats and the omnipresent sardine-box—all the wretched debris of the battle still littered the spongy earth as far as one could see." At one point, Bierce encounters a sergeant still alive but with part of his "brain protrud[ing] in bosses, dropping off in flakes and strings." A private wonders aloud if it would be more merciful to put the wounded man out of his misery, and Bierce answers with numb formality. "I told him I thought not; it was unusual, and too many were looking."[47]

At last, long after sunrise, he enters a dense forest in which a deposit of leaves had produced a highly combustible ground cover that had incinerated "part of an Illinois regiment" the day before: "The fire had swept every superficial foot of it, and at every step I sank into ashes to the ankle." Bierce marvels at how the saplings and trees had been mowed by bullets, before noticing a more gruesome harvest.

> Death had put his sickle into this thicket and fire had gleaned the field. Along a line…lay bodies half buried in ashes; some in the unlovely looseness of attitude denoting sudden death by the bullet, but by far the greater number in postures of agony that told of the tormenting flame. Their clothing was half burnt away—their hair and beard entirely; the rain had come too late to save their nails. Some were swollen to double girth; others shriveled to manikins. According to degree of exposure, their faces were bloated and black or yellow and shrunken. The contraction of muscles which had given them claws for hands had cursed each countenance with a hideous grin. Faugh! I cannot catalogue the charms of these gallant gentlemen who had got what they enlisted for.[48]

In the days following the Battle of Shiloh, Bierce's terse report on the death of an era would have seemed incomprehensible. The sardonic tone of the essay's final passage not only ushered in the flat, cynical understatement of the war literature that would become familiar in the next century; it also marked the moment when the war came to be seen as the termination of outmoded beliefs and ideals. Those beliefs and ideals included Christian piety, patriotic duty, and faith in human progress. To abandon them was the first step toward freeing oneself from the destructive past, Bierce implied, but it also meant killing off an earlier version of oneself. It meant, among other things, murdering "those years of youth when I was soldiering!"

CHAPTER 4

Telling It Slant

A WEEK AFTER Shiloh, a thirty-one-year-old woman in Amherst, Massachusetts, penciled her name onto a small rectangular card and then enclosed it in an envelope along with four poems and one of the most famous letters in American literary history:

> MR. HIGGINSON,
> Are you too deeply occupied to say if my Verse is alive?
> The Mind is so near itself—it cannot see distinctly—and I have none to ask—
> Should you think it breathed—and had you the leisure to tell me, I should feel quick gratitude—
> If I make the mistake—that you dared to tell me—would give me sincere honor—toward you—
> I enclose my name—asking you, if you please—Sir—to tell me what is true?
> That you will not betray me—it is needless to ask—since Honor is it's own pawn—[1]

The recipient of the letter was Thomas Wentworth Higginson, who lived in nearby Worcester and who happened to be the most notorious abolitionist in America. Higginson was athletic and brisk. He moved confidently, spoke with assurance. In his countenance was the hauteur of the fanatic. A former Unitarian minister who sought literary fame, he had been the most radical member of the Secret Six, the covert organization that had helped to fund John Brown's attack on Harpers Ferry. Within a year, he would make history by assuming command of the first black regiment in the Union army.

Reading Emerson at a young age, he later recalled, had been "a great event," "a revelation" that fundamentally altered his conception of life's meaning. Emerson broke sharply from "the comparative conventionalism of the [American] literature of that period," and his writing remained, even fifty years later, "starry with statements of absolute truth." The great man's essay "The American Scholar" had prompted within this young acolyte a powerful desire to combine action and reflection, thought and purposeful activity. (Thoreau felt Higginson patterned himself a little *too* closely on Emerson; after listening to one of Higginson's lectures, he complained of the similarity, wryly adding, "and I could not afford to be reminded of Christ himself.")[2]

Higginson preached and wrote, he lectured in a voice considered mellifluous and compelling, he sought to achieve nothing less than the goal proclaimed in the final lines of "The American Scholar," which was "the conversion of the world." The particular conversion he hoped to effect was the end, once and for all, of slavery. "We fight no longer with bayonets and bullets," he announced in 1853. "We have melted all our lead into type for 'Uncle Tom's Cabin.'" His efforts at eloquent persuasion were soon overshadowed by the urgency of the times. In 1854, he attained national notoriety by leading an inspired but poorly organized effort to rescue a fugitive slave named Anthony Burns. The runaway had escaped from Virginia by ship in 1853, arriving in Boston in the middle of winter. His owner, Charles F. Suttle, soon traveled north to reclaim his "property" under the provisions of the Fugitive Slave Act. Burns's arrest prompted a vehement public outcry in Boston and drew Higginson from his pulpit in Worcester. Following a protest at Faneuil Hall, he led a boisterous crowd to the Boston Court House, where Burns was imprisoned and awaiting a hearing. There, Higginson commanded an effort to batter down the door with a fourteen-foot beam. While rushing the frightened guards within, he received his first wound in the sacred fight for emancipation: a cut on the chin from a guard's cutlass. He fared comparatively well. A moment later, a shot was fired and a deputy marshal killed.[3] (See figure 4.1.)

Burns was returned to Virginia, and Higginson, along with the abolitionists Wendell Phillips and Theodore Parker, was indicted. But the brush with danger awakened something inside him, kindled his life with renewed purpose. The author and lawyer Richard Henry Dana Jr., who served as Burns's counsel, noted admiringly in his journal, "I knew [Higginson's] ardor and courage, but I hardly expected a married man, a clergyman, and a man of education to lead the mob."[4]

FIGURE 4.1 Anthony Burns (1855). Courtesy Library of Congress, Prints and Photographs Division (LC-USZ62-90750 [3-9]).

Inflamed with this sense of mission, Higginson next traveled to Kansas, where guerrilla warfare between pro- and antislavery forces had erupted in the aftermath of the controversial Kansas-Nebraska Act. He delivered knives, revolvers, and Sharps rifles to settlers opposed to slavery, and he wrote newspaper editorials announcing his belief that warfare would one day transform the nation into a utopia of freedom. On the flat prairies of Kansas, he also learned of the man with whom his name would become permanently associated. John Brown had traveled to the fledgling state to fight in the newest and most urgent front of the holy war against slavery. He soon consecrated his activities in blood, killing five proslavery settlers in Pottawatomie and terrifying much of the populace with his vigilante raids against anyone opposed to Kansas's entrance into the Union as a free state. In 1858, Higginson joined the Secret Six and encouraged Brown's plan to lead a slave insurrection at the federal armory in Harpers Ferry.

In an essay entitled "A Visit to John Brown's Household in 1859," Higginson assured his readers that the insurrectionist had not minded being hanged for his cause. "To the Browns, killing means simply dying—nothing more; one gate into heaven, and that one a good deal frequented by their family; that is all." The sentence was deliberately imprecise. Brown had been executed for his efforts to inspire a slave revolt, but he had certainly executed others in his single-minded effort to achieve the abolition of slavery. Was Higginson excusing these acts? Was the American scholar advocating violence to convert the world?[5]

Emily Dickinson, author of the breathless, gnomic letter to Higginson, was certainly aware of her correspondent's abolitionist activities. They had been extensively covered in the *Springfield Republican*, the most influential regional newspaper in New England, whose editor, Samuel Bowles, was a close friend of the Dickinson family and a possible candidate for one of her intense and unrequited infatuations (see figure 4.2).

But Higginson's abolitionism was not the primary reason she wrote to him. She sent her letter because she had read his essay for aspiring writers, "Letter to a Young Contributor," in the April 1862 issue of the *Atlantic*, and had felt a tingle of recognition. The article itself was pedestrian: "use black ink, good pens, white paper," Higginson solemnly advised at one point. But it was written by a notorious social rebel, an enemy of convention, a wild-eyed visionary who also valued poetry. In her teens, Dickinson had considered "words...cheap & weak. Now," she wrote, sometime in the 1850s, when she began to consider herself a poet, "I don't know of anything so mighty." Words had come to possess a hallucinatory appeal to her. They assumed depth and dimension, power and force. "Sometimes I write one," she confessed, "and look at his outlines till he glows as no sapphire."[6]

FIGURE 4.2 Emily Dickinson (ca. 1847).

These lambent, glowing words, which she collected from her "only companion," the dictionary, were secretly assembled into unforgettable poems at a tiny cherry desk in the second-floor bedroom of her father's house in Amherst. The Homestead, on North Pleasant Street, was formal, formidable, ostentatious, and private, much like the family it contained. Edward Dickinson, stiff and angular, a gimlet-eyed attorney who served as treasurer of Amherst College, ruled the home as if it were his well-regulated law office. Emily Norcross Dickinson, the poet's mother, was a ghostly presence, sickly and passive, often confined to her bedroom. The three children—Emily, Austin, and Lavinia—seem to have grown up trying simultaneously to please their father and to indulge their imaginative lives. "My Mother does not care for thought," Dickinson later confided to Higginson, "and Father, too busy with his Briefs—to notice what we do—He buys me many Books—but begs me not to read them—because he fears they joggle the Mind."[7]

From an early age, she had possessed a remarkable verbal facility and a slashing wit, but it wasn't until her late twenties that she began writing seriously. She had discovered her voice—a voice unparalleled in American literature, full of abrupt halts and catches, ringing with the unexpected, odd music of a rusted hinge, a screen door banging shut, a forlorn bird singing across a wintry meadow. Dickinson's poetry pauses and leaps, it halts and dashes forward, like a person crossing a brook from stone to stone; in the process, it mirrors a piercing, quick-silver intelligence relentless in its search for the correct word, the pre-cise image, the blinding insight.

Exceptional language use is by no means the only aspect of her poetry to command our attention. If Whitman's special burden was to create a unified poem out of the disparate and competing elements of American social life, Dickinson's was to produce something vital and new from the waning traditions and threatened beliefs of a previous generation. Each morning at the Homestead, Edward Dickinson began the day with a family prayer and a reading of scripture. Although he did not experience conversion until he was in his forties, he looked forward to joining his wife in heaven, where they might spend, he told her, "that eternal Sabbath of enjoyment, in company, which is possible to all who are redeemed." Elected as a member of the Whig Party to the House of Representatives, Edward proclaimed in 1855 that "by the help of Almighty God, not another inch of our soil *heretofore consecrated* to free-dom, shall *hereafter* be polluted by the advancing tread of slavery."[8]

His daughter, on the other hand, came to poetic maturity just as the old narrative of providential design had begun to lose much of its explanatory force. A magazine reviewer in 1858 acknowledged the extent to which religious belief recently had come under assault, lamenting "the existing forms and tendencies of unbelief." Emily's older brother, Austin, summed up his doubt and confusion in a letter to a girlfriend. "I ask myself, Is it possible that God, all powerful, all wise, all benevolent, as I must believe him, *could* have created all these millions upon millions of human souls, only to destroy them[?]"[9] The assault on piety felt by Austin and Emily Dickinson came from a wide range of sources: the Higher Criticism of German biblical scholars, the ascent of the scientific method, and the roiling upsurge of material wealth that tended to deflect thoughts from heaven. On the eve of the Civil War, it came increasingly to coalesce around a single figure: Charles Darwin.

On the Origin of the Species, Darwin's opus, was published in 1859, exactly six days after Emerson described John Brown as "the new saint awaiting his martyrdom, and who, if he shall suffer, will make the gallows glorious like the cross." While Brown outraged many with his claim to have acted under the inspired tutelage of God himself, Darwin disturbed many more by seeming to strip the universe of God altogether. His theory of natural selection replaced divine intention with chance and accident. According to an alarmed American religious press, *On the Origin of the Species* was a "sneer at the idea of any manifestation of design in the material universe." Its theories "repudiate the whole doctrine of final causes" and rendered obsolete "all indication of design or purpose in the organic world." As one indignant critic for the *Examiner* put it, Darwin's central idea was "neither more nor less than a formal denial of any agency beyond that of a blind chance in the developing or perfecting of the organs or instincts of created beings."[10]

Dickinson's poetry often dealt with an aloof and inscrutable God whose operations in the natural world seemed arbitrary, and even occasionally malevolent. "I have a king who does not speak," she wrote in the spring of 1860, lamenting God's stony silence, his undemonstrative nature so similar to her own father's. But though the deity of her parents' generation failed to speak to her, Dickinson longed to bridge the yawning gulf that separated her from his divine presence. Many of her best poems capture the metaphysical panic arising from her sense that the promise of heaven had been withdrawn inexplicably from human destiny. Heaven and earth, the transcendent and the human were portrayed time and again as antagonists, glaring at one another with suspicion:

> I had some things that I called mine—
> And God that he called his,
> Till, recently a rival Claim
> Disturbed these amities.[11]

Here, spiritual alienation is shown to be an unresolved property dispute, a violation of the contract between God and his people first invoked two centuries earlier in John Winthrop's sermon to the Puritans aboard the *Arbella*. "Thus stands the cause between God and us," Winthrop had asserted to New England's first settlers, confident as any litigator familiar with the fine print, "we are entered into

Covenant with him for this work."[12] In Dickinson's poem, the covenant has been smashed, broken, rendered null and void.

What distinguishes Dickinson from other nineteenth-century thinkers shaken in their faith is her insistence that *God*—not his creation—should be held accountable. The estrangement between the Father and his people was not the result of a sinful lapse in piety, as so many of the era's ministers claimed. It was rather the byproduct of a perplexing silence, a cruel indifference, from the one who was supposed to be concerned for his abiding creation:

> Of God we ask one favor, that we may be forgiven—
> For what, he is presumed to know—
> The Crime, from us, is hidden—[13]

A prediction of Kafka's later works, this poem describes a nightmare reality in which God's creatures are accused of breaking an unnamed law, presumably that of being alive. Here, as in so many other poems, Dickinson revealed just how difficult it was for her to imagine creation in terms other than the ones inherited from traditional religion while at the same time expressing profound anxiety that this religion was being undermined by science, history, and the poet's own disappointing spiritual experience.[14] This is what Dickinson means when she writes, "He put the Belt around my life—/...And turned away, imperial," or when she describes nature as a "Haunted house," suggesting that the world, empty of God and no longer a place wherein the Lord might interpose his precious blood, nevertheless remains inhabited by the ghostly memories of his presence.[15]

These observations are typically delivered in an indirect, sidewise perspective that she referred to as "slant":

> Tell all the truth but tell it slant
> Success in Circuit lies
> Too bright for our infirm Delight
> The Truth's superb surprise
> As Lightning to the Children eased
> With explanation kind
> The Truth must dazzle gradually
> Or every man be blind.[16]

This candescent poem about the nature of truth is also about the best way to convey that truth. A blinding revelation, a complete reconfiguration of the understanding, truth is a lightning flash that obliterates everything previously known as fact. The premise is Emersonian, the conclusion is not—for language, according to Dickinson, can never entirely capture truth's radiance. Words may strike at "Truth's superb surprise," but only by approximation, indirection, metaphor, obliquity. Poetic language is an imprecise medium, opaque and murky, a filter between truth's "dazzle" and our "infirm Delight."

It was through this refractive medium that she started to hypothesize about the real causes of the war. Dickinson's poetry from this period reveals her sense that the appalling violence that had begun to engulf the nation was at least in part a reaction to religious doubt. Holy warfare enabled Americans who felt abandoned by God to demonstrate their commitment to true Christian faith. It provided them with a crusade, a test to prove their loyalty and devotion. It offered an opportunity to reclaim their Father's aloof and contrary love.

This longing for a crusade could be found in countless sermons, theological tracts, and articles in the nation's religious press. Before the war, the *American Theological Review* noted, "The plot of the world's great drama has long been thickening; but everything indicates that its denouement is at hand." The *National Preacher* beseeched its readers to make "[o]ne strong, united earnest effort to return to God in the spirit of a true consecration." The war was a "great national baptism," according to the Reverend William Patton, who spoke before the Presbyterian General Assembly in 1863. Its very impulse and spirit would allow God to "so pour out his spirit...that millions of immortal beings will be converted, and the nation stand redeemed and sanctified."[17]

Amid this thickening plot, this gathering of forces, Dickinson performed a singular and audacious act of bravery. She sent four poems to a man she had never met. A man who was famous. An author. He would become her judge and confessor.

In the spring of 1862, about the same time that he "took from the post office" a letter "postmarked 'Amherst,' and...in a handwriting so peculiar that it seemed as if the writer might have taken her first lessons by studying the famous fossil bird-tracks in the museum of that college town," Thomas Wentworth Higginson was experiencing doubt about only one thing: what to do with his life.[18]

His faith in heaven and providence was unassailable. He believed America had been created by God to be a special instrument of divine fulfillment, a pattern of liberty for the rest of the world. As a young man, he had fervently longed for a "dawning age of Faith...this great period of commencing reconstruction to be embodied in a new social organization." His first published essay appeared in a journal called *Present*, dedicated to "advanc[ing] the Reign of Heaven on Earth." "I think the world is growing better all the time," he wrote to a friend at the start of the war, expressing his confidence that America was but a foretaste of eternal paradise. "Death is only a step in life," he elsewhere explained, "& there is no more reason why we should fear to go from one world into another than from one room to another." The next world would be characterized by "triumph without armies," a place "where innocence is trained in scenes of peace." As he put it in the epilogue of his only novel, *Malbone*, written well after the war: "Were this life all, its very happiness were sadness. If, as I doubt not, there can be another sphere, then that which is unfulfilled must find completion."[19]

Higginson's confidence in heavenly completion animated others in his set of friends. Another member of the Secret Six, Samuel Gridley Howe, was married to Julia Ward Howe, author of "The Battle Hymn of the Republic," which had been published earlier that year in the February issue of *Atlantic*. The poem was written shortly after she had reviewed troops outside Washington, D.C., and had witnessed a group of soldiers spontaneously singing "John Brown's Body." One of her companions, the transcendentalist minister James Freeman Clarke, had said, "Mrs. Howe, why do you not write some good words for that stirring tune?" As if prompted by a higher author, Howe recalled, the work composed itself while she slept that night. When she awoke, the "long lines of the desired poem began to twine themselves in my mind," and she soon "scrawled the verses almost without looking at the paper." The opening line—"Mine eyes have seen the glory of the coming of the Lord"—communicated the central theological premise for the war: a charitable God had willed the bloody conflict into existence as a preface to heaven's imminent glory.[20]

The question tormenting Higginson in the spring of 1862 was whether he could best usher in the impending reign of heaven by enlisting in the Union army or by focusing on his career as an author. The previous autumn, he had written an artistic credo in his field book: "To enjoy life & to write a few perfect sentences, & then to die is all I ask. It is not for power I seek this, nor even for the relief of self-expression,—but let me feel that I have achieved beauty & I am content." Literature, he confessed, transported the mind "into sublimity, by conforming the show of things to the desires of the soul."[21] Properly employed, literature indicated the way things *ought* to be, thereby directing the reader toward desirable ends.

But if literature was a form of activism, activism was also a form of poetry. The strain of aestheticism expressed in the field book ran counter to Higginson's long-standing belief that revolutionary action was needed to perfect the world. Wishing to complete the sacred mission begun by John Brown and to participate in a holy war that promised the spread of liberty, he was loath to do so as long as the Lincoln administration remained uncommitted to the slavery issue. "Slavery is the root of the rebellion," he announced, sounding much like his hero Emerson, "and so War is proving itself an Abolitionist, whoever else is."[22]

As he waited for this issue to resolve itself, he indulged his curiosity in the strange correspondent from Amherst. He asked for a photograph. Dickinson replied with a verbal portrait, describing herself as "small, like the Wren, and my Hair is bold, like the Chestnut Bur—and my eyes, like the Sherry in the Glass, that the Guest leaves—." Indulging a lifelong propensity to flirt with admiring women, Higginson asked about her friends, trying to determine her marital status. "You ask of my Companions," Dickinson promptly wrote back. "Hills— Sir—and the Sundown—and a Dog—large as myself, that my Father bought me—." She was, in other words, unattached.[23]

As for her poems, Higginson offered a decidedly more restrained response, apparently calling them "spasmodic" and "uncontrolled" and suggesting she refrain from publication, at least for the moment. Her reaction was to send more poems—and then *more* poems—each propelled by its own urgencies, each flushed with life and rich with verbal play, each utterly sui generis—all the while claiming that publication was the furthest thing from her mind. Flattering Higginson's self-image as a dispenser of wisdom, she asked her new "master," her "Preceptor," if a fresh batch of poems was "more orderly," before abruptly confessing, "when I try to organize—my little Force explodes—and leaves me bare and charred—."[24]

The image was taken directly from the war. Dickinson followed the news of battles and military commissions assiduously, reading the four newspapers and numerous journals to which her father subscribed. Her sensitive antennae were attuned to the village telegraph as well, picking up the names of the local dead and wounded, absorbing the town gossip that drifted up from the dim parlor below her bedroom. On the last day of 1861, she had sent her cousins Louise and Frances Norcross the following letter:

> Mrs. Adams had news of the death of her boy to-day from a wound at Annapolis. Telegram signed by Frazer Stearns. You remember him. Another one died in October—from fever caught in the camp. Mrs.

Adams herself has not risen from her bed since then. "Happy new year" step softly over such doors as these! "Dead! Both her boys! One of them shot by the sea in the East, and one of them shot in the West by the seas." ... Christ be merciful! Frazer Stearns is just leaving Annapolis. His father has gone to see him to-day. I hope that ruddy face won't be brought home frozen. Poor little widow's boy, riding to-night in the mad wind, back to the village burying-ground where he never dreamed of sleeping! Ah! the dreamless sleep![25]

The letter reveals how the poet relied upon current events to produce a dazzling array of rhetorical effects. The terse style of an official death announcement ("Telegram signed by Frazer Stearns") is followed by a paraphrase of Elizabeth Barrett Browning ("Dead! Both her boys! One of them shot by the sea in the East, and one of them shot in the West by the seas") before Dickinson at last invests the return of the soldier's spirit with all the tricked-up contrivances of a Gothic horror tale.

Yet, when the twenty-one-year-old son of Amherst College's president, Frazar Stearns, was killed three months later, this verbal panache was tempered by grief. "DEAR CHILDREN," Dickinson wrote again to her cousins:

> You have done more for me—'tis least that I can do, to tell you of brave Frazer—"killed at Newbern," darlings. His big heart shot away by a "minie ball."
>
> I had read of those—I didn't think Frazer would carry one to Eden with him. Just as he fell, in his soldier's cap, with his sword at his side, Frazer rode through Amherst. Classmates to the right of him, and classmates to the left of him, to guard his narrow face! He fell by the side of Professor Clark, his superior officer—lived ten minutes in a soldier's arms, asked twice for water—murmured just, "My God!" and passed! Sanderson, his classmate, made a box of boards in the night, put the brave boy in, covered with a blanket, rowed six miles to reach the boat,—so poor Frazer came. They tell that Colonel Clark cried like a child when he missed his pet, and could hardly resume his post. They loved each other very much. Nobody here could look on Frazer—not even his father. The doctors would not allow it.
>
> ... So our part in Frazer is done, but you must come next summer, and we will mind ourselves of this young crusader—too brave that he could fear to die. We will play his tunes—maybe he can hear them; we will try to comfort his broken-hearted Ella, who, as the clergyman said, "gave him peculiar confidence."
>
> ... Let us love better, children, it's most that's left to do.[26]

Dickinson's intimacy with the war—its minié balls, the recent battle at New Bern, North Carolina, and the perennial problem of preserving the remains of soldiers whose bodies had to be transported long distances for burial—provided her with an occasion to express pain. "Sorrow seems more general than it did," she wrote to her cousins, "and not the estate of a few persons, since the war began; and if the anguish of others helped one with one's own, now would be many medicines."[27]

While Higginson vacillated over the direction of his life, Dickinson, fueled by the pervasive pain she observed, entered the most creative phase of hers. Between 1861 and 1865, she produced some 800 poems, writing in the second-floor room late into the evening or, rising early, in the dim hours before dawn, anytime she could work undisturbed, anytime the house was still, producing one incisive, utterly original poem after another. During the bloodiest period of the war, which began in the fall of 1862 and would continue for the next year and a half, she sometimes wrote a poem a day, sometimes more, dozens of them about the war itself.

"It feels a shame to be Alive," written earlier that summer, is ostensibly about survivor's guilt. Our lives, the poem asserts, cannot possibly be worth the heroic sacrifice of others. All we can hope for is that these "Saviors" who have died nobly will encounter "Divinity" before the rest of us. But Dickinson's writing is "slanted" when it comes to describing "Battle's—horrid Bowl." The image recalls the meadows of Shiloh, the grisly crucible through which young men passed before becoming "Distinguished Dust." A tension between the horrors of battle and a consoling lesson is never resolved. Elsewhere, in "They dropped like Flakes—," Dickinson describes the war dead through the threadbare images of snow, stars, and "Petals from a Rose"—staples of the lyric tradition in poetry that prove inadequate to the subject matter at hand. The wholesale, anonymous deaths of young men in combat, their bodies scattered over hills and fields like nature's leavings, appear in another poem, "My Portion is Defeat—today—":

> 'Tis populous with Bone and stain—
> And Men too straight to stoop again—
> And Piles of solid Moan—
> And Chips of Blank—in Boyish Eyes—
> And scraps of Prayer—
> And Death's surprise,
> Stamped visible—in stone—[28]

The war dead, transformed by rigor mortis into statuesque rigidity in this last poem, appear throughout Dickinson's work of the period, puncturing the grand narratives and high-minded ideals used to justify the war. The images of the dead also convey the poet's anger and sorrow at recent events. "It don't sound so terrible—quite—as it did—," she writes, anatomizing the mood swings that accompany the news of sudden death. The poem's narrator "run[s] it over—'Dead,' Brain—'Dead,'" trying to assimilate the knowledge conveyed by telegraph or newspaper. She labors to convince herself that the news is not as bad as it seems. "I suppose it will interrupt me some," she admits, "Till I get accustomed"; then, she concedes that if "A trouble looks bitterest" while seen "full in the face," it will perhaps be necessary to "Shift it—just—."[29]

"It don't sound so terrible" aims for the consoling message that time softens all grief. Ultimately, it suggests just the opposite. A year was the traditional time of mourning in antebellum society. It was also, the poem points out with grim irony, long enough to get accustomed to pervasive bloodshed: "How like a 'fit'—then—/ Murder—wear!"[30]

In the autumn of 1862, Higginson settled his invalid wife and her menagerie of cats into a boardinghouse and left for Camp John E. Wool, just outside of Worcester, to form a regiment and at last participate in the great revolution of his time. "No prominent anti-slavery man has yet taken a marked share in the war," he observed, only partially exaggerating when he added, "there are a great many in this and other States who would like to go if I do. I have made up my mind to take part in the affair, hoping to aid in settling it quicker."[31]

What had convinced him to enlist was Antietam. The battle, near Antietam Creek in Maryland, had occurred in September 1862 and was the culmination of a most discouraging summer for the Union. Under the new command of Robert E. Lee, a shy and even timid man who led his forces with breathtaking boldness, the Confederacy's Army of Northern Virginia had effectively reversed the momentum of the war. During the Seven Days Battles, which began during the last week of June among the swamps and thickets near the Chickahominy River, Lee attacked fiercely and ruthlessly, decisively beating the Union's Army of the Potomac at Gaines' Mill and driving it from the southern capital of Richmond into a humiliating retreat.

Unable to sleep during the week of battles in June and increasingly weighed down by the Union's ineffectual military leadership, Abraham Lincoln began to reconsider his strategic options during the summer of 1862. He would later say, according to the *New York Times*, that he had no desire "to carry out this war for the purpose of elucidating a theory." But circumstances had changed, and the battle, he noted with grim humor, could no longer be fought "with elder-stalk squirts, charged with rosewater." It was time that southerners understood "that they cannot experiment for ten years trying to destroy the government, and if they fail still come back to the Union unhurt."[32]

On July 13, he privately informed two members of his cabinet, William H. Seward and Gideon Welles, of his plan to issue an emancipation proclamation that would deprive the enemy of its chief human resource. A week later, the topic was taken up with the entire cabinet. Much to everyone's surprise, it was promptly approved, with the proviso that the proclamation be postponed until after the Union had scored a major military victory.

That victory did not come until September, when Lee's forces and McClellan's Army of the Potomac collided near the village of Sharpsburg, Maryland. Once again, there was a church—a small clapboard church of the Dunkard sect—around which much of the fighting occurred. Once again, a cornfield was littered with bodies. Men fought one another in close combat, using their bayonets, killing in a frenzy, a delirium. Haystacks were torched, clouding the battlefield in a thick canopy of smoke that caused the sun to burn a smudged, sullen red. "My God, such confusion," wrote a soldier from the Fifteenth Massachusetts. George Whitman, who was present at Sharpsburg and who fought near the famous battle around Burnside's Bridge, wrote to his family in Brooklyn, "The way we showered the lead across that creek was noboddy's business."[33] (See figure 4.3.)

In London, where he followed the conflict as though it just might elucidate a theory, Karl Marx declared that Antietam "has decided the fate of the American Civil War." Marx had long believed that the war would spell the end of slavery. In August, he wrote to his collaborator, Friedrich Engels, "A single negro regiment would have a remarkable effect....A war of this kind must be conducted on revolutionary lines while the Yankees have been trying to conduct it constitutionally." From his distance, Marx had no way of knowing how costly the war had become. Antietam was the single bloodiest day in U.S. history, a massacre that lingered like a bad dream for its survivors. "Every battle makes me wish more and more that the war was over," wrote Robert Gould Shaw, the young man who had grown up on Staten Island next door to Theodore Winthrop. "It seems almost as if nothing could justify a battle like that of the 17th, and the horrors inseparable from it."[34]

FIGURE 4.3 Confederate dead at Antietam (September 1862). Photograph by Alexander Gardner. Courtesy Library of Congress, Prints and Photographs Division (LC-B8171-0557).

Ghastly as Antietam turned out to be, it was also, at least technically, a victory for the Union. Lee's exhausted troops, while not completely destroyed, were sufficiently battered to pull out of northern Maryland and retreat under cover of darkness. They were still retreating when Lincoln announced that slavery would be abolished in the rebellious states unless those states returned to the Union by January 1, 1863.

"We shout for joy that we live to record this righteous decree," wrote the abolitionist Frederick Douglass when the news reached him. Emerson was likewise exultant, noting in his journal that Lincoln's announcement would define "every man's position" once and for all. The draft proclamation had finally forced all Americans to side either for or against slavery, bringing the issue into each and every home and showing "us that the battleground is fast changing from Richmond to Boston." It seemed "to promise an extension of the war," Emerson added. "For there can be no durable peace, no sound Constitution, until we have fought this battle, & the rights of man are vindicated."[35]

The events of September 1862 ended Higginson's vacillation. If "I do not [go to war]," he had fretted during the summer, "I shall forfeit my self-respect & be a broken man for the remainder of my days." With the administration's shift in war aims, he now plunged into the heady business of recruiting a regiment, becoming the captain of the Massachusetts Fifty-first and reveling in the stiff, sweltering uniform he had especially tailored for his tall, lank frame. He immersed himself in the minutiae of military conduct and quickly found he had an aptitude for drills and marching. Higginson's townspeople would later recall how "day after day" in the late summer of 1862, "in the streets of

W. [Worcester] we used to see the indefatigable *Capt.* H. drilling his white company."[36]

He quickly grew attached to his men, delighting in their spirited singing and the impromptu square dances they held on the barracks floor as the New England evenings began to cool. Among the men who gathered in the golden circle of lantern light, he noted, were "grim & war-worn faces, looking as old as Waterloo" intermixed "with merely childish faces from school." What would the future hold for this odd assortment, Higginson found himself wondering. He was oddly consoled by the words of Theodore Parker, his mentor in the abolition movement, who had written, "All the great charters of humanity have been written in blood. It is plain now that our pilgrimage must lead through a Red Sea, wherein a Pharaoh will go under and perish."[37]

Until the Fifty-first was issued arms and given its assignment, Higginson tried not to worry. "I have always had a remarkable faculty of falling on my feet," he boasted to his mother, "& having got through Kansases & Court Houses unharmed, have the most entire faith in my having the same faculty" in war. In the meantime, he drilled his men. According to Charlotte Forten Grimké, a young schoolteacher in Worcester at the time, she had never seen a man "so full of life and energy." Higginson was a man transformed, she thought, "entering with his whole soul into his work" as he had a decade earlier during the Burns affair.[38]

When exactly Dickinson learned of her preceptor's decision to command a regiment is unclear. Throughout the summer, she wrote him quirky, coquettish letters in which the war seldom intruded. "You speak of Pippa Passes—," she noted, referring to Robert Browning's dramatic poem. "I never heard anybody speak of Pippa Passes—before." She confessed her preference for the work of Browning's wife, Elizabeth Barrett, and admitted to being frightened by Harriet Prescott Spofford's short story "Circumstance," which had been published in the *Atlantic* a year or so earlier. When "a sudden light on Orchards, or a new fashion in the wind troubled my attention," she told him, she felt "a palsy...the Verses just relieve." Poetry eased her anxiety, gave voice to her sense that the world made no sense. Still, she warned, he was not to read her poetry as autobiographical. "When I state myself, as the Representative of the Verse—it does not mean—me—but a supposed person."[39]

She repeatedly expressed gratitude for his comments about her poetry. "Thank you for the surgery—," she told him after his initial remarks about her poems, "it was not so painful as I supposed."

A subsequent batch apparently received more positive remarks from Higginson. "Your letter gave no Drunkenness," she informed him, "because I tasted Rum before—." She was referring to a young clerk in her father's office, long dead, who had first encouraged her to write by giving her a volume of Emerson's poetry. Yet she "had few pleasures so deep as your opinion, and if I tried to thank you, my tears would block my tongue—." Sending him yet another group of poems, she asked, "Are these more orderly? I thank you for the Truth—."[40]

In October, she sent a more plaintive note: "Did I displease you, Mr. Higginson? But won't you tell me how?" Quite likely, she knew about his military vocation; her uncle lived in Worcester, after all, and Higginson's activities were regularly reported in the *Springfield Republican*. But she was confused and upset by his decision to enter the fray. In "Letter to a Young Contributor," Higginson had seemed to value words over social and political concerns, weighing the merits of a "column of a newspaper or a column of attack" and finding the first every bit as valuable as the last. Shortly after sending her first letter to Higginson, she had written "The Soul selects her own Society," a paean to self-reliant friendship. In his reply, she had felt as if her soul had finally found its match, its mate, someone who understood the nature of writing, who knew that to write well, to tell the truth, however slant, was as courageous and heroic as fighting in any war. A hint of exasperation, then, a sense of betrayal, clung to Dickinson's terse missive.[41]

So did a whiff of fear. Terrified that Higginson might, like Frazar Stearns, "return frozen," or that his soul might sojourn back to New England and fret a Worcester graveyard, she was soon following the news of his regiment and redoubling her efforts to understand the meaning of the war. In an era rife with accounts of jagged wounds and shattered bones, Dickinson increasingly wrote poems concerned with the wounded and maimed. "The possibility to pass," she wrote,

> Without a Moment's Bell—
> Into Conjecture's presence—
> Is like a face of steel
> That suddenly looks into our's
> With a Metallic Grin—
> The Cordiality of Death
> Who Drills his welcome—in—[42]

As in so many other Dickinson poems, death appears here as a courtly gentleman, attractive and terrifying at the same time. But not even his calm demeanor and impeccable manners can camouflage the "Metallic

Grin" of bayonets, artillery shells, and minié balls. Poems like this one enabled Dickinson to enter into a wider communion of grief even from the seclusion of her father's house, to participate in a national bereavement shared by hundreds of thousands of families. But it did little to help her make sense of Shiloh's and Antietam's carnage within the moral framework of God's will. Nor did it help, as Dickinson continually reminded herself, that God refused to communicate his will in the first place. In Dickinson's poetry, the war allowed the spirit-hungry nation to "Read—Sweet—how others—strove—" and to consider "What they—renounced—/ Till we—are less afraid—." It also enabled the doubtful to feel "helped—/ As if a Kingdom—cared!"[43]

Poetry did not solve the riddle of suffering, nor did it crack the code of death. But it did mirror the way life could be fractured by loss. Hunched over her tiny desk in the southwest bedroom of her father's house, pausing only to warm herself at the Franklin stove, she wrote with renewed intensity as the year wound down. After Higginson joined the army and ceased writing to her, her poetic production leaped to five times the previous amount. Soon, she was writing more than forty poems a month, writing, as she would put it, like "a Soul at the 'White Heat.'"[44]

Tell me if my Verse is alive, she had implored Higginson in her first letter, written what now seemed a lifetime ago. *Tell me if they breathe. Tell me what is true.*

For some time, there would be no answer.

CHAPTER 5

Port Royal

T HERE WAS NOTHING to prepare Thomas Wentworth Higginson for the first day of 1863. Bright, sunny, ineffable: unlike any January morning in Massachusetts, unlike any winter in New England. The air was thick and soft, fragrant with jasmine and oleander, heavy as a curtain. Roses still bloomed in December. Spanish moss swayed like drapery, casting shadows on his tight, polished boots.

And the people. More than 1,000 soldiers and civilians were assembling in the small military camp just outside Beaufort, South Carolina, emerging from the deep, plum-colored shadows of live oaks and the tangle of vines, carried by steamboats that noisily paddled along the nearby river. Beginning at ten in the morning, Higginson wrote in his journal, "the road was crowded with riders & walkers—chiefly black women with gay handkerchiefs on their heads & a sprinkling of men. Many white persons also, superintendents & teachers." To feed this enormous gathering, a dozen oxen had been killed and barbecued. Large hogsheads of water were each mixed, according to an old slave recipe, with three gallons of molasses, a half pound of ginger, and a quart of vinegar, to provide the occasion's only beverage.[1]

Yet food was the last thing on most people's minds. They had gathered on this balmy, sun-filled day to celebrate a quiet and solemn act occurring several hundred miles to the north in the White House. Lifting his pen above a sheet of parchment unrolled by Secretary of State Seward, Abraham Lincoln had paused a moment and said, "I never, in my life, felt more certain that I was doing right, than I do in signing this paper."[2] He then affixed his name to the Emancipation

Proclamation. With a single stroke of the pen, some 4 million souls held in bondage throughout the rebellious states were slaves no longer. Jubilee had at last arrived.

Among the dignitaries attending the celebration in South Carolina were General Rufus Saxton, the earnest son of a transcendentalist who was now in charge of the Department of the South; Edward W. Hooper, a Harvard lawyer serving as Saxton's aide; Dr. William Henry Brisbane, an aging planter from the area who long ago had discerned the evils of slavery and freed everyone on his vast plantation; Charlotte Forten (later Grimké), a young African-American woman from Philadelphia who had journeyed south to teach the contrabands; and Higginson.

The events leading up to his arrival in this subtropical region were as filled with drama and coincidence as any scene from the novel he was then poring over, Victor Hugo's *Les Misérables*. "I had formed even in a short time a strong attachment to my own company," he recalled about the Fifty-first Massachusetts. One day, however, "when the governor of Rhode Island had made his first abortive suggestion of a black regiment, I had notified my young lieutenants, John Goodell and Luther Bigelow, that such an enterprise would be the only thing likely to take me from them." The words proved prophetic. While dining several days later with his fellow officers in the mess, he received a letter more momentous than the one he had opened six months earlier from Emily Dickinson. It was from the military governor of the Department of the South, and it offered him the command of a regiment of freed slaves in South Carolina.[3]

Earlier that fall, a limerick had appeared in the Boston papers and was soon picked up and reprinted throughout New England:

> There was a young curate of Worcester
> Who could have a command if he'd choose ter,
> > But he said each recruit
> > Must be blacker than soot,
> Or else he'd go preach where he used ter.

The offer from Rufus Saxton seemed to Higginson a special providence, the fulfillment of destiny. Before accepting, he had caught a tramp steamer to South Carolina to inspect the camp for himself. He spoke with Saxton and the other men in charge, and he recalled Emerson's counsel in "The American Scholar" that one's life work should entail "the study and the communication of principles, the making of those instincts prevalent, the conversion of the world." "I had been an abolitionist too long," he later recalled, "and had known and loved John Brown too well, not to feel a thrill of joy at last on finding myself in the position where he only wished to be." He accepted the commission.[4]

And now, little more than a month later, he stood on the parade ground of Camp Saxton, conscious of his excellent carriage and the handsome impression he made in his officer's uniform, deeply aware of the significance of this ceremony, which commemorated the end of the most corrupt and exploitative social system in the history of the world. Nearby, a crowd of reformers, ministers, philanthropists, and educators had gathered beneath a canopy of live oaks, perspiring in the heat. The band of the Eighth Maine wheezed out a medley of patriotic tunes. Then, silence fell as a solemn invocation was made from the wooden platform filled with speakers. The Emancipation Proclamation was read aloud by Brisbane, who had set free his own slaves decades earlier and whose voice quavered with emotion. The Reverend Mansfield French, editor of *The Beauty of Holiness*, an evangelical journal in New York, presented the regimental colors to the First South Carolina Volunteers— Higginson's new regiment, composed of freedmen (see figure 5.1).

Throughout these ceremonies, the African-American soldiers, somber in their dress uniforms, held rifles upright in their white-gloved hands. As soon as French quit speaking, Higginson took the regimental flag in order to present it to the color guard. But before he could hand it off, there "followed an incident so simple, so touching, so utterly unexpected and startling, that I can scarcely believe it on recalling, though it gave the key-note to the whole day." Higginson energetically waved the flag, aware that "now for the first time [it] meant anything to these poor people," when "there suddenly arose, close beside the platform, a strong male voice (but rather cracked and elderly), into which two women's voices instantly blended, singing, as if by an impulse that could no more be repressed than the morning note of the song-sparrow."

> My Country, 'tis of thee,
> Sweet land of liberty,
> Of thee I sing![5]

Higginson stood motionless, erect, his angular face partially hidden by the folds of the regimental flag. He struggled with his emotions. To him, the spontaneous outburst of song seemed to emanate from "the choked voice of a race, at last unloosed." Looking to his side, he noticed "a little slave boy, almost white," who had joined in the singing.[6] "Just think of it," he noted in his journal later that night, unable to sleep in

FIGURE 5.1 African-American soldiers at Beaufort, South Carolina.
Courtesy Library of Congress, Prints and Photographs Division
(LC-B82201–341 [4–5]).

his candlelit tent on the lush grounds of the Smith plantation, "the first
day they ever had a country, the first flag they had ever seen which
promised anything to their people."[7] (See figure 5.2.)

For abolitionists throughout the nation—earnest, idealistic, inflexible,
and often militant—New Year's Day 1863 marked the fulfillment of a

FIGURE 5.2 "Emancipation Day in South Carolina." *Frank Leslie's Illustrated Newspaper*, January 24, 1863.

dream to alter the meaning of the war as well as the broader destiny of the nation. Henceforth, the fighting between North and South was no longer simply an affair to restore the Union. It was a concerted effort to end the pernicious, soul-killing institution of slavery. "From the first," recalled Frederick Douglass, the great abolitionist writer who had escaped from his master a quarter of a century earlier to become one of the most influential black men in the nation, "I, for one, saw in this war the end of slavery."[8] Never doubting that sectional violence would rid the nation of its original taint, Douglass had waited impatiently for the Lincoln administration to come around to his position.

On the first day of 1863, he remained fearful that the president whom he had alternately praised and condemned in his abolitionist newspaper over the past two years might still change his mind and rescind the proclamation. Douglass was scheduled to speak at Boston's Tremont Temple, a cavernous former theater converted into a Baptist church. It was a cold, snowy day, and the packed audience huddled close to stay warm. Anxiously, Douglass awaited confirmation that "the war was to be conducted on a new principle, with a new aim," before taking the pulpit. At last the news arrived, traveling along a chain of people from the telegraph office through Boston's streets to the church door. Hearing that Lincoln had signed the proclamation, Douglass felt as though the nation had been struck by "a bolt from the sky, which would rend the fetters of four millions of slaves."[9] He stood before the congregation and led them in singing the Charles Wesley hymn "Blow Ye the Trumpet Blow," with its refrain, *The year of jubilee is come!*

A short distance away, in the same Music Hall where his lecture "Moral Forces" had been delivered the year before, Emerson read a new poem to celebrate the occasion. The program at the Music Hall once again reflected the cultural pretensions of Boston's Brahmin class. It began with Beethoven's overture to *Egmont* and concluded with Rossini's overture to *William Tell*. Emerson's poem, entitled "Boston Hymn," was a pleasant surprise to most of the 3,000 gathered. He had declined to have his name printed on the program, worried he might be unable to write a poem worthy of the occasion. He had fretted and stewed, making desultory attempts here and there in his poetry notebooks, and then suddenly, in a creative heat two days before the event, he wrote a twenty-two-stanza poem that would become an instant classic. Reprinted throughout the North, recited by schoolchildren, the poem traveled with remarkable speed. Within days of its introduction, the black soldiers in South Carolina under Higginson's command were singing all twenty-two stanzas as they drilled on the golden sands of Hilton Head beach.

The speaker of Emerson's poem is none less than God himself. In terse, austere lines, he describes Boston's citizens as the heirs of militant Puritanism. Having valued religious and civic freedom two centuries earlier, they are now asked once again to wage a righteous and unrelenting war upon evil. In the most memorable quatrain, Emerson turns on its head the debate about whether slaveholders should be compensated for their lost "property." The speaker of "Boston Hymn" decisively objects:

> Pay ransom to the owner
> And fill the bag to the brim.
> Who is the owner? The slave is owner,
> And ever was. Pay him.[10]

According to one of the listeners at the Music Hall, Emerson spoke "the last two words with such energy and emphasis that the audience felt something like an electric shock." The poem's conclusion was met with cheers and a standing ovation. Later in the evening, Emerson read the poem at the home of abolitionist George L. Stearns, one of the Secret Six. This time, his audience was smaller, but certainly no less committed to the abolitionist cause. Seated in the parlor were Wendell Phillips, Bronson and Louisa May Alcott, and Julia Ward Howe, who recited her own famous "Battle Hymn." After Emerson's recitation, Phillips unveiled a marble bust of John Brown.[11]

For Douglass and Emerson, Lincoln's proclamation meant the war had at last become holy, redemptive. It meant that the Union cause had finally aligned itself with larger "moral forces"—both men frequently employed the phrase—that would ensure victory in a universe conducing to good. But in many ways, the Emancipation Proclamation was less a promise than a threat, a "lever" of war, in Lincoln's phrase, issued to weaken a recalcitrant enemy. Freeing only those slaves in the rebellious states and therefore those least likely to be advantaged by it, the proclamation had little power to alter the racial prejudices prevalent even among the most fervent abolitionists.

None of this was immediately evident to those who had joined Thomas Wentworth Higginson in the exciting new experiment being conducted in the cotton-rich low country of Beaufort and Port Royal. The camp was located in the Sea Islands, a string of tidal islands that runs along the coast of Georgia and South Carolina. Toward the end of 1861, these islands had been captured by the federal army in one of the few northern successes of that year. The town of Beaufort, abundant in slaves and cotton, possessed the finest natural harbor on the southern Atlantic coast. As soon as the U.S. Navy secured a beachhead there, the army quickly conquered the remaining nearby islands.

What they found was completely unexpected. Cotton and rice plantations, warehouses, resorts, even entire villages had been vacated by white owners fleeing northern occupation. Left behind were stately plantation houses filled with fine English furniture, old paintings, Sevres china, pianos that refused to stay in tune in the humid climate. Also left behind were hundreds of field hands and other slaves, who found themselves without a white master for the first time in their lives. Soon, displaced blacks from as far away as Florida were drawn to the safe haven provided by the Union military bases, swelling the African-American population to approximately 10,000. The great historian and civil rights activist W. E. B. DuBois, imagining this migration forty years later, wrote, "They came at night, when the flickering camp-fires shone like vast unsteady stars along the black horizon: old men and thin, with gray and tufted hair, women, with frightened eyes, dragging whimpering hungry children; men and girls, stalwart and gaunt,—a horde of starving vagabonds, homeless, helpless, and pitiable in their dark distress."[12]

These refugees almost immediately attracted the attention of northern reformers. Relief associations were formed in Boston, New York, and Philadelphia, and a small army of the charitably minded flocked to Port Royal to help. The southward flow reminded some observers of the heyday of transcendentalism, when a disparate group of reformers and visionaries had shared millennial hopes in a series of improbable schemes. John Murray Forbes, a Massachusetts industrialist who accompanied the first wave of reformers to South Carolina (his son William Hathaway Forbes would marry Emerson's daughter, Edith, before the end of the war), described the relief workers as "bearded and mustached and odd-looking men, with odder-looking women.... You would have doubted whether it was the adjournment of a John Brown meeting or the fag end of a broken down phalanstery!"[13]

Calling themselves "evangels of civilization" and proudly adopting the term applied by conservative newspapers, "Gideonites" or, later, "Gids," these reformers, educators, radicals, social theorists, and philanthropists flocked to the displaced black population in South Carolina, energized by the chance to elevate "the lowest of their race in America," as one liberal publication depicted the freedmen and -women, in a "work of civilization" that would show "conclusively that the best way to educate a man for freedom is to make him free." The Virginia author Rebecca Harding Davis captured the enthusiasm for slave rehabilitation in a short story entitled "Out of the Sea." In it, she created a reformist heroine whose credentials included being "over thirty, an eager humanitarian, [and one who] had taught the freedmen at Port Royal." The Reverend Joseph P. Thompson, a popular pastor of the Broadway Tabernacle Church in New York City, suggested to his parishioners that they "adopt the jubilant style of the freedman at Port Royal, who, putting on his old master's best attire, 'just to save it from the moths,' came into the national camp, singing and shouting, and averred, that '*he neber enjoyed religion so much afore in all his life.*'"[14]

Throughout the summer of 1862, as the Union had faced a series of losses in Virginia, Port Royal was viewed with increasing hope by progressive northerners who dreamed of a new social order founded on principles of equality. The poet John Greenleaf Whittier expressed this view in "At Port Royal," which juxtaposed the fires set by fleeing slaveholders with the blaze of inner worth that illuminated the abandoned slaves:

The lurid glow falls strong across
Dark faces broad with smiles;
Not theirs the terror, hate, and loss
That fire yon blazing piles.[15]

As hopeful as Whittier and other abolitionists were, however, the success of the Port Royal experiment was by no means assured. "Two problems are concerned in the social problem of our time," wrote one of the participants in an 1863 piece for the *Atlantic* called "The Freedmen at Port Royal." "One is, Will the people of African descent work for a living? and the other is, Will they fight for their freedom? An affirmative answer to these must be put beyond any fair dispute before they will receive permanent security in law or opinion."[16]

Higginson's new commander, Brigadier General Saxton, had decided to try answering the second question. Saxton was the military governor of the Sea Islands and the first Union commander to muster ex-slaves into the U.S. Army. Short, fat, and bald, he was a Unitarian and a Republican whose favorite authors, not surprisingly, were Emerson and Higginson. Saxton understood that to convince skeptical northerners about the freedmen's willingness to fight, he would need a commander sympathetic to the cause of black suffrage, someone who could also inspire confidence in the ex-slaves. He was aware of the publicity that would be attached to the appointment of a man notorious for his association with John Brown and for his articles in the *Atlantic* about the slave insurrectionists Denmark Vesey and Nat Turner.

Until he received the momentous letter from Saxton, Higginson "had always looked for the arming of the blacks, and felt a wish to be associated with them."[17] Traveling south to learn more about the commission, he had been assured that the African-American regiment would not only harvest abandoned crops and improve derelict plantations but also reoccupy the islands. In this last duty, he saw the chance to lead his men in military glory. He saw an opportunity to write an epochal chapter in the history of emancipation. Promptly resigning his commission in the Fifty-first Massachusetts, he hastened south to the country of his enemy.

None had argued so proudly or so insistently that contrabands and free black men would fight to secure their freedom than Frederick Douglass. In speeches delivered throughout the churches and lyceums of the North, in articles published with increasing regularity in his perennially underfunded newspaper, the *Douglass Monthly*, he asserted that the

FIGURE 5.3 Frederick Douglass (ca. 1879). Courtesy National Archives.

government policy to ignore slavery was incompatible with the successful prosecution of the war. As the Lincoln administration gradually came to accept emancipation as a "military necessity," Douglass became the foremost advocate for arming former slaves and allowing them to fight for their freedom. *"Let the slaves and free colored people be called into service, and formed into a liberating army,*" he proclaimed, "to march into the South and raise the banner of Emancipation."[18] (See figure 5.3.)

At the time he penned these words, Douglass had for twenty years been the most famous black man in America. Bolstered by his notoriety as an abolitionist speaker aligned with William Lloyd Garrison, his *Narrative of the Life of Frederick Douglass, an American Slave, Written by Himself* sold more than 30,000 copies in the five years after it was published in 1845. A decade later, when he revised and expanded the autobiography, now titled *My Bondage and My Freedom*, he signaled a major change in his thinking. No longer was he a follower of Garrison, who viewed the Constitution as a compromise with slavery and refused to take seriously political action as an engine for social reform. Rather, Douglass had come to view the Constitution "in its letter and spirit, [as] an anti-slavery instrument," and therefore felt called upon to insist that his fellow citizens redeem the meaning of America by freeing *all* its peoples.[19]

Douglass shared with Emerson and Higginson a belief that freeing the slaves accorded with a higher law. "There are powers above those of the Government and the army," he asserted in 1861, "a power behind the throne, greater than the throne itself." Elsewhere, he admitted that the very fact of slavery violated "the natural operation of the eternal laws of the universe." But unlike Emerson and Higginson, his view of emancipation emerged from lived experience—hard won, achieved through risk and suffering—rather than from a high-minded moral philosophy from the ancient Greeks and the German Romantics. Slavery was, in his words, "soul murder," a "moral blight," a "soul plague and withering curse." It was nothing less than the theft of the self. At stake in emancipation was the redemption of the nation, which had been founded on the promise of liberty and equality for all. Even more important was the resurrection of souls, the recovery of personhoods.[20]

Douglass's oft-repeated argument that slaves and free black men would take up arms and fight for the Union was grounded in his own experience as a young slave raised in Maryland's Tidewater region near the Chesapeake. A rebellious young man, at times nearly sick with his yearning for freedom, he had been sent to a "negro-breaker" named Edward Covey at the age of sixteen. Douglass's account of his fight with Covey, first detailed in the *Narrative*, is one of the most electrifying moments in American literature:

> [B]ut at this moment,—from whence came the spirit I don't know—I resolved to fight; and suiting my action to the resolution,

I seized Covey hard by the throat....He held on to me, and I to him. My resistance was so entirely unexpected, that Covey seemed taken all aback. He trembled like a leaf. This gave me assurance, and I held him uneasy, causing the blood to run where I touched him with the ends of my fingers....He asked me if I meant to persist in my resistance. I told him I did, come what might; that he had used me like a brute for six months, and that I was determined to be used so no longer.[21]

At this moment, a slave named Bill stepped unwittingly into the stalemate.

Covey said, "Take hold of him, take hold of him!" Bill said his master hired him out to work, and not to help to whip me; so he left Covey and myself to fight our own battle out. We were at it for nearly two hours. Covey at length let me go, puffing and blowing at a great rate....The whole six months afterwards, that I spent with Mr. Covey, he never laid the weight of his finger upon me again.[22]

For Douglass, this epic battle "was the turning point in my career as a slave." It not only structured the meaning of his life, but it did much the same for his understanding of race relations in the United States. Abolition, he believed, could not be accomplished through moral suasion or legislative maneuvering alone. Rather, it had to be secured through an adversarial culture, through resistance: a fight in which life itself was risked but in which the slave might achieve "manhood" through combat.[23]

In the dozens of editorials Douglass wrote for his newspaper during the first three years of the Civil War, a visceral antipathy toward southern slaveholders fires nearly every word. The owners of human property are "pestiferous" villains who "know no law, and will respect no law but the law of force." They have "muzzled the mouth of all our large cities, and filled the air with whines for compromise," their actions roused by "the quenchless fire of a deadly hate, which spurns all restraints of law and humanity." They are, Douglass accuses, "[p]roud, grasping, ambitious, nursed in lies and cruelty," bearing "blackened hearts and bloody hands," poisoned by "perfidy and ingratitude."[24]

There was something deeply personal here. The blistering screeds against white masters not only reflected Douglass's resentment toward those who had deprived him of twenty years of freedom as he grew up on the shores of Maryland. It also expressed his bitter rage against Aaron Anthony, a white master rumored to be his father. The young Frederick had been conceived by this man in the full knowledge that he would be consigned to a life of slavery. The obverse of William Faulkner's Joe Christmas in *Light in August*, who is haunted by the unverifiable gossip that he possesses "nigger blood," Douglass would never know for certain the identity of his father. But his presumed parentage by a white slaveholder and a slave mother was the source of scalding resentment his entire life, the irritant and source of his most scathing criticism of the hypocrisy surrounding the slave system.

He understood better than most the belief that African Americans "had no rights which white men are bound to respect," the considered opinion of Supreme Court chief justice Roger Taney during the notorious *Dred Scott* decision of 1857. He understood how such claims masked destructive human relationships. Reversing Hawthorne's depiction of slavery as a "monstrous birth" visited upon American shores by accident, Douglass portrayed slaveholders as the "monster parents" of the Civil War. Speaking in 1862 at a Fourth of July gathering in Yates County, New York, Douglass told his audience, "*Your* fathers drew the sword for free and independent Government." The use of the second person in this statement portrayed the speaker as an orphan deprived of the promise of freedom exemplified by the nation's founders. But the war was the continuation of "the tremendous struggle, which your fathers and my fathers began eighty-six years ago." It promised to provide a legitimate paternity to all American citizens, black and white, free and enslaved. In a deft rhetorical pivot, Douglass announced, "The claim of *our* fathers upon our memory...are founded in the fact that they wisely, and bravely, and successfully met the crisis of their day."[25]

The speech reconfigured the American dream, placing Douglass within its promise of opportunity and equality while excluding the slaveholders' interests. "What is a slaveholder but a rebel and a traitor?" he asked in an 1861 editorial, arguing that the Confederacy and the slavocracy were inextricably linked, "[for a] man cannot be a slaveholder without being a traitor to humanity and a rebel against the law and government of the ever-living God." It followed that "[t]o fight against slaveholders, without fighting against slavery, is but a halfhearted business, and paralyzes the hands engaged in it."[26]

Douglass was by no means the only black intellectual, writer, and activist to participate in defining the meaning of the war and in contributing to the Union cause. Henry Highland Garnet, Martin R. Delany, Charlotte Forten Grimké, and many others transformed their lived experience as former slaves and free blacks into advocacy for the great cause of emancipation. For them, abolition was not an abstraction but a precondition for full involvement in life. Within this community of African-American intellectuals, there were disagreements over pressing issues such as black nationalism, black militancy, slave insurrections, and the proper reading of the Constitution. But the black vision of freedom, a vision of hope fused with understandable caution, enabled them to view the war as a historic opportunity for the transformation of self and society.

Douglass's utterances from the period are of particular interest not only because they are so powerful rhetorically, but also because they seem to anticipate the course of history. By the summer of 1862, as Union losses piled up, more and more people began to accept the idea that had once seemed but an improbable fantasy hatched by a fringe group of radicals. In July, Congress passed the Second Confiscation Act, which authorized the enlistment of blacks. A month later, General Saxton received permission to raise five regiments in the Sea Islands, and by November he had appointed Higginson as commander of the First South Carolina Volunteers. Shortly after Lincoln signed the Emancipation Proclamation, Douglass exclaimed that "the most hopeful sign of the times" was the "growing disposition to employ the black men of the country in the effort to save it from division and ruin." Eagerly, he looked southward for signs that the black population would engage in the epic struggle as he had once fought with Covey.[27] (See figure 5.4.)

Although Higginson believed he "had been an abolitionist too long...not to feel a thrill of joy" at the prospect of commanding a black regiment, he soon encountered unexpected difficulties. Many of the freed people in Port Royal remained understandably suspicious of whites. Their distrust had been inflamed by fleeing landowners, who warned that mercenary northerners would masquerade as reformers in order to sell them to Cuba. Susie King Taylor, a fourteen-year-old black girl living in Savannah during the early years of the war, remembered being warned by southern whites "not to go to the Yankees, for they would harness [blacks] to carts and make them pull the carts around, in place of horses." As a result of these and similar warnings, fewer black men volunteered to serve in the Union army than had been initially hoped.[28]

Susan Walker, one of the first wave of Gideonites, noted in her journal that she had "tried in vain to inspire a desire to fight but none [of the contrabands] wish to volunteer." She thought they might "be forced to fight, but none will volunteer to leave their homes," and

FIGURE 5.4 Recruiting poster for African-American troops. Courtesy
Rare Book, Manuscript, and Special Collections Library, Duke University.

she concluded, "This is a sad truth and full of deep meaning." When
he attempted to convince a student named Billy to enlist, educator
William Allen was told by the young man that he "would rather be a
slave all his life than fight." Allen confided, "I wish sincerely that
something would turn up to make these men more willing to fight for
their freedom." Describing a recruitment meeting in which a northern
white woman "made an appeal to the mothers, urging them not to
keep back their sons from the war fearing they might be killed but to
send them forth willingly and gladly...to fight for liberty," Charlotte
Forten worried that the speech did little to ameliorate the "good deal
of distrust about joining the regiment."[29]

Another difficulty, which Higginson tried not to think too much
about, was the personal danger in which he had placed himself by
accepting his commission. "[W]e all fought," he later wrote, "with ropes
around our necks, the Confederate authorities having denied to officers
of colored regiments the usual privileges, if taken prisoners, and having
required them to be treated as felons." Writing about Higginson, John
Greenleaf Whittier admitted, "I feel the greatest admiration for his

FIGURE 5.5 Thomas Wentworth Higginson in uniform.

heroic self-devotion, and yet I tremble in view of its peril. He will be a marked man, and especially exposed." How strange, Whittier continued, "to think of him so fresh, so beautiful in his glorious manhood, with his refinement, culture, and grace—leading that wild African regiment to avenge the wrong of two centuries of slavery! How this one act of his is making his name historic."[30] (See figure 5.5.)

Higginson responded to the threats and difficulties of his situation by drilling his men. And he wrote. Northern newspapers received regular dispatches from Beaufort, long missives filled with buoyant if mildly questionable claims about the heroism of his men. In truth, despite the difficulties, he was having the time of his life. He had liberated a piano from an abandoned plantation house, and sometimes in the evening, as the sea breeze blew through the veranda at headquarters, he played a waltz. With the excitement of a tourist visiting an exotic locale, he reveled in the Sea Islands' climate, the fecund tang of the sea, the lush flora and alien fauna. "Coming from the blustering and bleak March winds of New York," wrote a correspondent for *Harper's*, "the climate here is enchanting…the skies have a tropical radiance…[t]he air is full of the multitudinous song of birds." A reporter for the *Continental Monthly* observed, "The climate in winter is delightful," before including a catalog of botanical rarities and a hymn to the island's quality of air.[31]

Higginson was no different. His journal is full of horticultural descriptions, detailed, whimsical records of "the mighty limbs of a great live-oak, with the weird moss swaying in the smoke, and the high moon gleaming faintly through," and of the campsite "embowered in wild-plum-blossoms, small, white, profuse, and tenanted by murmuring bees." He lingered over sounds: the "wild and desolate cacophony of sea-fowl" reminded him of the "cry of a myriad of lost souls"; the revelatory song of the mockingbird, its "notes seeming to trickle down through the sweet air from mid the blossoming boughs," filled him with wonder, as did the "wild killdeer plover," which "flit[ted] and wail[ed] above us, like the haunting souls of dead slave-masters."[32]

He drank in the "[q]uantities of roses & magnolias" surrounding the camp and congratulated himself on "[t]his charming life among Cherokee roses & peach blossoms." "In the retrospect," he confided in *Army Life in a Black Regiment*, a memoir he would complete after the war, "I seem to see myself adrift upon a horse's back amid a sea of roses." In the evenings, after the piano, he occupied himself by reading *Les Misérables*, writing letters to his wife and mother, snacking on the ginger biscuits, chocolate, and prunes that arrived in packages from home.[33]

Beyond commentary on the vegetation and his daily activities, Higginson filled the pages of his diary with observations of his men. Furtively, he collected the words to slave spirituals.

> Often in the starlit evening, I have returned from some lonely ride by the swift river, or on the plover-haunted barrens, and, entering the camp, have silently approached some glimmering fire, round which the dusky figures moved in the rhythmical barbaric dance the negroes call a "shout," chanting, often harshly, but always in the most perfect time,

some monotonous refrain. Writing down in the darkness, as best I could,—perhaps with my hand in the safe cover of my pocket,—the words of the songs, I have afterwards carried it to my tent, like some captured bird or insect, and then, after examination, put it by.[34]

The slave spirituals made musicologists of several Gideonites. Lucy McKim, who would later marry the son of William Lloyd Garrison, gathered and described the songs she heard in Port Royal into the first serious collection of spirituals, *Slave Songs of the United States*, published in 1867. Charlotte Forten, the young poet who had traveled south to teach, was particularly stirred by the eerie and beautiful singing. Leaving her steamer for the low sandy beach near Beaufort, she described "the rich sonorous tones of the boatmen" who rowed her to the abandoned plantation that would become her temporary home. "Their singing impressed me much. It was so sweet and strange and solemn. 'Roll, Jordan, Roll' was grand, and another

'Jesus make de blind to see
Jesus make de deaf to hear
Jesus make de cripple walk
Walk in, dear Jesus,'

and the refrain

'No man can hender me.'"[35]

Higginson found in the spirituals the same exotic wildness he enjoyed in the dense, mysterious surroundings of the low country. Just beyond the borders of the camp was a thick canopy of trees, rhododendrons in bloom, blackberry brakes: a tapestry of greens, yellows, and reds. Vines crept up the porches and columns of abandoned houses, pried into the clapboard sheathing, as if nature were intent on swallowing whole the discarded morsels of human cultivation. Something about this fertile profusion reminded him of the singing of the men, which ignored "the long and short metres of the hymn-books" and instead "always gladly yield[ed] to the more potent excitement of their own 'spirituals.'"[36] It seems not to have occurred to him that the rough metrics and unfinished, improvised quality of the slave chants shared characteristics with the neatly copied poetry he continued to receive from Emily Dickinson in Amherst.

As winter turned to spring, Higginson's regiment grew in size and competence. In blazing heat, the men marched up and down the sandy beach of Hilton Head, the dark blue of their uniforms blending with the ocean and sky. "Today in looking at my best company drilling with the musket," he wrote, "it suddenly occurred to me that all soldiers were not black & it seemed as if a white company would look very odd." Writing to his mother, he claimed that life in camp was "as good as anything we have had, were only the zest of immediate danger added."[37]

In the spring of 1863, immediate danger was 500 miles to the north, where despite the perpetual problems of sickness, malingering, and desertion, both armies were preparing for what would become an epic series of clashes at Chancellorsville, Vicksburg, and Gettysburg. Feeling isolated from the action, Higginson continued drilling his men, convinced that the discipline he instilled had already provided them with an Emersonian self-reliance unattainable to slaves. Longing to put this discipline to the test, he lobbied to lead his regiment on a military expedition and was soon heading a trip up the St. Mary's River along the border of Georgia and Florida to recruit more blacks for the army.

Armed with the regimental flag and miniature copies of the Emancipation Proclamation, Higginson and his men traveled aboard a gunboat, flanked by two other ships, into the thick, musky atmosphere of Florida. One night, sometime around midnight, he and a small detachment of men went ashore, hoping to surprise the enemy just outside of Township Landing. The maneuver went awry. Some of his men fired at a rebel cavalry unit before receiving a command and promptly found themselves in a firestorm. "Perhaps at the first shot a man fell at my elbow," Higginson recalled. "I felt it no more than if a tree had fallen,—I was so busy watching my own men and the enemy, and planning what to do next."[38] Through the murk, a Confederate officer took aim at Higginson but was shot by three men from the First South Carolina, who pulled their triggers a split second before the sniper did.

The next day, a former slave, now a corporal in Higginson's unit, took his commander to the Georgia plantation where he had been raised. He showed Higginson the fields where he had labored and the small, cramped building equipped with stocks and chains where slaves were punished. Higginson promptly confiscated some shackles and chains as evidence of the "infernal barbarism" of slavery.[39]

Soon, the expedition began its return, having confiscated forty bushels of rice, some sheep, and sundry other provisions (but not nearly as many recruits as Higginson had hoped). Steaming down the sluggish St. Mary's, they were fired upon by rebel artillery hidden among the bluffs. Bullets rattled the sides of the gunboat, sounding like hail, and the captain of the steamer was killed. He "was not among my soldiers,"

Higginson noted, "and yet he was killed." For a moment, Higginson allowed himself to think about the man's "wife and children, of whom he had spoken," wondering how the family would survive without their husband and father. But "one learns to think rapidly in war," he continued, "and cautioning the Major to silence, I went up to the hurricane-deck…to see where we were."[40]

Although the trip was but a footnote to the great machinations of war occurring farther north, Higginson was ecstatic at the demeanor of his men. No one doubted "that the key to the successful prosecution of this war lies in the unlimited employment of black troops," he wrote to General Saxton.

> Their superiority lies simply in the fact that they know the country, while white troops do not, and, moreover, that they have peculiarities of temperament, position, and motive which belong to them alone. Instead of leaving their homes and families to fight, they are fighting for their homes and families, and they show the resolution and the sagacity which a personal purpose gives.[41]

Higginson's second and more significant expedition occurred in March, when he led his troops even farther south, to Jacksonville, Florida, which he was ordered to secure and occupy. Susie King Taylor, the young woman who had been warned against northern interlopers while a girl in Savannah, had since married a soldier in Higginson's regiment and enlisted as a laundress. In her remarkable narrative about her wartime experiences, *Reminiscences of My Life in Camp with the 33rd United States Colored Troops, Late 1st S.C. Volunteers*, she described how she accompanied the men to Jacksonville, which was soon captured. Higginson's men confiscated timber and railroad iron, and they also recruited fugitive blacks for a second regiment in South Carolina. Again, there was skirmishing with Confederates. According to Taylor, a small band of rebels hid "behind a house about a mile or so away, their faces blackened to disguise themselves as negroes." When Higginson's unit cautiously approached, "the firing was opened and several of our men were wounded and killed."[42]

According to Taylor, "the rebels shelled directly toward Colonel Higginson's headquarters," the bombardment so heavy "that the colonel told my captain to have me taken up into town to a hotel, which was used as a hospital." "I shall never forget that Dantean monster," Higginson later wrote about the artillery, "rearing its black head amid the distant smoke."[43] He remained mute, however, about the many troops under his command who broke and fled toward the transports at the wharves during the first day's battle. Nor did he dwell on what proved to be the most controversial aspect of the expedition.

The First South Carolina had occupied Jacksonville for several weeks, working alongside white troops from the Sixth Connecticut and the Eighth Maine. "It was the first time in the war (so far as I know)," Higginson reported, "that white and black soldiers had served together on regular duty." This example of interracial service was abruptly broken, however, when Higginson's troops were suddenly ordered to evacuate. The men, he wrote, were "disappointed and amazed," and that morning there "occurred an act on the part of some of the garrison most deeply to be regretted." The act was "not to be excused by the natural indignation at their recall,—an act which, through the unfortunate eloquence of one newspaper correspondent, rang through the nation,—the attempt to burn the town."[44]

On March 28, 1863, Jacksonville burned to the ground, its small downtown consumed by a "roar of the flames, and the rolling clouds of smoke." Churches, warehouses, and cottages were destroyed, as were fragrant orange groves. The question was, *who* burned it? If Higginson's black troops were responsible—as was immediately asserted by northern Democrats, who continued to argue that a war to liberate the slaves was a violation of the Constitution and a transgression of the natural order of racial hierarchy—then the Port Royal experiment had proven a failure. Higginson quickly collected testimonials from war correspondents, who exonerated the black troops of any responsibility in the destruction of Jacksonville and placed the blame squarely on white soldiers serving in the town. According to the *New York Times*, "It is certainly unfortunate that we should have among us a class of patriots who will twist and exaggerate an insignificant affair like this into one of the most shocking Union atrocities—to the infinite infamy of our army and the disgrace of the whole nation."[45]

Yet there is some reason to question Higginson's account. Writing a history of the St. Johns River, which flows through Jacksonville, the novelist James Branch Cabell described Higginson's brief adventure in Jacksonville as a "career of arson and theft," imparting a final image of Higginson drawn from the charismatic commander's own journal. "In the garden of his former headquarters," Cabell wrote, Higginson "with a poetic touch, culled for his lapel a white tea-rosebud, to be a memento of Jacksonville, which he left on fire."[46]

Even before Higginson's second expedition, Charlotte Forten had written of the abolitionist's peculiar fondness for arson. "The Colonel seems to have entered into firing houses at St. Mary's with great zest," she recorded in her diary on February 21, 1863. "We were laughing and talking about it when he turned to me with great gravity...and said, 'Now Miss Forten, what in your opinion is the best place to begin with in setting a house on fire?...some authorities say to the leeward, others to the windward. I've tried both and I don't see that it makes any difference.' "[47]

Higginson's third and final expedition came one week after Gettysburg. The three-day battle in Pennsylvania, fought July 1–3, 1863, resulted in a staggering 51,000 dead and wounded, and would become the most famous battle of the war. Decisively ending Robert E. Lee's bold invasion into the north, Gettysburg marked yet another turning point in the conflict. Walt Whitman, having relocated to Washington, recalled watching a Fourth of July parade on Pennsylvania Avenue when he suddenly noticed an enormous placard proclaiming "Glorious Victory for the Union Army!" He walked to the armory hospital with "several bottles of blackberry and cherry syrup," which he mixed with ice water and distributed to the wounded in celebration.[48]

Higginson's expedition was more modest. Its purpose was to destroy a railroad bridge and, once again, to gather as many recruits from the abandoned slave population as possible. Accompanied by 300 men, he traveled aboard the *John Adams* with two smaller vessels up the Edisto River, a sluggish, winding waterway overhung with dense vegetation. At Wiltown, the expedition's three boats came under fire. Higginson sounded a hasty retreat, but the boats caught and snagged on stakes hidden by the enemy in the brackish river. With his tugboat trapped during a falling tide, he next ordered the vessel abandoned and burned. Just as the tug was being deserted, a barrage of artillery hit Higginson's boat. A "few casualties occurred," he remembered, "and those instantly fatal. As my orderly stood leaning on a comrade's shoulder, the head of the latter was shot off."[49]

That sentence is the most understated in Higginson's entire oeuvre. Earlier that spring, in a spirited moment of derring-do, he had reconnoitered enemy camps by swimming across the channel at Hilton Head in the middle of the night. In his account of the adventure, he recalled "the smooth, eddying currents," "so still and lovely," which imbued him with the feeling that he had entered "some magic crystal, of which I was the enchanted center." But as he drew closer to the enemy shore, his mood drastically changed. Aware that his "unfortunate head" had become a vulnerable target above the waterline, he was seized by terror. Heart racing, he imagined his skull had "gradually assumed to its inside a gigantic magnitude," had enlarged to monstrous proportions.[50]

Something of this sense of horror returned now as the head of the soldier standing near him was blown cleanly from the man's shoulders. Although barely touched by a projectile, Higginson was mysteriously wounded. "I myself felt a sudden blow in the side," he recalled, "as if from some prize-fighter, doubling me up for a moment." The wound "proved afterwards to have been produced by the grazing of a ball, which, without tearing a garment, had yet made a large part of my side black and blue." Still later, he would remark that he "must have been grazed by grapeshot or an exploded shell. This was to have found myself only half an inch, yet, in Mercutio's phrase, it was enough."[51]

Years later, Higginson's enigmatic correspondent from Amherst confessed, "If I feel physically as if the top of my head were taken off, I know that is poetry." The incident on the Edisto River had the reverse effect on Higginson: it deprived him of life's poetry, left him spiritless, depleted, without his usual recourse to jaunty prose.

He was, quite literally, shell-shocked, stunned by the proximity of death. Although he could joke "in the words of one of the men, 'I'se been a sickly person, eber since de expeditious,'" it would be years before he fully regained his health.[52] He lingered in a military hospital for more than a month, eventually requesting a furlough to see his wife and mother. Soon after the visit, he resigned his commission and moved to Newport with his wife, where the two convalesced in the ocean breeze.

On the way home, he had reported more bad news to his mother. It involved another African-American regiment, the Massachusetts Fifty-fourth, led by the soft-spoken, dark-haired scion of a prominent abolitionist family, Robert Gould Shaw. Higginson had gotten to know the young commander in June, when Shaw traveled south to train his men in South Carolina. In truth, he was faintly jealous of the youth. The Fifty-fourth had received far more attention and encouragement from the nation's men of letters, primarily because it originated in Massachusetts. But now was no time for rivalry or ill feelings. "The 54th was badly cut up," Higginson informed his mother as he made his way north, "& Shaw certainly killed."[53]

CHAPTER 6

Fathers and Sons

Nor far from Higginson's destination in Newport stood a stately stone house at 465 Spring Street. For the past several years, it had been a boisterous place. Henry James Sr. liked to boast that he had purchased it "at half its worth"—if true, one of the only sound investments he ever made in his long, interesting, and thriftless life.[1] During the summer, as the sea air rustled the hydrangeas and made Newport among the most pleasant places to live in America, the towering gambrel-roofed home roared and clattered with raucous debate.

The James children would become known for their brilliance. William, the oldest son, slender and acerbic, his mind darting like a hummingbird from idea to idea, had only recently abandoned his dream of becoming a painter in order to devote himself "quite positively and before everything [to] Science, physical Science, strenuous Science."[2] (He would eventually become a psychologist and, still later, one of the nation's most influential philosophers.) Henry, the next oldest, always more dilatory, more plodding, more cautious and attuned to subtle distinctions, had recently suffered an "obscure hurt" while helping to put out a stable fire and was quietly nursing his aspirations to become a novelist. Alice, the witty sister, the only daughter, was just beginning her career as a lifelong diarist and invalid.

But during the tumultuous summer of 1863, with the nation plunged in the middle of an unrelenting war, it was the two youngest sons, Wilky and Bob, who seemed the most interesting and dynamic. Both had attended the "transcendental" Sanborn School in Concord with Emerson's and Hawthorne's children and with the attractive daughters of John Brown. Emerson's son Edward once visited the James family in Newport after the school year had ended and described how the "'adipose and affectionate Wilky,' as his father would call him, would say something and be instantly corrected by the little cock-sparrow Bob, the youngest." Voices would rise and in the excitement of debate the combatants would begin waving their silverware. "'Don't be disturbed, Edward,' interposed the genial Mrs. James, 'they won't stab each other. This is usual when the boys come home.'"[3]

Often as not, the discussion was about the war. The boys shared the unwavering abolitionism of their father, who on July 4, 1861, had delivered an address to the citizens of Newport on precisely that topic. The elder James was famously abstruse. William once noted about his father's thought, "Suffice it that many points which before were incomprehensible to me because doubtfully fallacious—I now definitely believe to be entirely fallacious." On that occasion of the nation's birthday, Henry Sr. had invoked the religious mystic Emanuel Swedenborg to claim that freedom was "identical with the God-made constitution of the human mind itself." The promise of liberty for all would be consummated in the violent termination of slavery, an act that would propel American society "from appearance to reality, from passing shadow to deathless substance," helping it to achieve the millennial utopia portended in the Declaration of Independence and the Constitution.[4]

It was a lesson Wilky especially took to heart. Recalling that he had been "brought up in the belief that slavery was a monstrous wrong," Wilky convinced his father, who had discouraged William and Henry from enlisting, to allow him to join the Massachusetts Forty-fourth and then the Fifty-fourth, the first African-American regiment to form in the free states. He was seventeen. Wilky's enlistment endowed him with instant glamour and authority in the family. He seemed ripe with "romantic chances," according to his novelist brother, Henry, who gathered in the parlor with his parents and William and Alice to read aloud the letters sent from the front.[5]

"Today is Sunday," Wilky wrote shortly after leaving camp in the late spring of 1863, "and I've been reading Hugo's account of Waterloo in *Les Misérables* and preparing my mind for something of the same sort. God grant the battle may do as much harm to the Rebels as Waterloo did to the French. If it does the fight will be worth the dreadful carnage it may involve." Venturing farther south to Charleston, he found the once-elegant port city, with its airy verandas

FIGURE 6.1 African-American soldiers at Fort Wagner (1865). Courtesy Library of Congress, Prints and Photographs Division (LC-B811-3491).

and skyline full of steeples, "more forsaken and stricken than I can describe." Like a sign from the Old Testament, the birthplace of the rebellion now resembled "some old doomed city on which the wrath of God has rested."[6]

Not long after this letter arrived, the house on Spring Street took on a different tone. It became hushed, tense, the quiet punctuated only now and then by a feverish shout. On July 18, while serving as an adjutant to Robert Gould Shaw, the commander of the Fifty-fourth Massachusetts, Wilky had led his men up the sandy ascent to Fort Wagner, a battery fortification on Morris Island, South Carolina, less than a hundred miles north of Port Royal. There, he had met raking rifle and artillery fire. When he was halfway up the hill, a shell tore into his side. Fueled by adrenaline, he got back up and continued the ascent. Then, he was struck in the ball of his right foot by a second shell. "[F]altering with shock," as he later described it, he toppled over and clawed his way from the fort in order to avoid being captured.

The wounds were grave. By the time Wilky was transported to the field hospital in Port Royal, both his side and ankle had become dangerously infected. He lay beside hundreds of other injured and dying soldiers in makeshift cots, sweating in the subtropical heat, until at last he was recognized by a family friend, Cabot Russell, who had traveled from Boston to search for his own son. (He was unsuccessful.) Russell took charge of Wilky's return to Newport, remaining at the young man's side when emergency surgery was performed to remove a shell fragment from his foot. So precarious was the soldier's condition that, when he arrived at last in Newport, the doctors insisted that his stretcher not be moved from where it had been set down inside the entranceway of 465 Spring Street.

Overnight, the James house became a hospital. William watched over his comatose brother, changing bandages and, in a brief return of his old ambitions, drawing Wilky's unconscious face. Wilky's return and convalescence had a profound effect upon Henry, as well. "Clear as some object presented in high relief against the evening sky of the west," he wrote a half century later, "is the presence for me beside the stretcher on which my brother was to lie for so many days before he could be moved."[7]

Henry Sr. was particularly distraught. To a friend, he reported, "Poor Wilky cries aloud for his friends gone and missing." One night, the wounded boy suddenly sat up. "Ah father," he announced, half delirious,

it is easy preaching faith in God's care, but one night it was hard to practice it. I woke up lying in the sand under my tent, and slowly recalled all that had happened, my wounds, my fall…my feeble crawling to the ambulance…sick and faint for loss of blood. As I lay…wondering whether I should ever see my home again, a groan beside me arrested my attention, and turning my head I discerned…a poor Ohio man with his jaw shot away, who finding that I was near to him and unable to move, crept over on me and deluged me with his blood. At that I felt—

"Here he stopped too full to proceed," Henry Sr. continued sadly, "and I suppose he was going to say, that then he felt how hard it was to hope in God."[8]

* * *

Back in March, around the same time Thomas Wentworth Higginson was leading his troops into the heat of Jacksonville, Emerson had received a request to help raise funds for the Massachusetts Fifty-fourth, Wilky James's regiment. Emerson was an obvious choice for the request, his view of the war having become something like a categorical imperative. Moreover, he was a long-time friend of the Shaw family, who lived near his brother William and whose son Robert had been selected to lead the historic regiment. Yet the appeal to speak at a fundraiser on behalf of the first black regiment from the North prompted something of a personal crisis in Emerson. Under the journal heading "Negro Soldiers," he wrote a series of comments in what his editors described as "uncharacteristically passionate and ungrammatical language."[9] At times, the clotted and incomplete sentences threatened to dissolve into incoherence. For one of the only times in his life, Emerson was at a loss for words.

In the spring of 1863, it seemed as though he had finally witnessed the fruition of his youthful vision of human transformation. The long-awaited work of conversion had begun with the signing of the Emancipation Proclamation. Everywhere, portents suggested that slavery would soon be consigned to history. Yet something about the chance to speak on behalf of Massachusetts's first black regiment gave Emerson pause, made him hesitant, uncertain, filled with uncharacteristic doubt.

For one thing, death had intruded into his thoughts. Death made him scratch out words and ransack his library in an effort to restore his habitual optimism. He could not help dwelling upon all the young men who had hoped to "restore the spirit of the American constitution" to their country, soldiers who had died bravely on the battlefield, sacrificing themselves for the "purpose to end slavery at the earliest day." Too many boys and young men had "died for the largest & noblest sentiment," he admitted, many of them of "the best blood of our educated counties [and the] objects of the most romantic hope & love, poets & romancers themselves."[10] All of these precious lives were martyrs in the battles of Shiloh and Antietam; victims of dysentery, typhus, and other rampant infections in unsanitary field hospitals; prisoners of war now starving in barbaric camps throughout the South.

These dark musings were preparation for a question Emerson almost dared not ask: Would the black regiments be capable of redeeming the sacrifices of these men? Would they fight valiantly in order to secure their freedom, or would they, as some claimed, malinger, desert, or refuse to fight during actual combat? Emerson had no tolerance for the extreme pronouncements of anti-abolitionists such as Horatio Seymour, reelected as New York's governor in 1862, who called the arming of black soldiers "a proposal for the butchery of women and children, for scenes of lust and rapine, of arson and murder unparalleled in the history of the world." But Emerson was prepared to admit that a race of people subjugated and debased by centuries of slavery might not be ready for the responsibilities that accompanied freedom. From South Carolina had come reports that the fugitive slaves flocking to the Sea Islands and mustering into the Union army were "an abject race, more docile and submissive than those of any other locality."[11]

Sitting at the round table in his book-lined study, his notebook open before him, Emerson strived to allay these doubts. He quoted his friend Massachusetts governor John Albion Andrew, who had recently informed him that many of the state's free blacks had promised to "enlist if you send us out for freedom & not if you send us out to return slaves." Reflecting the racial stereotypes of his period, he struggled to list racial attributes that seemed to promise the success of the newly formed regiment. "Negroes good soldiers," he wrote, "they love music, dress, order, parade."[12]

Then, something rather surprising happened. Emerson abruptly quit arguing with himself. He sat back in his rocking chair, picked up his pen, and wrote a poem that seemed to cut the Gordian knot of his reflections:

> I am not black in my mind
> But born to make black fair:
> On the battlefield my master find,—
> His white corpse taints the air.[13]

It is difficult to overstate just how revolutionary are these four lines in Emerson's thinking. They blaze with an insight impossible to him even six months earlier. Belonging to a Romantic poetic tradition that had emerged a half century before with Wordsworth's *Lyrical Ballads*, Emerson had populated his poetry with a person whose interior life once would have been considered unworthy of poetic representation: a black soldier stationed somewhere in the South. The quatrain gave voice to the voiceless, expression to one whose thoughts few had bothered to consider before. It transformed the once-powerless and mute speaker into a radiant and articulate being. And it confronted the most appalling subject to haunt the white imagination: the killing of masters by slaves.

Black insurrection had long been a primal fear troubling and roiling the genteel surface of antebellum culture. Beneath the exuberant claims of Manifest Destiny, beneath the optimistic assertions of a progressive democratic society, there lurked a gut-deep dread that the nation could be destroyed by those excluded from full participation in society should they decide to revolt. The fear was strongest in the South, which still recalled with horror the slave uprising led by Nat Turner in 1831, when a small band of slaves and freedmen embarked on a two-day killing spree that left fifty-seven white men, women, and children dead. But the fear was widely evident in the North, as well. "If you desire negro citizenship," Stephen Douglas told an audience in one of his famous debates with Lincoln, "if you desire them to vote on an equality with yourselves, and to make them eligible to office, to serve on juries, and to adjudge your rights, then support Mr. Lincoln and the Black Republican party." When the audience began to shout "Never, never," Douglas continued to play upon his listeners' fear of black insurrection. The "signers of the Declaration of Independence had no reference to negroes at all when they declared all men to be created equal. They did not mean the negro, nor the savage Indians, nor the Feejee Islanders, nor any other barbarous race."[14]

Even in the context of war, black-against-white violence was a taboo subject. The immensely popular *Frank Leslie's Illustrated Weekly*, a pictorial newspaper crammed with battle scenes by illustrators who traveled with the Union army, provided its readers with numerous pictures of African-American soldiers during the first half of 1863. It showed these soldiers drilling, marching, even charging into battle. It also showed them being hacked and bayoneted by enemy troops. Never, however, did *Leslie's* portray black soldiers killing or even engaging in hand-to-hand combat with white combatants.

Emerson's poem broke new ground for him in terms of subject matter, but he wrote it with mixed feelings. The clue is in the poem's final image. He had previously written that slavery poisoned the element so often associated by nineteenth-century Romantics with *spiritus* and inspiration: air. Now, in this poem, he attempted to fumigate the fetid atmosphere of U.S. history, to eliminate the stink and rot of a society based on human property, to restore the freshness and freedom upon which the nation had, in theory at least, been built. But this purification came at a cost. The nation found itself burdened with yet another corpse: the decomposing body of southern society.

Writing some forty years after the formation of the Massachusetts Fifty-fourth, W. E. B. DuBois marveled, "How extraordinary....The slave pleaded; he was humble; he protected the women of the South, and the world ignored him. The slave killed white men; and behold, he was a man."[15] Emerson's quatrain pulsed with this insight also, but it ended less triumphantly. Sitting in his study and trying to write a speech on behalf of the Fifty-fourth, he seemed to have recognized that his longing to convert the world had helped to blow a hole in the culture. The atmosphere of American life, tainted by violence and death, was a shared inheritance, a mutual grief, a national defeat. And all of this, he had sadly begun to realize, was bequeathed to the next generation.

As with Walt Whitman and Thomas Wentworth Higginson, Theodore Winthrop and Moncure Daniel Conway, Emerson had inspired a cohort of talented young people who believed that ideas—-*ideals*—mattered more than things. Oliver Wendell Holmes, the towering, lanky son of the Boston wit who would one day become an eminent Supreme Court justice, revered Emerson's iconoclasm and disdain for social convention. If the transcendentalist had brought Whitman "to a boil," Holmes claimed that he "set me on fire," and admitted even in his late eighties, "The only firebrand of my youth that burns as brightly as ever is Emerson."[16]

Holmes was a close friend of Charles Russell Lowell, son of Charles and Anna Lowell, at whose house the Emerson daughters stayed while attending the Agassiz School in Boston. Lowell would become a colonel in the Army of the Potomac and toward the end of the war would lead Herman Melville and others on an expedition through the woodlands of Virginia in search of Confederate guerrillas. A decade earlier, Lowell had delivered a commencement oration at Harvard entitled "The Reverence Due from Old Age to Youth." The speech was pure Emerson. "[C]hange is indeed the only constancy," he maintained, "the world always advanced by impossibilities achieved." It was therefore imperative that members of the older generation look toward the "fresher and purer ideals" cherished by the young if they hoped to improve or even remake the world.[17]

Of all the young soldiers influenced by Emerson, the most famous by far was Lowell's brother-in-law Robert Gould Shaw. Handsome, small, lithe, with a luxuriant mustache he cultivated to promote the gravitas necessary for his military rank, Shaw was the son of wealthy New York abolitionists whose home on Staten Island abutted that of Theodore Winthrop. As a boy, he had been tutored at the utopian community in Roxbury, Massachusetts, Brook Farm, while his father, Francis Shaw, wrote polemics on behalf of the working class. But it was his mother who exerted the strongest influence on his life. Sarah Shaw was an ardent follower of Emerson and the abolitionist William Lloyd Garrison. She made certain that her children grew up imbibing the enlightened atmosphere of her friends Lydia Maria Child and Harriet Beecher Stowe, whose *Uncle Tom's Cabin* the young Robert read over and over again.

Like Oliver Wendell Holmes and Charles Russell Lowell, Robert Gould Shaw enlisted almost immediately after the firing on Sumter, joining the same regiment as Theodore Winthrop. He fought at Antietam, where he received a minor wound and was promoted to captain. He remembered, in the aftermath of the battle, crossing into "a large open field, and such a mass of dead and wounded men, mostly Rebels, as were lying there, I never saw before; it was a terrible sight, and our men had to be very careful to avoid treading on them; many were mangled and torn to pieces by artillery." Shaw was surprised by "so many young boys and old men among the Rebels," and thought it "hardly possible that they can have come of their own accord to fight us."[18]

Soon after the Emancipation Proclamation was signed, Shaw had been asked to lead the Massachusetts Fifty-fourth, the first African-American regiment assembled north of the Mason-Dixon line. Initially reluctant to assume command, he overcame his fear that white soldiers would not fight alongside blacks, persuaded in large part by his mother's convictions. "Well!" she wrote to him after he accepted the commission. "I feel as if God had called you up to a holy work. You helped him at a crisis when the most important question is to be solved that has been asked since the world began."[19]

After training his men throughout the frigid early spring of Massachusetts, Shaw and the Fifty-fourth traveled to South Carolina, where they soon drilled in proximity to Higginson and the Port Royal Gideonites. Charlotte Forten was particularly smitten by the young commander. "I am perfectly charmed with Col. S.," she confessed in her journal, "he seems to me in every way one of the most delightful persons I have ever met. There is something girlish about him, and yet I never saw anyone more manly. To me he seems a perfectly lovable person." In July 1863, as the battle at Gettysburg raged, she found herself "more than ever charmed with the noble little Col. What purity, what nobleness of soul, what exquisite gentleness in that beautiful face!"[20]

When white troops were ordered to Charleston as part of a new offensive to retake Fort Sumter, Shaw complained to General George C. Strong, his brigade commander, requesting "that the colored soldiers should be associated as much as possible with the white troops, in order that they may have other witnesses besides their own officers to what they are capable of doing." Soon, his regiment was ordered to James Island, near the southern city. Thomas Wentworth Higginson met with Shaw at Beaufort just before he departed and remarked upon the "watchful anxiety in his look." "I trust God will give me strength to do my duty," Shaw confided to a friend, adding, "If I could only live a few weeks longer with my wife, and be at home a little while, I might die happy, but it cannot be. I do not believe I will live through our next fight."[21]

He was correct. On July 18, Shaw led his troops in an assault on Fort Wagner, just outside Charleston, accompanied by two brigades of white soldiers. The assignment was a suicide mission. Soldiers clambered up the sand walls leading to the fort, waving the regimental colors and screaming at the enemy. Others followed with Enfield rifles. All met heavy fire from above. Wilky James recalled how the "battle line melted away" and quickly became "a phalanx of defeat and death." From his vantage below the first wave of attackers, he could see Shaw struggle up the parapet of the fort, sword in hand, then halt as if frozen when a bullet struck him in the chest.[22] (See figure 6.2.)

FIGURE 6.2 Lithograph depicting the death of Robert Gould Shaw at Fort Wagner. Courtesy Library of Congress, Prints and Photographs Division (LC-USZ62-1288).

Horace Greeley's *New York Tribune* compared the battle at Fort Wagner to Bunker Hill. The *Boston Commonwealth*, reporting that Confederate gravediggers had buried Shaw and 800 other Union soldiers in a mass pit and left them "mouldering in the ground," tacitly linked this common burial to the memory of John Brown. The English novelist and ardent abolitionist Elizabeth Gaskell beseeched American readers to "remember the name of the late Colonel Robert Gould Shaw as the name of one who gave up his life for what he believed to be right." Privately, Lydia Maria Child consoled the young man's mother with the thought that her son had "died nobly in the defense of great principles, and has gone to join the glorious army of the martyrs." Francis Shaw, the slain man's father, struggled to find consolation in the loss of his son. "We do thank God," he admitted, "that our darling...was chosen, among so many equals, to be the martyred hero of the downtrodden of our land."[23]

Shaw's brief career with the Fifty-fourth quickly became the subject of occasional verse throughout the North. In the *Continental Monthly*, Isabella McFarlane struck a characteristic note in a long ballad, which began:

> Loud rang the voice of the chieftain,
> As the Fifty-fourth rushed on:
> Charge on the guns of Wagner,
> Charge—and the fort is won![24]

Emerson, who had spoken on behalf of the Fifty-fourth and followed its movements with great interest, also felt moved to commemorate Shaw's death in poetry. His contribution to the young man's memory, a poem entitled "Voluntaries," appeared in the October 1863 issue of the *Atlantic Monthly* and eulogized an entire generation of young men who had given their lives in order to realize transcendental ideals. The "[n]ew generation [is] better than the last," he wrote in his journal around this time, honoring Shaw and other slain sons of Boston. "If our brothers or children are killed in the battle," he continued, "we owe to them the same courage & selfrenunciation in bearing well their death, which they showed us in sacrificing themselves."[25]

But once again, a gloomier strain ran through these musings, a dark lake that had suddenly opened in his mind. He weighed how many more men would die "with Winthrop, Lowell..., Shaw...," and noted, "As we live longer, it looks as if our company were picked out to die first, & we live on in a lessening minority." He recalled those who had died in the past several years, including Thoreau, who remained present in his thoughts, spectrally "erect, calm, self-subsistent before me," and his beloved aunt Mary Moody Emerson. He recalled his two brothers, Edward and Charles, dead for two decades but "of a class of forgotten but wonderful young men, burning too fast to live long" and reminding him now that the war was "blot[ting] out one generation." He followed these melancholy reflections with a list of those "I have lost."[26]

It was not Shaw's death alone that prompted these somber thoughts. It was something closer to home. For another young man—eager to fight for the triumph of the higher law, eager to exhibit "courage & selfrenunciation" even if that renunciation meant "bearing well [his] death"—was on Emerson's mind: his youngest child, Edward.

Born in 1844, the same year that his father's *Essays: Second Series* was published, Edward Emerson had been raised to the kind of privilege only available to a small clique of northeastern intellectuals. He had played games with Henry Thoreau and attended the schools of the famed naturalist Louis Agassiz and the transcendentalist Franklin B. Sanborn. The proud owner of a pony, Edward loved giving rides to his friends and classmates, who included Una and Julian Hawthorne and the young Alcott sisters. In the summers, he swam with Wilky and Bob James in the grassy Concord River, which meandered sluggishly through town, or hiked the woods surrounding Walden Pond and explored ancient Indian sites.

He was particularly drawn to military heroism, an allure to which none of the Emerson children were immune. Writing in January 1861 after Lincoln's election, Ellen Emerson, the oldest child, confessed that she had "always wanted to know how to fight, and felt an exultation at the prospect of war, and when Father reads of the Romaic lady with her apron full of cartridges I always envy her." As she wrote this letter, the seventeen-year-old Edward was outside in the cold, practicing his "Fencing and Broadsword."[27] The two of them studied Greek that year by translating *The Iliad*, a work whose bristling war scenes thrilled the entire family (see figure 6.3).

The only son of the nation's most famous thinker and writer, Edward increasingly dreamed of distinguishing himself on the field of combat much like Achilles and Hector. Once the war commenced, this dream only intensified. Through the Boston newspapers, he followed reports of every battle; he kept informed about dozens of young men of his acquaintance who had enlisted; he longed to lead a regiment in the greatest conflict of his times. During the summer of 1862, when he turned eighteen, he drilled with the Concord militia beneath the town's

FIGURE 6.3 Edward and Edith Emerson with their father. Courtesy
Concord Free Public Library.

great elms, marching along the dusty streets and thoroughfares to the
beat of a snare drum. Nearby, his mother and sisters prepared first aid
kits, knitted socks, and gathered information about friends and rela-
tives on the front. "Here in Concord we all agree that we have had the
pleasantest summer that has been known in years," Ellen wrote,
describing "a more intimate and social town-feeling, caused by the war
probably," than she could recall.[28]

But there was an obstacle to Edward's dream, an old family wound
that had never completely healed. In 1842, two years before he was

born, Edward's older brother, Waldo, had died of scarlet fever at age five. Emerson and his wife, Lidian, were stunned by the loss, their happiness demolished. Louisa May Alcott, nineteen at the time, visited the family the next morning to inquire about the little boy and would never forget how "his father came to me, so worn with watching and changed by sorrow that I was startled and could only stammer out my message." Emerson himself could barely speak. "Child," he managed at last, "he is dead." Alcott believed it "was my first glimpse of great grief." Lidian Emerson was nowhere to be seen when Alcott paid her visit. She had retreated to her bedroom. "Grief, desolating grief came over me like a flood," she later wrote, "and I feared that the charm of earthly life was forever destroyed."[29]

Emerson struggled to lessen his heartache through work. "In the death of my son, now more than two years ago," he wrote in his great mid-career essay "Experience," "I seem to have lost a beautiful estate,— no more. I cannot get it nearer to me."[30] The essay was in part an effort to purge sorrow, to apply the consolations of philosophy to his anguish. But despite such efforts, the Emerson household was diminished in the wake of Waldo's death. For months afterward, Lidian could not help bursting into tears. Years later, Emerson, still bereft, visited the family vault in the nearby cemetery and opened his dear boy's casket in order to glimpse him one last time.

"The one thing we watch with pathetic interest in our children," he noted when Edward was six, "is the degree in which they possess recuperative force." Waldo's death had filled Emerson with a sense of life's fragility, an anxiety he had never before known but that would henceforth attend the upbringing of his other children. Thinking of his surviving son and two daughters, he observed, "If they lose their spirit and remember the mischance in their chamber at home,—it is all over with them, they have a check for life. But if they have that degree of buoyancy and resistance that makes light of these mishaps…the scars rapidly cicatrize and the fibre is all the tougher for the wound."[31]

The war, especially the formation of the Massachusetts Fifty-fourth, had dredged up these feelings once again for Emerson. The reasons for this were complex. In the spring of 1861, Edward's oldest sister, Ellen, had written enthusiastically of his desire to enlist, commenting that "the idea of Edward's coming to it, if this lasts long enough, is…charming." A year later, she wrote to her brother: "My dearest boy, I don't *know* how you feel nor what you plan, but I have little doubt that I guess right and Mother's decree that you shall not enlist will be a great trial to you. She says that when emancipation is proclaimed you may."[32]

Lidian Emerson, an even more committed abolitionist than her husband, had "always a realizing and practical sense that this War is wholly directed and controlled by God." Confident that it was only a matter of time before the fighting would center upon "the establishment of *Universal* Freedom," she had forbade Edward's enlisting until the war was fought for emancipation. "The dear boy wants to enlist," she admitted, "but I will never consent to it till the War is avowedly for Universal Freedom."[33]

The crisis for the Emerson family thus followed the signing of the Emancipation Proclamation. Even after his father's poem celebrating the historic event, even after the speeches and parties commemorating Lincoln's historic action, Edward remained enrolled at Harvard. He did so, reluctantly, at his father's request. It made no sense, Emerson argued, to enlist before the young man had completed the academic year. After all, the war showed no signs of abating; there was still plenty of time to taste glory. But when the school year ended, just around the time the Massachusetts Fifty-fourth was being deployed to South Carolina, Emerson changed tack and argued that Edward was too frail to survive the rigors of camp life. The boy must consider his health, he argued, for there would be no benefit in enlisting to fight if he were to spend the entire time in a military hospital.

Emerson was torn, split by warring impulses, self-divided. Edward's desire to enlist had reignited the old anxiety toward his only surviving son. But this anxiety clashed sharply with his faith in moral forces and in the noble correctness of the Union cause. Even death, he had argued in his lectures on the war, contributed to the upward-trending direction of the universe. The inner conflict between his highest ideals and his love for Edward had been at the core of the journal entry "Negro Soldiers," and it would become the great private drama of his war years, a tension that would push him in first one direction, then another. Writing to a friend whose son had announced his intention to enlist, Emerson spoke on behalf of patriotism and the moral sentiment: "I believe all wise fathers are coming to feel that they have no right to dissuade their sons from this career." But to his brother William, he was more candid, fretting about Edward's plans: "if...he shall insist, like his cousin, on going to the war, & to such a war!"[34] He could not finish the sentence. Like Abraham of the Old Testament, he found himself caught between obedience to God's will and a powerful and abiding love for his son.

The dilemma prompted a series of rationalizations, equivocations, and arguments with himself. "The war has cost us many valuable lives," he admitted, "but perhaps it has compensated us, by making many lives valuable that were not so before." He tried to diminish the terrors of Antietam and Gettysburg: "It is never quite so dismal weather out of doors as it appears from the house window. Neither is the battlefield so horrible, nor wounds, nor death, as we imagine." But the thought of sacrificing his son caused him to recoil from these propositions. "Faults lay on either side the Trojan towers," he wrote in 1862, alluding to *The Iliad* to suggest that the war was the product of human shortcomings, not progressive history.[35] When friends in New Bedford lost their son to a Louisiana sharpshooter, he wrote the grieving family a note that reflected a shift from transcendental optimism to stoic forbearance.

"The soldier & the soldier's father & mother must have rehearsed this dread contingency to themselves quite too often," he began, "not to know its face when it arrives." The war, Emerson asserted, taught "selfrenouncement." Recently, a mutual friend, the "mother of Capt. James J. Lowell who fell on the peninsula," had visited him in Concord, and during her stay Emerson had "found in her not so much grief, as devotion of herself & all her family to the public service." He admired Mrs. Lowell's indomitable conviction, her forbearance and enduring acceptance, and he sought to extrapolate from her example some advice that would make the loss more bearable. "I think daily that there are crises which demand nations, as well as those which claim the sacrifice of single lives. Ours perhaps is one,—and that one whole generation might we consent to perish, if, by their fall, political liberty & clean & just life would be made sure to the generations that follow."[36]

The statement is characteristic Emerson but for a single word: *perhaps*. Gone was the famous optimism, the unshakable conviction in the Union cause, replaced by a hesitancy he seldom revealed in public. Emerson suggested that, while it was quite possible the war was worth the sacrifice of a generation, he could no longer be entirely certain. More remarkable, the letter was written six months *after* the signing of the Emancipation Proclamation—precisely when the shift in war aims had seemingly validated the cause of liberty.

One night at dinnertime, just after Antietam, Edward Emerson had come to the family table with his face distorted. The news had reached Concord that young James Lowell had been killed and Oliver Wendell Holmes critically wounded. Edward could not contain himself. "Oh don't you envy them?" he cried out, alarming the rest of the family.

"Don't you envy them? Wounded for their country! They can feel that it has cost them something."[37]

He continued to drill with the Concord militia, continued to practice fencing and to study military strategy. In order to toughen himself for combat, he camped with friends in the White Mountains and hiked the countryside surrounding Concord. Yet he did not enlist. "Edward has again asked to join the Army," Lidian wrote to Ellen, glossing over the tensions in the house surrounding the topic. Tacitly, she sided with her son:

> Your Father's great unwillingness to have him lose his next college year, is what keeps E. undecided. He is very much distressed (Edward) with the conflict between duty and inclination. He longs to go to war and thinks it will be the best possible thing for him, besides being, in a sense his duty; but your Father thinks it is rather his duty to stay and complete his education—and do the best he can for the world as a civilian.[38]

Years later, Ellen Emerson offered her own explanation for why Edward never served.

> He never stopped trying to get leave to go to the war, and the slaves being free Mother gave her consent, Father too; and when he was off at last Mr. [John Murray] Forbes waylaid him and said to him, "I am not half the man I was, since Will went to the war. If Malcolm should go too, I think my usefulness would be ended. You are your Father's only son. I leave it to you to judge whether your Father's services to your country or those that you could offer would be of most value."

According to Ellen, "[D]ear Edward gave up his heart's desire just as he had at last attained it, and came home to the friends he had just said goodbye to, and told them he would not go. How grateful were Father & Mother to Mr. Forbes!"[39]

Like the neat denouement of a parlor drama, Ellen's account resolved her brother's dilemma between filial obligation and national duty by showing the two opposing pressures to be one and the same. In relieving his father's anxiety, Edward was helping the nation. The only problem is that the story doesn't entirely square with the facts. Ellen claimed that Edward enlisted soon after the Emancipation Proclamation, "the slaves being free." But Lidian's letter to Ellen, which described her son as still agitating to join the army, was written in 1865. Further calling into question whether Edward actually enlisted or not is a letter Ralph Waldo Emerson wrote toward the end of 1863.

The letter was addressed to Edward Hallowell, recently promoted to colonel and put in command of the Massachusetts Fifty-fourth after the death of Robert Gould Shaw. Emerson was responding to Hallowell's request in late October to ask permission to invite Edward to join the heroic black regiment. Out of courtesy and respect for a national figure, Hallowell wished to broach the idea with the father first. It is not entirely clear whether Emerson consulted with Edward about the opportunity, or whether he even informed him about the letter. What is clear is that he declined the honor on his son's behalf:

> I thank you for the high honor you do my son in the proposal contained in your letter, and I feel that you have every right to make this claim on me. What right has to you & your comrades, it has to him. I believe that he too is quite well persuaded of that fact. But he is not quite yet worth the sending as a soldier. With a taste for rough life, he is of a delicate health, & very easily disordered....
>
> In his wish to go to war, I believe, Edward prefers the cavalry service, and is aiming at that. He has just been active in getting up a petition of his class & of all the classes to the college gvt. for the establishment of a compulsory drill; and he has been seeking private instruction in sabre exercise. As he is thus preparing to answer your question in his own way, I think you must give him a little more time, and he will be a soldier better worth having.
>
> In this state of the matter, I hope you will not make any proposition to him at this moment, since I fear the proposition would make his stay in college useless, if it did not take him out of college. With renewed thanks to you for the considerate manner in which you have acted towards us, and with respect,
>
> R. W. Emerson[40]

Robert Gould Shaw was killed at Fort Wagner exactly one week after Edward Emerson's nineteenth birthday. Reflecting on her son's birth, Lidian Emerson wrote to him, "I realized with joy and gratitude the greatness of the gift which God in indulgent kindness had given us, after he saw best to call Waldo to himself."[41] Emerson, with equally turbulent emotions, wrote one of his most moving Civil War poems, "Voluntaries," about Shaw's martyrdom, with its famous stanza:

> So nigh is grandeur to our dust
> So near is God to man,

When Duty whispers low, *Thou must*,
The youth replies, *I can.*[42]

The poem begins aboard a slave ship traversing the Middle Passage from Africa to the United States, where imprisoned slaves are shown to possess little more than a "wailing song" transmitted from "Hapless sire to hapless son." From there, the scene abruptly dissolves into the U.S. Senate, where "Great men" adjourn, "Building for their sons the State." Slavery is a *shared* inheritance, Emerson suggests, bequeathed to white and black sons alike. Having refused "to break [its] chain," the

FIGURE 6.4 Robert Gould Shaw in uniform. Courtesy Boston Athenaeum.

current generation is warned by the stern voice of "Destiny": " 'Pang for pang your seed shall pay, / Hide in false peace your coward head, / I bring round the harvest-day.' "[43]

Into this deplorable historical impasse enters the mythic figure of Shaw, a "generous chief" who arrives "To lead him willing to be led." "Stainless soldier on the walls," Emerson writes,

> Knowing this,—and knows no more,—
> Whoever fights, whoever falls,
> Justice conquers evermore,
> Justice after as before,—
> And he who battles on her side,
> God, though he were ten times slain,
> Crowns him victor glorified,
> Victor over death and pain.[44]

In many ways, the poem anticipated Lincoln's comments at Gettysburg, when the president stood near the spot where some 8,000 bodies had fallen in July 1863 and announced, "The brave men, living and dead, who struggled here, have consecrated [this cemetery] far above our power to add or detract." Three days of butchery had not only protected the recent and fragile Emancipation Proclamation, Lincoln suggested, it had helped to preserve the ideal of self-government, a "government of the people, by the people, and for the people."[45]

The speech crystallized a new vision of the war and of the Union. It proclaimed to a grieving nation that the dead had been sacrificed for a noble cause, that henceforth all battles in the interminable, bloody conflict would be waged in the spirit of the Declaration of Independence and the Constitution, waged to free all Americans, black and white, from tyranny. Emerson's "Voluntaries" had been written in the same spirit. It portrayed Shaw's death as the price exacted to free all Americans. It ennobled the war dead in a dirge as stately and reserved as a Greek elegy. But the author who had begun his literary career proclaiming, "Our age is retrospective. It builds the sepulchers of the fathers," would write some thirty years later in a much different tone. Sadness, strident optimism, uncertainty, and a profound ambivalence run like crosscurrents through "Voluntaries." All he had once longed for, Emerson seems to have realized, would be built upon the sepulchers of the sons.

CHAPTER 7

Phantom Limbs

W ALT WHITMAN WAS standing in a deserted battlefield on
Christmas Day 1862, scribbling in a small notebook. Dead
horses and mules littered the countryside. Splintered
stumps stood where fine, stately oaks and maples had recently grown.
The earth, loamy, damp, and smelling of minerals, was churned from
artillery.

Standing in the aftermath of battle, Whitman could "hear plainly
the music of a good band, at some Brigadier's headquarters, a mile
and a half away." He continued: "Then the drum tap from one
direction or other comes constantly breaking in. . . . I hear the sound
of bugle calls, very martial, at this distance." Something about the
music altered his mood, made him both pensive and hopeful. The
landscape was suddenly transformed. "Amid all this pleasant scene,
under the sweet sky and warm sun, I sit and think over the battle of
last Saturday week."[1]

That battle was Fredericksburg: the Union debacle in which his
brother George had been wounded, the battle that would end the
year with yet another northern defeat. Gunfire had been so heavy,
according to a Confederate survivor, that "a chicken could not live in
that field when we open on it." Whitman would later describe it as
"the most complete piece of mismanagement perhaps ever yet known
in the earth's wars." To a visitor at the White House, Abraham
Lincoln offered this assessment: "If there is a worse place than Hell,
I am in it." The president had recently fired the inert and unrespon-
sive McClellan and replaced him with Ambrose Burnside to lead the
Army of the Potomac. That choice proved disastrous. By no means a

military strategist, Burnside impetuously led 122,000 troops across the Rappahannock in the hopes of attacking Fredericksburg. General Lee was waiting for him, his troops heavily fortified, entrenched on high ground. Marching into this trap, the Union suffered 13,000 casualties.[2]

In Brooklyn, Whitman had happened across his brother's misspelled name in the list of casualties printed by the New York newspapers after the battle. He immediately left home, presumably encouraged by his family, and boarded a train to Washington. Somewhere along the way, his pocket was picked, and for the next few days he wandered penniless through the capital's thirty or so hospitals. He searched without success for George, haunting the teeming wards and makeshift infirmaries that had been set up throughout the city in tents, old taverns, and even the Greek-columned U.S. Patent Office. Finally, he borrowed enough money to take the train to Falmouth, Virginia, closer to the battlefield.

There, he stumbled into the chaos of defeat. The Army of the Potomac had been torn to shreds in its misguided assault upon the entrenched Confederate positions on Marye's Heights, near Fredericksburg. Now, the wounded lay in makeshift clusters, awaiting treatment. Men leaned against trees and tents, wrapped in blankets, their heads bandaged, their clothes caked with dirt and blood. In this place of misery, Whitman soon found George, whose injury turned out to be slight. The poet left no description of the brief reunion that followed, but promptly wrote to his mother to inform her of the good news. Then, he strolled from camp to camp, asking questions, taking notes. He spoke with men clustered around fires and watched wagonloads of the injured depart for Washington. He stepped inside the hospital tents, where doctors were soaked to the skin in blood. One of the first things he encountered outside the field hospital was a somber row of "[s]everal dead bodies…each cover'd with its brown woolen blanket."[3] (See figure 7.1.)

The sight of these bodies, which he hastily recorded in a small, hand-sewn notebook, would become the source for one of his most moving war poems, "A Sight in Camp in the Daybreak Gray and Dim." The poem opens with its speaker emerging "so early sleepless, / As slow I walk in the cool fresh air the path near the hospital tent." The morning stroll is abruptly terminated when the speaker discovers "Three forms…untended lying":

Over each the blanket spread, ample brownish woolen blanket,
Gray and heavy blanket, folding, covering all.

FIGURE 7.1 *Burial of Soldiers, Fredericksburg, Va.* Courtesy Library of Congress, Prints and Photographs Division (ca. 1863) (LC-B811-2509).

Curious I halt and silent stand,
Then with light fingers I from the face of the nearest the
    first just lift the blanket;
Who are you elderly man so gaunt and grim, with well-gray'd hair,
    and flesh all sunken about the eyes?
Who are you my dear comrade?

Then to the second I step—and who are you my child and darling?
Who are you sweet boy with cheeks yet blooming?
Then to the third—a face nor child nor old, very calm, as of beautiful
    yellow-white ivory;

Young man I think I know you—I think this face is the face of the Christ himself,
Dead and divine and brother of all, and here again he lies.⁴

In the early days of the conflict, Whitman had rather blithely announced that the war could not be conveyed by "dainty rhymes or sentimental love verses." The clash of a mighty nation was too massive, too epic, too freighted with masculine heroics to be entrusted to just any "pale poetling seated at a desk lisping cadenzas piano." The war, he wrote, awaited "a strong man erect, clothed in blue clothes, advancing, carrying a rifle on [his] shoulder," to sing its bold meanings.⁵

Early in the war, he had aspired, however vicariously, to *be* that "strong man." After "A Sight in Camp in the Daybreak Gray and Dim," he would no longer hope for that. The poem is light-years ahead of the simplistic boosterism of "Beat! Beat! Drums!" and it is different in tone and intention from the earlier poetry of *Leaves of Grass*. Gone are the expansive catalogs, the imperious persona, the unbounded optimism, and the overbearing insistence on union and harmony. The speaker of "A Sight in Camp" is more concerned with the human toll of a disastrous battle. When its narrator lifts "with light fingers" the coarse blankets draping the dead, he has no idea who or what he will find. No longer can he assume that the reality of his situation will coincide with his wishes. Only after studying the "gaunt and grim" face of a stranger does the speaker recognize the common humanity shared by dead and living alike. "Who are you my dear comrade?"

Stepping away from the row of the dead, Whitman encountered something even more disturbing: a pile of refuse stacked as high as his shoulders. The tang of blood was in the air, mixed with wood smoke and gunpowder, and upon closer inspection the pile of offal turned out to be "a heap of feet, legs, arms, and human fragments, cut, bloody, black and blue, swelled and sickening." There was, he wrote, "a full load for a one-horse cart."⁶

For weeks and months to come, the image returned to him, unbidden, in vivid flashes, horrible. His description of the heap of severed limbs appeared in letters home, in notebooks, and eventually in the memoirs he published after the war. It changed his entire perspective, reoriented his vision. The poet who had sung hymns to the wholeness of the human form, who had praised "the body electric," would soon turn his attention to the disfigured and maimed, to men who lay in the hospitals with arms and legs missing, bodies resembling meat, men who lay inert beneath the coarse woolen blankets, quietly suffering, the dying and the dead.

Some of the wounded men Whitman observed near Fredericksburg were transported north to a small hospital in Georgetown, where they were tended by a pert, irrepressible, and ironic nurse who had just left Concord—that "famous land," as she sarcastically described it, "of Emerson, Hawthorne, Thoreau, Alcott, & Co." Like so many young, idealistic New Englanders, Louisa May Alcott had considered traveling to Port Royal to teach the contrabands, but these plans did not work out, and she finally volunteered for hospital work. "I've often longed to see a war," she confided in her journal, explaining her decision and at the same time expressing a lifelong impatience with the constrictive role of women in the nineteenth century. "I long to be a man; but as I can't fight I will content myself with working for those who can." She arrived in Washington several days before "the Burnside blunder" to begin her duties in one of the city's many hospitals.[7] (See figure 7.2.)

She was thirty, bright, ambitious, deeply frustrated. She envied and adored her younger sister Anna, recently married. She longed to travel, to see the world beyond the provincial confines of Concord and Boston and to experience the charms of London and Paris, the Nile and the Levant. She dreamed of acting, writing, meeting new people. Most of all, she resented the burdens placed upon her family by its putative head, the transcendentalist Bronson Alcott, whose improvidence was even more legendary than his incomprehensible lectures. Since her early teenage years, Louisa had indulged in reveries that involved the writing of bestsellers, the making of huge fortunes after she had become the next Harriet Beecher Stowe. But despite her best efforts, the world had so far remained unimpressed. "Stick to your teaching," advised James T. Fields, editor of the *Atlantic*, with whom she boarded in 1862 while serving as a schoolmistress in Boston. "You can't write."[8]

Nothing in her Concord upbringing, with its transcendental schools and strawberry parties, its self-conscious eccentrics and intellectual self-satisfaction, had quite prepared her for the Union Hotel Hospital, where she was assigned to work as a nurse in the winter of 1862. A hastily remodeled tavern in Georgetown, the place was dank, grubby, still reeking of beer. Alcott began her first shift "sitting all day between a boy with pneumonia and a man shot through the lungs."[9] Both breathed horribly; both sounded as if they were drowning.

The ward to which she was assigned had once been a ballroom and was intended to hold roughly forty patients. That capacity was quickly

FIGURE 7.2 Louisa May Alcott.

exceeded. On Alcott's third morning in Washington, before she had even
fully unpacked and become acclimated to her new duties, a panicked
orderly announced the arrival of the ambulances from Fredericksburg.
Alcott watched in horror as the hospital quickly filled with young men
"so riddled with shot and shell, so torn and shattered" as to have "borne

suffering for which we have no name." The sick and wounded were carried in, a few raving, a few groaning with each jolt of the litter. Most, however, bore their injuries with stoic, white-lipped silence. The novice nurse shuddered at the "sight of several stretchers, each with its legless, armless, or desperately wounded occupant."[10] Handed a bar of brown soap and a towel, she was told to thoroughly bathe the dirty, wounded soldiers.

These descriptions would appear in *Hospital Sketches*, Alcott's lightly fictionalized account of her experiences as a nurse. Originally written as letters to the Alcott family in Concord, they were soon reprinted in the *Commonwealth*, a Boston abolitionist newspaper published by her old schoolteacher, Franklin Sanborn, where their huge popularity almost immediately prompted a book contract and then publication between hard covers in late 1863. With the appearance of *Hospital Sketches*, literary success had arrived at last. Years later, Alcott savored her heated reply to James Fields when he had counseled her to abandon her literary aspirations: "I won't teach, I can write, and I'll prove it."[11]

Part of what made *Hospital Sketches* so popular was its narrator: a thinly disguised version of the author herself whose nom de guerre is Tribulation Periwinkle and whose place of work is a fractious hospital she calls Hurly-Burly House. Modeled on the hyperbolic narrators of Dickens, Trib converts the sorrowful realities of war into an effective blend of melodrama and comedy. Her crisp vignettes of wounded soldiers are always presented within a sentimental framework that assures the book's readers that human suffering is but a precondition for heavenly reward.

But the book was also a success for its vivid portraits of an increasingly growing segment of the population: the severely wounded, the maimed and disfigured, the permanently disabled. "[N]ot two years since," Oliver Wendell Holmes put it six months before the publication of *Hospital Sketches*, "the sight of a person who had lost one of his lower limbs was an infrequent occurrence. Now, alas! there are few of us who have not a cripple among our friends, if not in our own families."[12]

Alcott portrayed this new class of people in a tone that oscillated between humor and compassion. One night in the dim hospital ward, Trib sees "a one-legged phantom hopping nimbly down the room." It is a Pennsylvania soldier, delirious from "wound-fever," wearing only a sheet and his military cap. "When sane," Alcott wrote, "the least movement produced a roar of pain or a volley of oaths." Now, mad with pain and fever, the young man stood in the moonlight, "balancing himself on one leg, like a meditative stork, [and plunging] into an animated discussion of the war, the President, lager beer, and Enfield rifles." On another occasion, encountering a young sergeant "with one leg gone, and the right arm so shattered that it evidently must follow," Trib discovered not so much a shattered veteran as a colorful character absorbed in a comical metaphysics: "'Lord! What a scramble there'll be for arms and legs, when we old boys come out of our graves, on the Judgment Day." The speculative soldier wonders "if we shall get our own again? If we do, my leg will have to tramp from Fredericksburg, my arm from here, I suppose, and meet my body, wherever it may be."[13]

The soldiers Alcott described had emerged from the blood-soaked inferno of a field hospital, the victims of new technologies of killing. The minié ball, a rifled .58-caliber bullet that was heavy, slow-moving, and devastating, did not simply pierce the flesh. It tore jagged holes in the body, demolished bone and tissue. "The shattering, splintering, and splitting of a long bone by the impact of the minie or Enfield ball were, in many instances, both remarkable and frightful," wrote a doctor familiar with these wounds, "and early experience taught surgeons that amputation was the only means of saving life."[14]

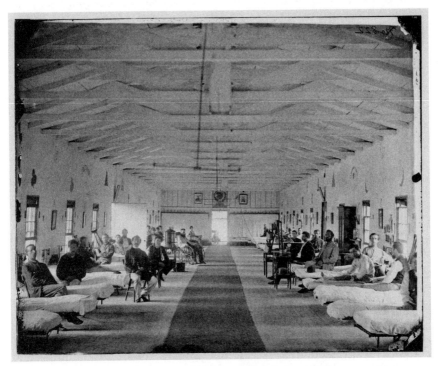

FIGURE 7.3 A Washington hospital. Courtesy Library of Congress, Prints and Photographs Division (LC-B817-7822).

Walt Whitman would observe many such operations when he returned in early 1863 to Washington, where he began ministering to "the great army of the wounded" whom he found in the city's hospitals. After witnessing the aftermath of Fredericksburg, he had discovered a new vocation, a calling every bit as significant and compelling as poetry. He would attend the sick and wounded. He would care for the damaged. He would serve as surrogate family. In this modest way, he would heal the nation. "To-day after dinner," he recorded in his notebook,

> Lewy Brown had his left leg amputated five inches below the knee.... I was present at the operation.... The surgeon in charge amputated, but did not finish the operation, being called away.... Lew bled and they thought an artery had opened. They began to cut the stitches again and make a search, but after some time concluded it was only surface bleeding.... I could hear his cries and sometimes quite loud, and half-coherent talk.

Whitman attended the recovering man that evening, noting his pale, drawn face and the way the patient felt "oppressed for breath, with deathly feeling...in the stomach &c & great pain in the leg. As usual in such cases," he added, "he could feel the lost leg very plainly."[15]

The possibility of losing a limb haunted many soldiers. In the weeks before great battles, Robert Gould Shaw and Charles Russell Lowell both practiced writing with their nondominant hand; the odds were simply too great they might lose an arm (or leg) in combat. Civil War diaries and letters were filled with accounts of wounded men begging their doctors not to remove a limb. In one case, an artillery corporal wounded in the leg at Hatcher's Run borrowed a pistol from a soldier and placed it under his pillow. "The man who puts a hand on me dies," he announced to the surgeon who told him the leg would have to be removed.[16]

By 1862, the vast number of amputations in the Union army had prompted Surgeon General William Hammond to call for the scientific study of battlefield wounds. He ordered surgeons to forward severed limbs to Washington and to have postoperative photographs taken when possible. Soon, thousands of arms and legs were being sent north in kegs containing the preservatives saltwater, rubbing alcohol, or sometimes even whisky. The amputated limbs were numbered and described in detail in a series of books entitled *Histories of Specimens*. As the war progressed, the specimens, as well as surgical equipment, shrapnel fragments, and photographs of wounds, came to form the core holdings of the Army Medical Museum in Washington.

FIGURE 7.4 Silas Weir Mitchell.

Less than thirty miles away from the army museum, in a leafy, peaceful northern Philadelphia suburb, the first specialist in the treatment of amputees was writing about his experiences. Silas Weir Mitchell is best remembered as the proponent of the "rest cure," a regimen of inactivity for patients with nervous diseases that was portrayed with scathing disdain in "The Yellow Wallpaper," a classic proto-feminist short story written in 1891 by one of Mitchell's patients, Charlotte Perkins Gilman.

But in 1863, Mitchell had been recently appointed to be the acting assistant surgeon in Philadelphia, a position he carried out with energy and ingenuity. A decade earlier, he had studied with the renowned French physiologist Claude Bernard in Paris, where he learned to apply the principles of scientific investigation to medicine. Returning to Philadelphia, he had set up a practice and, simultaneously, began performing research projects that would make his reputation among a tiny cadre of knowledgeable scientists. (He was especially known for his analysis of the effect of snake venom on the nervous system.) In 1862, his wife died of diphtheria; after a period of mourning, he signed up to become a contract surgeon for the Union army. His first assignment was Gettysburg.

The famous battle had ended the day before he arrived. The view as he approached the battlefield was like a medieval morality painting. Eight thousand bodies lay strewn on hills. Pieces of human beings hung in the branches of trees. Overwhelmed burial crews labored to retrieve the remains and cover as many as possible with several inches of soil. Arms and legs, occasionally faces, stuck out of the dirt. Those yet to be buried blackened and deliquesced in the July heat. Nearby residents wore camphor-soaked handkerchiefs covering their faces. Three weeks later, a Gettysburg banker wrote that "my attention has been directed to several places where the hogs were actually rooting out the bodies and devouring them."[17]

Scattered about the battlefield lay nearly 30,000 wounded men—far more than the small army of doctors and surgeons could handle. The stink was unbearable. Mitchell recalled that he "smelt nine hundred smells," and he expressed dismay at "dead Confederates…with arms and legs in rigid extension—a most horrible memory." He proceeded to amputate.[18]

Within months of Gettysburg, he had assumed command of Turner's Lane Hospital, a bucolic collection of buildings on the outskirts of Philadelphia officially known as the U.S. Army Hospital for Diseases of the Nervous System. There, he identified a condition that would later be called *shell-shock* and that included mental and physical collapse caused by proximity to traumatic events. (Thomas Wentworth Higginson continued to suffer from this condition around the time Mitchell and his team of physicians were identifying it. Throughout the autumn of 1863, he recuperated in a boardinghouse in Newport.)

What interested Mitchell most, however, were those soldiers who had nerve damage caused by bullet and artillery wounds.

"No sooner did [these] patients begin to fill our wards," he wrote in his pioneering *Gunshot Wounds and Other Injuries of the Nerves*, "than we perceived that a new and interesting field of observation was here opened to view." Among those who filled the hospital, Mitchell continued, "were representatives of every conceivable form of nerve injury, from shot and shell, from sabre cuts, contusions, and dislocations." Many suffered from a condition he was the first to label *causalgia:* an intense burning sensation caused when nerves are severed or destroyed by bullets or shattered bones. "Perhaps few persons who are not physicians," Mitchell noted with characteristic understatement about the condition, "can realize the influence which long-continued and unendurable pain may have upon both body and mind."[19]

The pain was often greatest, Mitchell observed, in soldiers who had lost a limb. During the next year, he treated literally thousands of these men, meticulously recording their symptoms and treatments each evening when he had concluded his rounds at the wards. A collection of case studies from this clinical work was included in Mitchell's 1871 masterwork, *Injuries of Nerves*, which served as a standard neurological text well into the first decade of the twentieth century. "Nearly every man who loses a limb carries about with him a constant or inconstant phantom of the missing member," Mitchell wrote, coining the term *phantom limb* to describe the strange feeling experienced by so many amputee veterans as "a sensory ghost of that much of himself."[20]

So palpable, so *real* was the sense of the missing limb that many of Mitchell's patients accidentally injured themselves when they momentarily forgot they were amputees. A man with a missing leg got up in the middle of the night and promptly fell over. Another "attempted," Mitchell reported, "when riding, to pick up his bridle with the lost hand, while he struck his horse with the other, and was reminded of his mistake by being thrown." Yet a third patient tried to pick up his fork at every meal with his missing hand, "and was so disturbed emotionally at the result as frequently to be nauseated."[21]

Gunshot Wounds and Other Injuries of the Nerves was Mitchell's first important work to emerge from his practice at Turner's Hospital, but his second appeared in the *Atlantic Monthly*. Like so many of his era, he longed for the plaudits of literary fame. He would complain that no book describing "the personal life of a war surgeon" had been written, arguing that such a work "would have its romance, its pathos, its humor."[22] His story in the *Atlantic* was an effort to change that. It was called "The Case of George Dedlow."

George Dedlow, the narrator of Mitchell's first work of fiction, is, like his creator, the son of a physician and an assistant surgeon in the Union army. Unlike Mitchell, however, Dedlow is wounded in a series of skirmishes and battles in the war's western theater. Having enlisted in the Twenty-first Indiana Volunteers, he is ambushed outside a Tennessee log cabin and shot in both arms as he tries to tear down a fence to escape. Mitchell describes the wound and resulting causalgia with clinical precision: "The right hand and forearm were cold and perfectly insensible," he reports. Captured by the Confederates and thrown into a wagon, Dedlow soon feels "in my dead right hand a strange burning...as if the hand was caught and pinched in a red-hot vice. Then in my agony I begged my guard for water to wet it with."[23]

Dedlow is sent to a rebel hospital, where he suffers among the rows of nameless patients. One day, he describes the burning sensation to a mysterious visitor, who uses the occasion to offer a religious homily: "[S]uch will you be if you die in your sins; you will go where only pain can be felt. For all eternity, all of you will be as that hand,—knowing pain only." Is the religious stranger a ghost from the past, an emblem of an earlier piety, or a modern-day prophet of doom? Mitchell's story never fully answers that question. But the pain in Dedlow's arm isn't eased by the purgation of sin, but rather by the arm's removal. As soon as it is amputated—without the benefit of ether since the Confederate hospital is without adequate medical supplies—Dedlow feels "a strange lightening of the pain through the limb....This was followed by instant, unspeakable relief, and before the flaps were brought together I was sound asleep." Looking at "the arm which lay on the floor," he remarks to himself, "There is the pain, and here am I. How queer!"[24]

Eventually exchanged, furloughed, and returned to duty, Dedlow takes part in the September 1863 Battle of Chickamauga. There, again, he is wounded. Knocked unconscious by an artillery blast, he awakens beneath a tree some distance from the fighting, only to discover that both his thighs have been hit. Just as he is about to call for help, a towel soaked in chloroform is clamped over his mouth and when he next comes to, he is in a hospital, this time suffering from a sharp cramp in his left leg. He calls out to an attendant to massage the calf:

> "Calf?" said he, "you ain't none, pardner. It's took off."
> "I know better," said I. "I have pain in both legs."
> "Wall, I never!" said he. "You ain't got nary leg."[25]

Now missing three limbs, Dedlow is transported to Hospital No. 2 in Nashville, where his recovery is halted when an epidemic of hospital gangrene spreads through the wards and eventually requires that his remaining arm—still suppurating from its earlier wound—be removed at the shoulder joint. "Against all chances I recovered," he recalls, "to find myself a useless torso, more like some strange larval creature than anything of human shape."[26]

The rest of the story chronicles Dedlow's move to Turner's Hospital in Philadelphia, which, as he notes, "was then known as the Stump Hospital." "It was filled with men who had lost one arm or leg, or one of each, as happened now and then...but none, like myself, stripped of every limb." Nearly all of the patients experience sensations in their missing limbs. Some patients feel only a thumb; others suffer pain along an entire arm; still others feel as though a missing foot is situated at their knee. Dedlow himself feels "a most acute pain in my left hand, especially the little finger," and occasionally at night, "would try with one lost hand to grope for the other."[27]

Slowly, he heals. But as he grows more accustomed to his surroundings, he finds himself increasingly "disturbed by the horrible variety of suffering around me." There is a man who "walked sideways; there was one who could not smell; another was dumb from an explosion." One man's injured shoulder blades stand out so far that he is called Angel. War's horrors are not to be found on the battlefield, Mitchell suggests, but in the surgical inferno of the hospitals.

Soon, a strange affliction begins to distress Dedlow. "I found to my horror that at times I was less conscious of myself, of my own existence, than used to be the case....I felt like asking some one constantly if I were really George Dedlow or not....At times the conviction of my want of being myself was overwhelming, and most painful."[28] Losing so much of his body diminishes Dedlow's sense of selfhood. Realizing that "one half of me was absent or functionally dead," he wonders just "how much a man might lose and yet live....I thus reached the conclusion that a man is not his brain, or any part of it, but all of his economy, and that to lose any part must lessen this sense of his own existence."[29] Lying in bed and observing his fellow patients, Dedlow wonders how these diminished, mutilated soldiers will fit into a postwar nation.

Increasingly "moody and wretched," Mitchell's narrator meets another casualty, who belongs to "the New Church"—a spiritualist group that claims to summon the dead during its quasi-religious séances. "It's a great comfort for a plain man like me," announces this wounded believer, "when he's weary and sick, to be able to turn away from earthly things, and hold converse daily with the great and good who have left the world."[30] (Mitchell's story was intended to be an entertainment, but here it gently explores the nature of faith in a moral universe upended by war.) Skeptical, Dedlow agrees to attend the New Church's "circle," a gathering in a member's house, where a medium offers to summon dead friends and family members from the other side. The quadruple amputee agrees, and soon the medium raps twice: apparently, two spirits are present in the room. When the medium asks their names, she receives a series of irregular raps that turn out to be Morse code: "UNITED STATES ARMY MEDICAL MUSEUM, NOS. 3486, 3487."[31]

"Good gracious!" Dedlow announces, "they are *my legs! my legs!*" What follows, he continues,

> I ask no one to believe except those who, like myself, have communed with the beings of another sphere. Suddenly I felt a strange return of my self-consciousness. I was re-individualized, so to speak. A strange wonder filled me, and, to the amazement of every one, I arose, and, staggering a little, walked across the room on limbs invisible to them or me. It was no wonder I staggered, for, as I briefly reflected, my legs had been nine months in the strongest alcohol. At this instant all my new friends crowded around me in astonishment. Presently, however, I felt myself sinking slowly. My legs were going, and in a moment I was resting feebly on my two stumps upon the floor. It was too much. All that was left of me fainted and rolled over senseless.[32]

The Case of George Dedlow" was a sensation; dozens of *Atlantic* readers sent contributions to the fictional narrator in care of "Stump Hospital," believing that the wounded man was a real person. Others wrote asking for contact information; they, too, had suffered grievous wounds in the war and wished to share their story with the unfortunate narrator.

It was precisely this kind of literary success that Walt Whitman hoped to achieve when he moved to Washington early in 1863, shortly after his brother George returned to the front. He was certainly aware of Alcott's *Hospital Sketches;* in the fall of that year, he wrote to James Redpath, the abolitionist publisher who had brought out Alcott's volume, proposing to write his own book about Washington's hospitals: "My idea is a book of the time, worthy of the time—something considerably beyond mere hospital sketches—a book for sale perhaps in a larger American market." The politically radical Redpath understood his business, as evidenced in his shrewd response: Whitman's book might be of interest, he conceded, but there was "a lion in the way—$."[33]

Accordingly, Whitman concentrated on his poetry. He wrote lines in snatches as he watched over feverish patients, bathing their temples in vinegar or offering them dippers of water. He wrote late at night when he returned to his tiny boardinghouse room at 394 L Street. The poems he produced during this period were different from the literary productions of Alcott and Mitchell; they required neither sentimental charity nor ghostly visitations to locate significance in the endless suffering of the Union army. They required instead only the detailed observations of Whitman himself.

He had boasted, soon after becoming a fixture in Washington's hospitals, that he supplied "to some of these dear suffering boys in my presence & magnetism that which doctors nor medicines nor skill nor any routine assistance can give." To Emerson, he admitted, "The first shudder has long since passed over, and I must say I find deep things" in the hospitals, "unreckoned by current print or speech." Thousands of "American young men, badly wounded, all sorts of wounds," he continued, had opened for him "a new world...giving closer insights, new things, exploring deeper mines than any yet." This newly discovered world of pain endowed Whitman with an empathetic experience of suffering: "I sometimes put myself in fancy in the cot, with typhoid, or under the knife, tried by terrible, fearful tests, probed deeper, the living soul's, the body's tragedies, bursting the petty bonds of art."[34]

After years of feeling unappreciated by a national audience, Whitman had found communion, a sense of purpose in the most unexpected of places. Soon after arriving in the capital city, he got a part-time job working in the army paymaster's office, which allowed him plenty of leisure to walk the streets, observing the war-torn capital. "Shed hospitals covered acres on acres in every suburb," one Washington resident recalled about the city at this time. "Churches, art-halls and private mansions were filled with the wounded and dying of the American armies. The endless roll of the army wagon seemed never still. The rattle of the anguish-laden ambulance, the piercing cries of the sufferers...made morning, noon and night too dreadful to be borne."[35]

Sometimes in the evening, Whitman strolled to the White House, gazing at the "palace-like, tall, round columns, spotless as snow," admiring "the tender and soft moonlight, flooding the pale marble, and making peculiar faint languishing shades, not shadows," beneath the cool marble columns of the Capitol building. In the summer and

FIGURE 7.5 Walt Whitman in Washington (1862). Photo by Mathew Brady. Courtesy Brady-Handy Photograph Collection, Library of Congress (LC-BH82-137).

fall, President Lincoln left Washington each evening to sleep at the pastoral Soldiers' Home, founded in 1851 for retired and disabled veterans of American wars. Whitman saw him each morning on his return. "Mr. Lincoln on the saddle generally rides a good-sized, easy-going gray horse, is dress'd in plain black, somewhat rusty and dusty, wears a black stiff hat, and looks about as ordinary in attire, &c., as the commonest man."[36] The longer Whitman stayed in Washington, the more he became impressed with the careworn president.

"I see very plainly ABRAHAM LINCOLN's dark brown face," Whitman recalled years later in his *Memoranda during the War*, published in 1875. The president haunted his memory with his "deep-cut lines, the eyes, always to me with a deep latent sadness in the expression." The two men, he claimed, had "got so that we exchange bows, and very cordial ones." Occasionally, he saw Lincoln with his wife, Mary Todd Lincoln, still clad in mourning after the death of their son Willie, riding through Washington in a barouche, the equipage "of the plainest kind, only two horses, and they nothing extra."[37]

Mostly, though, Whitman spent his time in the hospitals. Although each hospital varied in size and capacity, most resembled the one on Seventh Street, a "collection of barracks-like one-story edifices" containing roughly eighty patients each, "half sick, half wounded." The interior was little more than whitewashed boards, bare wooden floors, rows of narrow iron bedsteads on either side. "You may hear groans or other sounds of unendurable suffering from two or three cots," Whitman wrote, "but in the main there is quiet—almost a painful absence of demonstration." He admired the stoicism and toughness of the patients, their "fortitude to bear" suffering. One man, J. L., a Brooklyn boy "with an amputated arm, the stump healing pretty well," had caught Whitman's attention before he moved to Washington. "I saw him lying on the ground at Fredericksburgh [*sic*] last December, all bloody, just after the arm was taken off. He was very phlegmatic about it, munching away at a cracker in the remaining hand." Stoic and cheerful, J. L. recovered from the operation and continued to talk of fighting more Confederates.[38]

What most captured Whitman's sympathy was the loneliness and social destitution of the sick and wounded. Many were "entirely without friends or acquaintances...no familiar face, and hardly a word of judicious sympathy or cheer, through their sometimes long and tedious sickness, or the pangs of aggravated wounds." From his paltry earnings at the army paymaster's office, Whitman purchased horehound candy and blackberry preserves for the sick and wounded. He distributed

tobacco, brandy, peaches, tea, oysters, flannel underwear, handkerchiefs, socks, newspapers, razors, and combs. For many soldiers, he
wrote letters home. In these chatty missives, he informed distant rela-
tives of the location and medical condition of son, husband, father.[39]

In the friendships he made, Whitman found renewed life, cause for
hope. "I find it refreshing," he affirmed again and again, "these hardy,
bright, intuitive, American men." Some of those he encountered had
"been in every battle since the war began." There hung about these
men "something majestic," making the hospital neither "the repulsive
place of sores and fevers, nor the place of querulousness, nor the bad
results of morbid years which one avoids like the bad s[mells]."
Providing succor to so many had lifted "the corner in a curtain [and]
vouchsafed me to see America."[40]

Yet *seeing* America was not the same as *healing* America. Confident
as he was in his ability to help individual soldiers, he was no longer so
certain about the role of poetry in this healing. Whitman's Civil War
verse, first gathered in *Drum-Taps* and published in 1865, would
eventually be incorporated into the ever-burgeoning *Leaves of Grass*.
Much of this material, including his most famous poem of profound
suffering, "The Wound-Dresser," expresses the inadequacy of language to comfort the sick and dying. "I am continually lost at the
absence of blowing and blowers among these old-young American
militaires," he admitted, referring to the refusal of most veterans to
brag or even talk about their experiences. Increasingly, Whitman's
earlier hymns to the body gave way to graphic accounts of the stricken
human form:

> From the stump of the arm, the amputated hand,
> I undo the clotted lint, remove the slough, wash off the matter and
>   blood,...
> I dress a wound in the side, deep, deep,
> But a day or two more, for see the frame all wasted and sinking,
> And the yellow-blue countenance see.[41]

The narrator of "The Wound-Dresser" recalls how at the start of
the war he had been "Arous'd and angry...I'd thought to beat the
alarum, and urge relentless war." But like the Whitman who had written "Beat! Beat! Drums!" this speaker is soon worn out by war's relentless suffering. "I resign'd myself," he says, "To sit by the wounded and
soothe them, or silently watch the dead."[42] Perhaps not surprisingly,
this narrator is haunted by terrifying dreams. In these recurrent night-
mares, he is forever

Bearing the bandages, water and sponge,
Straight and swift to my wounded...
Where they lie on the ground after the battle brought in,
Where their priceless blood reddens the grass the ground,
Or to the rows of the hospital tent, or under the roof'd hospital,
To the long rows of cots up and down each side I return,
To each and all one after another I draw near, not one do I miss,
An attendant follows holding a tray, he carries a refuse pail,
Soon to be fill'd with clotted rags and blood, emptied, and fill'd again.[43]

The poet who had tried to bridge the chasm between art and life, body and soul, now wrote poems that seemed simply wounded. Whitman's wartime verse was populated by "Surgeons operating, attendants holding lights," who left behind "the smell of ether, the smell of blood." These profoundly anguished poems were strewn with "bloody forms," "[s]ome on the bare ground, some on planks or stretchers, some in the death-spasm sweating."[44]

On occasion, flashes of the earlier Whitman burst through: "Must I change my triumphant songs?" he interjects, as if despairing that the radiant optimism of *Leaves of Grass* is lost forever. "Must I indeed learn to chant the cold dirges of the baffled? / And sullen hymns of defeat?"

Yet despite the transformations wrought in himself and in America, he found hope in the hospitals. The dimly lit wards illuminated areas of compassion he scarcely knew existed. "O the sad, sad things I see," he wrote to his mother, "the noble young men with legs & arms taken off—the deaths—the sick weakness, sicker than death, that some endure, after amputations." To these young men, the wound dresser was

faithful, I do not give out,
The fractur'd thigh, the knee, the wound in the abdomen,
These and more I dress with impassive hand, (yet deep in
My breast a fire, a burning flame.)
...
I sit by the restless all the dark night, some are so young,
Some suffer so much, I recall the experience sweet and sad,
(Many a soldier's loving arms about this neck have cross'd and rested,
Many a soldier's kiss dwells on these bearded lips.)[45]

These examples of faith and generosity, Whitman hoped, would help to restore the country to peace and wholeness. But they came at an enormous personal price. After five months of visiting the hospitals, Whitman began to complain of "quite an attack of sore throat &

distress in my head." Friends warned him that "I hover too much over the beds of the hospitals, with fever & putrid wounds, etc." His head ached; his joints throbbed; there was a humming in his ears. One day, he cut his hand and immediately bandaged the appendage with elaborate care, fearful he might contract hospital gangrene.[46]

After a year, he was no longer the robust man who had once impressed friends and strangers with his animal health. He had perceptibly aged. Doctors examined him and diagnosed "hospital malaria," "hospital fever," or "hospital poison." They ordered him to quit the hospitals. In the summer of 1864, Whitman finally acquiesced and boarded a train to Brooklyn, where he recuperated for six months under his mother's care before returning to Washington. In the interval, his hair turned completely white. He kept the pallor of the wounded, the fever-bright eyes.

Yet he could not quit "these thousands, and tens and twenties of thousands of American young men, badly wounded, all sorts of wounds, operated on, pallid with diarrhea, languishing, dying with fever, pneumonia, &c.," all of which opened "a new world somehow to me, giving closer insights, new things, exploring deeper mines than any yet, showing our humanity." A gift, both precious and dangerous, had been bestowed on him.

> He refused to relinquish it.[47] "What did I get?" he asked rhetorically, many years after his time in the hospitals. Well—I got the [soldier] boys, for one thing: the boys: thousands of them: they were, they are, they will be mine....then I got Leaves of Grass: but for this I would never have had Leaves of Grass—the consummated book (the last confirming word)....You look on me now with the ravages of that experience finally reducing me to a powder. Still I say: I only gave myself: I got the boys, I got the Leaves of Grass. My body? Yes—it had to be given—it had to be sacrificed: who knows better than I do what that means?[48]

One answer to that question was Louisa May Alcott, whose health was even more greatly compromised by her hospital work. Within six weeks of arriving at the Union Hotel Hospital, she had contracted typhoid pneumonia, a serious illness that left her with great racking coughs and a perilously high fever. To compound matters, the garret room in which she slept had five broken windowpanes, and the January air blustered and whistled into the tiny space as she grew progressively weaker.

Alcott's supervising nurse, who had contracted the same illness and would die within days, managed to telegraph Bronson Alcott in

Concord, informing him of his daughter's condition. The old transcendentalist canceled a speaking engagement and caught the first train to Washington. The journey was delayed by fog in New Jersey, so that when at last he arrived in Georgetown he hurried up the stairs to Louisa's room, afraid of being too late, and found, in a narrow iron bed like those in which the war casualties lay, a woman he scarcely recognized. She was thin, barely conscious, pale as death. "Come home," he said.[49]

Concord was beside itself with the news. Emerson sent a maid to help the family, and Sophia Hawthorne hurried next door to offer them food. She returned to the Wayside reporting that strong, rosy-cheeked Louisa had been replaced by a skeletal wraith. Her son Julian, who was particularly close to the young woman, could scarcely look at the "hollow-eyed, almost fleshless wreck" his friend had become.[50] Nathaniel wrote to James T. Fields to say that the publisher's former tenant might not survive.

The treatment for typhoid at the time was "heroic" doses of mercurous chloride, also known as calomel, a chalky, acrid substance that caused patients' "faces to swell, their tongues to jut out of their mouth, and their saliva to gush forth at the rate of anywhere from a pint to a quart every twenty-four hours."[51] Although she survived, for the next twenty years, Alcott slowly deteriorated from the effects of mercury poisoning. She lost her teeth and hair. A scalding pain shot down her back and arms. She suffered a sore throat for months at a time. The bestselling author of *Little Women* and *Little Men* never recovered from the fever that plagued her for weeks after her return from Washington.

Delirious and raving in her old bed at the Alcotts' Orchard House, she believed she was back at the hospital in Georgetown, surrounded once again by the wounded and dying, overwhelmed by the suffering she was expected to ease. Here was Sergeant Bane, who was teaching himself to write with his left hand. Here was the Virginia blacksmith, John Suhre, whose chest had been torn open by artillery, his lungs exposed. She could not escape them, could not purge them from her memory. In her delirium, she thought a group of nurses and doctors from the Union Hotel Hospital had tricked her into joining them as they worshipped the devil. And in one terrifying dream, she imagined that the roof of Orchard House—the home that would be memorialized four years later in *Little Women*—had blown off, allowing the whole world, with all its misery, to come swirling in.

"I dwell in Possibility—" Emily Dickinson had boldly asserted late in 1862, at about the same time that Alcott was embarking upon her short-lived career as a nurse and Whitman was anxiously traveling to Fredericksburg: "a fairer House than Prose—." The boundless realm of her imagination, the scope of her poetic power, she claimed, was like a home in which the "everlasting Roof" was nothing less than "The Gambrels of the Sky—."[52]

But in 1864, Dickinson's world contracted on account of her health, and she found herself dwelling in a dismal, dark boardinghouse at 86 Austin Street in Boston, many miles from her father's austere mansion. Early in February, she consulted with the nation's preeminent ophthalmologist, Henry Willard Williams, about her eyes. In April, she returned, remaining under Williams's treatment for the next eight months.

Almost nothing specific is known about the mysterious condition that prompted this extraordinary measure. Dickinson's eyes ached; they could not tolerate light. To a poet who employed the term *eclipse* to refer to everything from God to love to pain, it was as if a planetary object had suddenly obscured the sun. She missed home, missed her family, missed the bright room on the southwest corner of the Homestead and the bureau in which she squirreled away her poetry. She feared she would go blind, would no longer "see to see." And in her crisis, she thought about Higginson.

Had he survived so far away in the unimaginable geography of Port Royal? Or had he joined the dead, those cadaverous "Men too straight to stoop again—"? To find out, she sent a letter to him after nearly a year of silence. Possibly, she had not heard of his injury on the Edisto River. Her eyes kept her from reading the tiny print of the reports in the *Springfield Republican*, and her concern with her health may have temporarily shut out the world. "Are you in danger," she wrote in June 1864, nearly a year after Higginson had been wounded. "I did not know that you were hurt. Will you tell me more?"[53]

Just as likely, she *had* known of Higginson's injury, had been informed by some friend or family member, and now used it as a pretext for resuming contact. From the dim isolation of her room in Cambridge, she confided that while her physician did not "let me go, yet I work in my Prison, and make Guests for myself." These guests—presumably her poems—were restive, seeking escape. She was asking, obliquely again, if he would care to resume a correspondence sundered by war, to read the poems that had emerged from her own and the nation's suffering.[54]

Convalescing in the crowded boardinghouse in Newport, Higginson obliged, resuming a remarkable relationship that would continue unabated for the next two decades. Gradually, he began to recover from the wound he had received in South Carolina. He strolled the cliffs overlooking the sea, attended parties and lectures, rode out to watch boys and adolescents marching and drilling in preparation for their turn at war. He tried not to think of the man decapitated but a yard from him, and he sought to assure himself that the cause for which he had fought since the 1850s justified such violence.

But he was in shock when he received Dickinson's letter. Like much of New England's literary establishment, he was adjusting to recent news that signaled the end of an era. As usual, Dickinson understood her audience and anticipated his emotions. Inserted into her letter was the disturbing piece of news: "Mr. Hawthorne," she wrote, "died."[55]

CHAPTER 8

The Man without a Country

B ACK IN 1862, after he had traveled to Washington to get a glimpse of the war, Nathaniel Hawthorne had returned to Concord with several souvenirs. One of these was the germ of an idea for an essay that eventually became "Chiefly about War-Matters." Another was a pair of portraits.

The first portrait was by the painter Emanuel Leutze, a German American whose artistic reputation, then as now, rested largely upon the monumental *Washington Crossing the Delaware*, completed in 1851. Leutze's most famous work had set the standard for American history painting. Its focus on an *exemplum virtutis*—an iconic hero engaged in significant action—was meant to enlarge the viewer's sense of national destiny. Universally praised when it was unveiled shortly after the Mexican-American War, the painting was described by *Literary World* as "incomparably the best painting yet executed for an American subject."[1]

Hawthorne had taken the opportunity to view the early stages of Leutze's *Westward the Course of Empire Takes Its Way* when he was in Washington. The vast, didactic painting was commissioned for the west stairwell in the House of Representatives, and Hawthorne watched, fascinated, as the painter climbed scaffolding to work on the huge mural for Congress. "It was delightful to see him so calmly elaborating his design to go on the walls of the Capitol," he wrote, "while other men doubted, and feared, or hoped treacherously, and whispered to one another that the nation would exist only a little longer, or that, if a remnant still held together, its centre and seat of government would be far northward and westward of Washington."

He was particularly impressed by Leutze's sense of purpose. "[T]he artist keeps right on, firm of heart and hand, drawing his outlines with an unwavering pencil, beautifying and idealizing our rude, material life, and thus manifesting that we have an indefeasible claim to a more enduring national existence."[2]

Hawthorne might as well have been speaking of himself. He, too, had devoted his professional life, albeit through the medium of language, to "beautifying and idealizing our rude, material life." He, too, had committed himself to revealing spiritual truths too often obscured by the commonplace. Within days of his visit to the Capitol, he sat for the artist, who kept his subject compliant with an abundant supply of cigars and champagne (see figure 8.1). "He is the best of fellows," Hawthorne informed James T. Fields, who had his own reasons for admiring the painter. A decade earlier, Leutze had painted a version of Hester and Pearl from *The Scarlet Letter* that had brought "tears of joy" to the publisher.[3]

One day before sitting for Leutze, Hawthorne was the subject of a different kind of portrait, this one produced at the Washington studio of Mathew Brady. Already a famous portrait photographer of the rich and famous, Brady would soon become known for his extraordinary visual record of the Civil War. A dervish of activity, Brady was in the field preparing to photograph the impending Peninsular War when Hawthorne appeared at his studio. A Scottish émigré named Alexander Gardner took Hawthorne's likeness instead. Under Brady's direction, Gardner would also create memorable and haunting images of the war. His photographs of dead soldiers in the fields of Maryland and Virginia, the silvery pallor of blank faces etched with dirt and gunpowder, have a calm immediacy that remains compelling to this day.

When Gardner's portraits arrived at the Wayside in Concord, Sophia Hawthorne expressed disappointment at the seated *carte de visite*. It was too dour, too stern. But she enthused over the "superbly handsome" imperial-size portrait of her husband, an image that reveals an entirely different subject than the one rendered by Emanuel Leutze.[4] Absent is the whimsical, poetic expression that emanates from the blue eyes of the painted Hawthorne. At a time when thousands of men were having tintypes made to chronicle their courage and patriotism, Hawthorne's photo image looks alarmed and wary. Devoid of the healthful flush and dreamy countenance of the painting, Hawthorne's photograph presents instead a guarded, aging author—a man fully twenty years older than the one in Leutze's portrait (see figure 8.2).

FIGURE 8.1 *Nathaniel Hawthorne* (1862), by Emanuel Gottlieb Leutze. Courtesy Creative Commons.

Most of the Civil War images taken by Brady's team of photographers were more difficult to produce than Hawthorne's portrait. It was a struggle to transport cumbersome photographic equipment onto the uneven, boggy terrain of battlefields. Once there, events happened too quickly for the laborious processes of daguerreotype photography to capture them. In a medium that still required rigid head braces to keep subjects motionless and, on the part of those subjects, intense concentration not to blink or move before the shutter finally closed, the frenetic movement of combat could not be secured. Battle scenes were conveyed to the public instead through a network of sketch artists

FIGURE 8.2 *Nathaniel Hawthorne* (1862), by Mathew Brady. Courtesy Frederick Hill Meserve Collection, National Portrait Gallery, Smithsonian Institution.

whose drawings were reproduced in rotogravure by the newspapers and weeklies.

Brady and his crew compensated for these difficulties in a number of ways. They relied on the conventions of landscape and historical painting to create familiar, static images that implied movement. More important, they photographed scenes and objects that didn't move. Brady's photographic plates worked superbly with stationary artillery pieces, composed groupings of men in camp, and cavalry officers sitting erect on their mounts. And they captured the strangely tranquil aftermath of battle: the shell-pocked buildings, the splintered trees, and especially the dead (see figure 8.3).

Brady's Civil War images entered the public consciousness late in the summer of 1862, when the photographer opened an exhibit at his Manhattan gallery entitled "The Dead of Antietam." The title picture, taken by Alexander Gardner two days after one of the bloodiest battles in U.S. history, single-handedly changed photographic subject matter forever. Even now, Gardner's photograph assaults the unprepared perceiver, shocking us with its grim immediacy. Mutilated corpses lie

FIGURE 8.3 *The Dead of Antietam.* Courtesy Library of Congress, Prints and Photographs Division (LC-B811-560).

scattered haphazardly along a fencerow, hemmed in on the left by a diagonal wagon road. But if the road and fence convey order and meaning, the jumble of bodies communicates just the opposite. The scene is inexplicable, incomprehensible. How could such a thing happen? How could human beings behave in such a way?

During the second half of the war, Hawthorne tried to answer these questions in the only way he knew: through writing. He struggled to respond to the aesthetic and moral challenges created by the war, working on a novel that he feared no one would care to read. And he worried that Gardner had captured something ominous in his photo portrait: the death of Romance.

Hawthorne was old—suddenly, insufferably old. Like Jean Valjean, the hero of the novel everyone was reading that year, *Les Misérables*, his hair had whitened almost overnight. He walked stiffly, moved with care. Moncure Daniel Conway observed that, soon after the war began, Hawthorne "was much aged in appearance."[5]

The legendary shyness that had imbued his public image with a Byronic gloom now contracted into a frigid solitude, a wintry aloofness. The gregarious Bronson Alcott, his house separated from Hawthorne's "by a gate and shaded avenue," tried repeatedly to halt the brooding man on his walks and to engage him in conversation. "I seldom caught sight of him," Alcott admitted, "and when I did it was but to lose it the moment he suspected he was visible; oftenest seen on his hilltop screened behind the shrubbery and disappearing like a hare into the bush when surprised."[6]

Alcott specialized in essays. So did Emerson. So had Thoreau and the long-dead Margaret Fuller. Each of them believed that literature was the expression of a singular personality; each of them offered a glimpse of the world through a single window. But Hawthorne crafted complex fictions that required the skillful choreography of numerous characters, multiple perspectives, competing outlooks. Henry James understood this when he described "Chiefly about War-Matters" as an "example of the way an imaginative man judges current events—trying to see the other side as well as his own, to feel what his adversary feels, and to present his view of the case." The English journalist Edward Dicey, who met Hawthorne in Washington in 1862, quickly discovered that the author's "mind was...always hovering between two views." Those who claimed that Hawthorne opposed the war, Dicey asserted, had it all wrong. "He sympathized with the war in principle; but its inevitable accessories—the bloodshed, the bustle, and, above all perhaps, the bunkum which accompanied it—were to him absolutely hateful."[7]

These same qualities were observed by the young novelist Rebecca Harding Davis when she visited Concord in 1862. Davis was the author of *Life in the Iron Mills*, published in the *Atlantic* a year earlier. The novella, widely regarded as the first work of realism in American writing, was admired by readers everywhere, including Emily Dickinson, who mentioned it the month the war began. It is the story of a poor but artistic man dehumanized by industrial labor, and its power and originality prompted Hawthorne to invite Davis, then thirty years of age, for a visit.

A native of Wheeling, Virginia (it became West Virginia after the war), much of Davis's childhood had been spent sitting in a cherry tree in her backyard, where she read Sir Walter Scott's *Waverley* novels and Hawthorne's tales with something akin to a thirst. She arrived in Concord excited to meet so many of her literary heroes, but was quickly disappointed. The "first peculiarity which struck an outsider in Emerson, Hawthorne, and the other members of the *Atlantic* coterie," she recollected, was "that while they thought they were guiding the real world they stood quite outside it, and never would see it as it was."[8]

As a southerner, Davis was more familiar with the human cost of the war than any of Concord's literary lions. One day during her visit, she found herself in the comfortable parlor of the Wayside, pelted with questions about slavery and the war by Emerson and Bronson Alcott. Stonewall Jackson had recently defeated the Union army in the Shenandoah Valley; Robert E. Lee had assumed command of the Army of Northern Virginia. Despite these apparent setbacks, Alcott stood in Hawthorne's parlor and "chanted paeans to the war, the 'armed angel which was waking the nation to a lofty life unknown before.'" Davis was having none of it.

> I had just come up from a border State, where I had seen the actual war: the filthy spewings of it; the political jobbery in Union and Confederate camps; the malignant personal hatreds wearing patriotic masks, and glutted by burning homes and outraged women; the chances in it, well improved on both sides, for brutish men to grow more brutish, and for honorable gentlemen to degenerate into thieves and sots. War may be an armed angel with a mission, but she has the personal habits of the slums. This would-be Seer who was talking of it, and the real Seer [Emerson] who listened, knew no more of war as it was than I had done

in my cherry-tree when I dreamed of bannered legions of crusaders *debouching* in the misty fields.

On the periphery of this discussion was Hawthorne, "lank" and "gray," who "sat astride of a chair, his arms folded on the back, his chin dropped on them, and his laughing, sagacious eyes watching us, full of mockery." He watched Alcott extemporize at length on the moral benefits of the war and then "gathered himself up lazily to his feet and said, quietly: 'We cannot see that thing at so long a range. Let us go to dinner.'" Davis remarked, "Mr. Alcott suddenly checked the droning flow of his prophecy and quickly led the way to the dining-room."[9]

Hawthorne had hoped to write the triumphant follow-up to *The Marble Faun*, to spend the remaining years of his life in bookish peace, climbing to his improbable "sky-parlour" each morning to write, walking along the promontory known as Revolutionary Ridge behind the Wayside, spending his evenings before the hearth, surrounded by family as he reread the complete works of Scott. The firing on Sumter had altered these plans, however, forcing him to abandon his tale about an American claimant who tries to repossess his ancestral English property. Gradually, the war made him doubt the utility and relevance of literature. It distracted his concentration, overtook his imagination, poisoned his fancy.

Nevertheless, by the time of Davis's visit he was dwelling on a new story—this one based on a tale Thoreau had told him long ago about the Wayside. He had recounted the legend to George William Curtis, the literary editor of *Harper's*, explaining that the Wayside house stood "within ten or fifteen yards of the Boston road (along which the British marched and retreated)" during the Revolutionary War. "I know nothing of the history of the house; except Thoreau's telling me that it was inhabited, a generation or two ago, by a man who believed that he should never die." Hawthorne joked that he sincerely hoped that the man had died, "else he may possibly appear, and disturb my title to the residence."[10]

Something about Thoreau's unlikely tale struck a chord. Perhaps it was the dying writer's poignant interest in a man convinced he would live forever. Perhaps it was Hawthorne's own sense of mortality. He daydreamed about the curious man, tried to imagine the unforeseen consequences of immortality. Slowly, he began to rough out a plot, to sketch a group of characters, building his story from the fragments of previous tales and notebook entries, resurrecting a well-worn image from his obsessive imagination: a flower that grew from the hillock of a grave. He had described just such a plant in *The Scarlet Letter*, where the spiritually desiccated Roger Chillingworth gathers "flabby" weeds from an unmarked grave in order to create a dubious potion for the guilt-ridden Reverend Mr. Dimmesdale. "[T]hese ugly weeds," Chillingworth confesses, "grew out of [the dead man's] heart, and typify, it may be, some hideous secret that was buried with him, and which he had done better to confess during his lifetime."[11]

Each morning now, Hawthorne mounted the steps to his tower and wrote. It wasn't easy, he complained, "when an earthquake is shaking one's writing-table." To James T. Fields, the man responsible for his fame, he prevaricated about the "instalment of the Romance" he had promised for publication in the *Atlantic*. "There is something preternatural in my reluctance to begin," he claimed. In truth, he had been working on his book for some time. "I linger at the threshold, and have a perception of very disagreeable phantasms to be encountered, if I enter." He complained that he found it impossible to write a "sunshiny" book.[12]

Always before, he had been able to transmute history into romance, action into narrative. Always before, he had divined in human folly the profound symbols of existence. But *The Elixir of Life*—the romance he began to write shortly after the Civil War began—was inert from the beginning. Plot and characters shifted repeatedly. Action occurred as if in a dream: intense but without purpose. The distinguished Hawthorne critic Edwin Haviland Miller described the voluminous manuscript the author produced throughout the war as laden with "corrections, interpolations, exclamations of frustration, and unanswerable questions as to plot, characterization, and motivation." The numerous drafts are marked with repeated cries of despair. "I find myself dealing with solemn and awful subjects," Hawthorne wrote midway into the second draft, "which I but partly succeed in putting aside." Elsewhere, he noted, "[T]elling a story with a voice, you can run off into any wildness that comes into the head; whereas the pen petrifies all such flights."[13]

Nothing seemed to work. "I do wish Providence would think me worthy of possessing a pen which I could write with," he groused to Fields toward the end of 1863. "I have bought what was purported to be a first-rate gold pen, but it has a trick of writing as if the paper were greasy."[14] But the problem wasn't his writing implements. It was the less-forgiving tool of his intellect.

At times, the war seemed to blunt his sensibilities entirely. "The play (be it tragedy or comedy) is too long drawn out," he complained to his Liverpool friend Henry A. Bright, "and my chief feeling about it now is a sense of weariness. I want the end to come, and the curtain to drop, and then to go to sleep." He felt increasingly out of step with his times, criticized for speaking the truth, incapable of accepting the glorious rhetoric of the Republicans. Referring to "Chiefly about War-Matters," he explained to Bright, "The war-party here do not look upon me as a reliably loyal man, and, in fact, I have been publicly accused of treasonable sympathies." The truth, however, was that he sympathized "with nobody and approve[d] of nothing; and if I have any wishes on the subject, it is that New England might be a nation by itself."[15]

Moncure Conway, always planted squarely in the center of Concord society, remembered Hawthorne during this period as having "no party,—then the equivalent to having no country."[16] He was alluding to Edward Everett Hale's short story "The Man without a Country," published in the *Atlantic Monthly* in December 1863 and even more popular than Davis's *Life in the Iron Mills*.

Edward Everett Hale was the nephew of Edward Everett, the great orator and statesman who delivered the two-hour stemwinder before Lincoln's 272-word masterpiece at the Gettysburg cemetery. Hale had been serving as a Unitarian minister at Worcester, Massachusetts, back in the 1850s, when he had received a letter from a twenty-four-year-old Emily Dickinson, who had written to inquire if her friend Benjamin Franklin Newton had died "peacefully." In Worcester, he was also a colleague of the young Thomas Wentworth Higginson.[17]

Like these friends and correspondents, Hale longed to make his name as an author. He encapsulated the creed of his literary milieu in a famous motto: "Look up and not down, look forward and not back, look out and not in, and lend a hand." And he wrote short stories. "The Man without a Country" resembled Silas Weir Mitchell's "The Case of George Dedlow" in that it employed a reportorial brand of realism that convinced many *Atlantic* readers the story was actually true. Philip Nolan is the tragic protagonist, a young army officer befriended by the traitorous Aaron Burr in the early years of the nineteenth century. When Burr is tried for treason, Nolan is hauled into military court as his accomplice. Following his testimony, the rebellious young man is asked if he has anything to say that might prove his loyalty to the United States.

"D—n the United States!" he cries. "I wish I may never hear of the United States again!" From the shocked silence of the courtroom, the judge replies with icy scorn, "Prisoner, hear the sentence of the Court. The Court decides, subject to the approval of the President, that you never hear the name of the United States again."[18]

The rest of the story chronicles the consequences of this unusual sentence. Nolan is condemned to spend the rest of his life aboard U.S. warships, never touching shore, never leaving the vessels. "[T]here was no going home for him," remarks the narrator, who becomes acquainted with the prisoner while serving in the navy, "even to a prison."[19] Nolan's newspapers and magazines are censored; books referring to the United States are banned. Even the sailors who guard him are prohibited from mentioning America in his presence.

The rigors of this punishment are not immediately apparent, but gradually they take their toll on the prisoner. Initially defiant, Nolan becomes homesick. Years pass, and he grows increasingly hungry for news of his birthplace. In one of the story's more poignant episodes, the banished man takes his turn reading poetry to a gathering of sailors. Unwittingly, he selects the fifth canto of Scott's "The Lay of the Last Minstrel." "[W]ithout a thought of what was coming," the narrator recalls, Nolan begins to recite:

> Breathes there the man, with soul so dead,
> Who never to himself hath said...
> This is my own, my native land![20]

Pale, shaken, realizing for the first time the extent of his alienation from a native land, Nolan quits reading, unable to continue.

As the first half of the nineteenth century gradually passes, the protagonist becomes a "gentle, uncomplaining, silent sufferer," said to have "*aged* very fast, as well he might." Decrepit, ailing, more desperate for home than ever, he addresses the narrator in a climactic scene of renunciation: "Youngster, let me show you what it is to be without a family, without a home, without a country. And if you are ever tempted to say a word or to do a thing that shall put a bar between you and your family, your home, and your country, pray God in His mercy to take you that instant home to His own heaven." When at last Nolan dies in his cabin berth, we learn that he has created a shrine to his forbidden nation. "The stars and stripes were triced up above and around a picture of Washington, and he had painted a majestic eagle," recalls the narrator. "The dear old boy saw my glance, and said, with a sad smile, 'Here, you see, I have a country!'"[21]

An allegory of rebellion and secession, Hale's story was immensely popular. It argued that repudiating one's country was treasonous, that it produced malaise, alienation, soul sickness. At the end of the story, the narrator feels pity for the dying man and tells him "everything I could think that would show the grandeur of his country and its prosperity." But, he sadly adds, "I could not make up my mouth to tell him a word about this infernal Rebellion!"[22]

Hawthorne's novel was set during the Revolutionary War—a substitute for the present national crisis. His protagonist, Septimius Felton, paces the hillside behind his house, brooding over the destruction of his country as British and revolutionary soldiers clash on the road below. The mortal combat sickens the young man, awakening in him the bitter knowledge that humans are endowed with a passion for killing, a fondness for extermination.

However much he disdains the battle below him, Hawthorne's hero cannot escape the fighting. In the heat of the skirmish, an English officer leads a charge up the hill and confronts the reclusive Septimius. The scene that follows might have been lifted directly from Hawthorne's favorite childhood author, Sir Walter Scott. Even by the standards of the revolutionary period, it is anachronistic, a courtly duel crammed with awkward action and improbable dialogue. Certainly, it bears no resemblance to the stark carnage photographed by Brady. Forced to defend himself, Septimius inadvertently wounds the officer, who exclaims that his desire to fight was but "a boy's play, and the end of it is, that I die a boy, instead of living forever, as perhaps I otherwise might."[23] With his last breath, he bequeaths to Septimius a mysterious manuscript containing the recipe for eternal life. In return, Septimius buries the English officer in a hillside grave, from which there soon sprouts the heart-shaped flower of immortality.

Hawthorne spent weeks on this scene. He wrote and rewrote, fiddled with dialogue. The problem wasn't with the mechanics of plot or character, but with his subject matter. Writing about the Revolutionary War forced him to consider the devastation of the current conflict. He struggled to view combat as noble and necessary, asserting at one point that war "is well ended, and performs its purpose, if any grand truth of morals or religion be but established by it." This could be said about the war that had liberated America, he knew, but he was less certain about the Civil War. Memories of his trip to Washington coupled with the grim accounts in the newspapers kept rising before him and clouding the charmed vision of his fancy. Warfare, Septimius angrily declares, is nothing nobler than a "great surge of bloody violence which we fling together." In a moment of revulsion toward the northern ministry, which continued to describe the war as the work of a superintending providence, Hawthorne wickedly sketched Septimius's solicitous preacher: gentle, meek, sage—who nevertheless assures his doubting parishioner that "to slay a fellow-man may be an act of worship."[24]

The authorial distance Hawthorne had cultivated when setting his tales in the Puritan past was no longer attainable. The war intruded, exploding plot, outflanking narrative, spoiling action. When Septimius leaves the familiar environs of Concord to visit a doctor in Boston who will help him to translate the secret formula of immortality, Hawthorne swerves into a meditation on the conflict between romance and realism. "[I]t seemed as if [Septimius] were coming out of a mist," he narrates,

> out of a mist, out of an enchanted land, where things had seemed to him not as they really were; where impossibilities looked like things of everyday occurrence; out of some region into which he had wandered unawares, and dreamed a life-like dream, most life-like in its force and vividness, most unlifelike by its inconsistency with what really is, with men's purposes, fates, businesses; into such a misty region had he been, and strayed many days, deeming himself at home; but now the mists were thinning away, he was passing the witch-like boundaries, and he might never find his way over them again.[25]

The passage describes the jarring experience Hawthorne had when he set aside his novel and traveled to Washington in 1862. He had departed from the "enchanted land" of home and imagination, propelling himself into what became a "great depression." Like Septimius, who had "flung himself so earnestly and entirely upon his strange purpose" of discovering the elixir of life, he had discovered that "when it seemed about to be removed from him, he felt that he must wander vaguely, stagger, go no whither, and finally sit down by the wayside, and remain there, staring at the wayfarers who *had* a purpose, until he died." Hawthorne here interjected a personal note: "I have had [this feeling] oftentimes myself, when long brooding and busying myself on some idle tale, and keeping my faith in it by estrangement from all intercourse besides, I have chanced to be drawn out of the precincts enchanted by my poor magic." The effect was painfully disorienting. Looking back, he continued, "I have thought, how faded, how monstrous, how apart from all truth it looks, being now seen apart from its own atmosphere, which is entirely essential to its effect."[26]

The passage is an obituary to romance. It reflects the sad recognition that Hawthorne's particular brand of writing is no longer tenable during the urgent conflagration of civil war. Not surprisingly, what little enchantment he had mustered for his story drained away soon after he wrote the confession. Describing Septimius in Boston,

Hawthorne essentially repeated the scenes of war he had witnessed during his trip to Washington:

> [Septimius] saw many tokens of what had been suffered...during the oppression, syncope, or feverish action, of the war still going on....here, for instance, were vacancies, over which the grass was beginning to grow, where wooden houses had been torn down for fuel for the soldiers;...here were maimed persons, limping along the streets; here was a sort of wildness in the look of many of the inhabitants, and elderly citizens, in powder, and ruffles at their sleeves, walked along as men in a dream, unable to realize what great change it was, that had put them into a new, uncomfortable world, since they were young; there seemed to be little business, only, several times, he heard the sound of a drum, and saw the drill of young men preparing for the army. For there seemed to be no other life than this—the purpose to kill one another.[27]

Gone was the courtly duel that had opened the romance; gone, increasingly, the hope for eternal life. Through 1863, Hawthorne's novel increasingly assumed the stark reality of a Mathew Brady photograph. Long passages were now devoted to "the lump of dead flesh, which a fly was already settling on," to "the ghastly armies of slain." Stumbling through the wreckage of a deserted city, Septimius discerns "in the dusk of the even'g on the road...now and then a dead man lying in the dust, now the smoking ruin of a house."[28]

Like Philip Nolan, the man without a country, Hawthorne grew weaker and older the longer he remained separated from his nation. Soon after his trip to Washington, he sent James Fields the photograph by Alexander Gardner, feebly joking, "My hair is not so white....The sun seems to take an infernal pleasure in making me venerable—as if I were as old as himself." Like all jokes, this one masked a deeper concern. By the end of 1862, when Concord was abuzz with the news that Louisa May Alcott had become a nurse and joined the great cause in Washington, Sophia Hawthorne wrote to her daughter Una, "Julian came in with the portentous news that the battle has at last begun and Fredericksburg is on fire from our guns. So Louisa goes into the very mouth of the war." She then added, "Papa has not a good appetite, eats no dinners except a little potato. But he is trying to write, and locks himself into the library and pulls down the blinds."[29]

But no matter how Hawthorne tried to shutter out the world and retreat into the spectral confines of literature, his thoughts were drawn, much like Emerson's, to death and the departed. To Fields, he described his plan to open *The Elixir of Life* with a sketch about Thoreau because it "seems the duty of a live literary man to perpetuate the memory of a dead one, when there is such fair opportunity as in this case—but how Thoreau would scorn me for thinking that *I* could perpetuate *him!*"[30] No sooner had he written this, however, than his imagination began to fail him.

He tried diverting himself by converting extracts from his English notebooks into articles for the *Atlantic*. By the spring of 1863, at Fields's prompting, he agreed to publish them as a book. In July, he proposed to dedicate *Our Old Home*, as the volume was titled, to his long-time friend Franklin Pierce, the former president who had appointed him U.S. consul in Liverpool a decade earlier, making his life in England possible. This act of loyalty to a "dear friend" sparked a minor controversy among the abolitionist literati, who viewed Pierce as an unscrupulous collaborator with the proponents of slavery. Harriet Beecher Stowe, writing to Fields, expressed her incredulity at Hawthorne's act: "Do tell me if our friend Hawthorne praises that arch-traitor Pierce in his preface and your loyal firm publishes it. I never read the preface, and have not yet seen the book, but they say so here, and I can scarcely believe it of you....What! patronize such a traitor to our faces!" Emerson, less demonstrative, simply, and without a word to the author, scissored out the dedication from the book.[31]

In the midst of the furor, most readers overlooked a more significant remark buried in the preface. Noting that he had begun revising his English notebooks in the hopes of producing a work of fiction, Hawthorne announced that such an ambition was no longer possible. "The Present, the Immediate, the Actual has proved too potent for me," he explained. "It takes away not only my scanty faculty, but even my desire for imaginative composition."[32]

At the time it was written, the statement was more prediction than fact. Hawthorne had not abandoned *The Elixir of Life* narrative—*yet*—but he was continuing to have difficulty with it. Increasingly, sentences wandered, paragraphs ran out of gas. As if trying to spur on his flagging enthusiasm, Hawthorne changed the names and ages of his principal characters, tinkered with their descriptions. At last, he began to focus on the mysterious manuscript bequeathed to Septimius by the slain English officer. The manuscript, said to confer the secret of immortality to its successful interpreter, is mutilated and bloodied, torn and unreadable. Most critics accept without question the novel's premise that the manuscript contains the recipe for a potion to produce eternal life. But the actual contents of the document are never satisfactorily established, and Septimius is free to project any fantasy he wishes upon the bloodstained parchment.

Only toward the end of his second draft did Hawthorne himself seem to understand the significance of the document. After writing hundreds of pages that failed to generate suspense, he suddenly announced that the bloodstained manuscript might reveal "how a nation, not an individual being, might attain enduring existence on earth."[33] The wording echoed the statement he had made earlier about Emanuel Leutze's mural for the Capitol. There, the artist had labored away on his ambitious painting, oblivious to the great conflict raging beyond the magic circle of his imagination and "thus manifesting that we have an indefeasible claim to a more enduring national existence." The elixir of life, Hawthorne seemed at last to suggest, was nothing less than the Constitution: a scrap of parchment defaced by blood and war, yet promising the nation's eternal life if properly interpreted. That interpretation required the nation to once again inhabit the neutral territory in which multiple perspectives are honored, to think like a novelist and not through the egotistical prism of the essayist.

Upon reaching this insight, however, *The Elixir of Life* finally succumbed to narrative exhaustion. Perhaps the string of Union defeats and the mounting casualties of 1863 proved too much for Hawthorne's always precarious optimism. Perhaps he simply no longer felt strong enough, vigorous enough to write. Regardless, he sent his protagonist to Boston once more, then abruptly stopped writing. Septimius's "dream of everlasting life had failed him," he wrote. "Then what was his next choice? Was it not, to seek the readiest passage out of an existence?" How easy, Hawthorne mused,

> to find a battle field to die on; and perhaps, in the sweet exhilarating sense of living, with his fellow men—the free life of humanity, risking all, sacrificing all for the triumph of his country, and dying in the attainment of victory for her, there might be an intensity of life, into the few moments of which would be compressed all that heat, vigor, earnestness, which would have been thinly scattered over such an interminableness as he had dreamed of.[34]

Then, he abandoned the manuscript for good.

In March 1864, at the invitation of his old friend and publisher William D. Ticknor, Hawthorne made another trip south. Once again, the Union army had begun preparations for a spring offensive. This time, however, George B. McClellan was no longer commander of the Army of the Potomac. Ulysses S. Grant had been promoted to lieutenant general and had assumed command of all active Union forces. William Tecumseh Sherman was placed in charge of the Military Division of the Mississippi, assuming command of the Departments of the Ohio, the Tennessee, the Cumberland, and the Arkansas. Those who had fought at Shiloh, those who believed that ruthless attacks against and unconditional surrender by the enemy were the keys to success were at last in charge of the war's prosecution.

Unlike his trip to Washington two years earlier, Hawthorne journeyed this time purely for reasons of health. "Mr. Hawthorne has really been very ill all winter, and not well, by any means, for a much longer time," Sophia confided to Horatio Bridge. Her husband and her children were her world, and she steeled herself for his departure from the Wayside. Then in her fifties, she was still pretty, still finely featured, despite the lifelong poor health that forced her to take regular doses of opium and calomel—the latter concoction the same that had poisoned her next-door neighbor Louisa May Alcott. Since her marriage at the comparatively late age of thirty-two, Sophia had ceaselessly devoted herself to her husband, whom she believed to be a genius of the first order, a visionary poet of the human soul, and the only person in Concord who understood the social, political, and moral complexities of the war.[35]

"Mr. Hawthorne" was not "ill in bed," she confided to Bridge, but he was "miserable on a lounge or sofa, and quite unable to write a word, even a letter, and lately unable to read." Mustering up the courage to write as candidly as possible, she admitted that her husband "has wasted away very much, and the suns in his eyes are collapsed, and he has had no spirits, no appetite, and very little sleep.... The state of our country has, doubtless, excessively depressed him. His busy imagination has woven all sorts of sad tissues."[36]

Ticknor had promised the worried wife that the trip would lift Hawthorne's faltering spirits. There was to be no itinerary. The two friends would simply travel south, moving from place to place whenever they liked, enjoying one another's conversation and the increasingly lush and verdant bloom of spring. A change of scenery was bound to do the author good.

Stopping in Boston along the way, Hawthorne spent the night with James and Annie Fields, both of whom were shocked by his "invalid appearance." "He has become quite deaf," Annie remarked in her diary. "His limbs are shrunken but his great eyes still burn with their lambent flame." That evening, Hawthorne seemed troubled by pre-

FIGURE 8.4 James T. Fields, Nathaniel Hawthorne, and
William D. Ticknor. Courtesy National Portrait Gallery, London.

monitions of his mortality. "Why does Nature treat us so like children!" he complained. "I think we could bear it if we knew our fate. At least, I think it would not make much difference to me now what became of me." Throughout the night, Annie Fields heard him pacing in the bedroom down the hall, "heavily moving, moving as if waiting, watching for his fate."[37]

Once he began to travel, however, Hawthorne seemed to recover. By the time they reached New York, Ticknor noted an improvement in the author's appetite and sleep. He did not move so slowly, so heavily. And even history seemed on the mend; the Senate had just ratified the Thirteenth Amendment, making slavery and involuntary servitude illegal. (The House of Representatives would not pass the amendment until the following year.) The two men would have certainly discussed this momentous development, speculating on its consequences for the nation, but for one of those random occurrences that forever alters the trajectory of a life. On the carriage ride to Philadelphia, Ticknor lent his coat to Hawthorne, who had forgotten his, and promptly caught a cold. On April 10, the publisher died.

Stunned and unbelieving, Hawthorne sat in the dead man's hotel room in Philadelphia, waiting for family members to claim the body. He had known Ticknor since 1850, when Ticknor and Fields had contracted to publish *The Scarlet Letter*, thereby changing his fortunes forever and making him a literary celebrity. He had been friends with the man, had delighted in the commingling of their mutual prosperities, had applauded the recent purchase by Ticknor and Fields of the *Atlantic Monthly* and *North American Review*. And while the publisher was six years younger than Hawthorne, the author had looked to him nevertheless as an older, wiser brother.

Dazed and still distressed, he returned several days later to Concord, where no carriage awaited him. He walked to the Wayside pale, sweating, and shaking. "[A]s soon as I saw him," Sophia wrote to Fields, "I was frightened out of all knowledge of myself—so haggard, so white, so deeply scored with pain and fatigue was the face, so much more ill than I ever saw him before."[38] To soothe him, she read Thackeray aloud, not bothering to report the latest news that Confederate soldiers had slaughtered more than 200 African-American soldiers who had formally surrendered at Fort Pillow, Tennessee. The act was in retaliation for Congress's recent actions.

In *The Elixir of Life* manuscript now gathering dust in his study, Hawthorne had lamented what happened to his imagination whenever it stepped "beyond the limits of the spell." The experience he described was akin to shifting his glance from the enchanted colors of a Leutze painting and then gazing at the harsh pallor of a Brady photograph, and it was fatal to his particular brand of creativity. The result, he noted, was "sad destruction, disturbance, incongruity, impossibility, everything that seemed so true and beautiful in its proper atmosphere, and nicely adjusted relations, now a hideous reality."[39]

There was one final reworking of the elixir theme, a tale in which a charming elderly gentleman who feels "he had gone irrevocably out of fashion" is granted immortality from the beginning of the story.[40] This version, which Hawthorne titled *The Dolliver Romance*, seemed briefly to recharge him. The pacing and characterization were more sure-footed, the language brisk. All references to war had been eliminated; the narrative had finally freed itself from history and context.

Nevertheless, this version ultimately proved unsatisfactory. As early as 1863, when *Our Old Home* was published, Hawthorne had found himself "sadly content to scatter a thousand peaceful fantasies upon the hurricane that is sweeping us all along with it, possibly, into a limbo which our nation and its polity may be as literally the fragment of a shattered dream as my unwritten Romance." Fiction, he seemed to say, required protection from the kind of reality now imposing itself so violently upon the imagination. "The Present, the Immediate, the Actual," he admitted, "has proved too potent for me."[41]

With characteristically spare sorrow, Emily Dickinson had written to the traumatized Thomas Wentworth Higginson, "Mr. Hawthorne died." Others were more effusive, especially the New England literary community that soon gathered at the funeral service in Concord and the burial in the Sleepy Hollow cemetery. The transcendentalist minister James Freeman Clarke, who had married Hawthorne and Sophia two decades earlier, delivered a tribute to the dead man. He declared that "Hawthorne had done more justice than any other to the shades of life, shown a sympathy with the crime in our nature, &, like Jesus, was a friend of sinners." Once outside the church, Oliver Wendell Holmes couldn't help remarking on the bright, warm May day, which seemed to him to make the occasion "a happy meeting," nature's celebration of a life.[42] Franklin Pierce attended, accompanying the family, as did the Alcotts and James Russell Lowell. Hawthorne's fellow student at Bowdoin College Henry Wadsworth Longfellow would capture the day in verse. Less interested in the weather or the camaraderie of the occasion, the poet alluded to Hawthorne's unfinished life and manuscript:

There in seclusion and remote from men,
The wizard hand lies cold,
Which at its topmost speed let fall the pen,
And left the tale half told.[43]

Somewhat surprisingly, it was Emerson who found the occasion most sorrowful. "I thought there was a tragic element in the event," he admitted in his journal, speaking perhaps of his own sense of endings. Thinking about the man he had so recently welcomed back to America with a strawberry party, Emerson found himself almost unbearably saddened by "the painful solitude of the man—which, I suppose, could not be endured & he died of it. I have found in his death a surprise & disappointment. I thought him a greater man than any of his works betray, that there was still a great deal of work in him, & that he might one day show a purer power."[44]

As usual, Emerson had touched on something overlooked by most. With that sixth sense of the competitive writer, he had divined his neighbor's almost desperate desire to finish his romance. "I have fallen into a quagmire of disgust and despondency with respect to literary matters," Hawthorne complained a few months before his death. "I am tired of my own thoughts and fancies and my own mode of expressing them." Speaking to Fields about *The Dolliver Romance*, he admitted defeat: "I shall never finish it.... I cannot finish it unless a great change comes over me; and if I make too great an effort to do so, it will be my death; not that I should care much for that, if I could fight the battle through and win it, thus ending a life of much smoulder and scanty fire in a blaze of glory."[45]

The language in this last sentence precisely echoed that of Hawthorne's friend George William Curtis, who not so long before had eulogized Theodore Winthrop in the *Atlantic Monthly*. In 1856, Winthrop had asserted, "A man to be a complete man must sometimes come into collision with the great facts of reality." Winthrop had come into collision with those facts at Big Bethel, back in the early days of the war, when it seemed as if the fighting might provide a chance to prove one's heroism and redeem the nation—all within ninety days. If Winthrop had been "a lovely possibility before he went to war," Curtis wrote, his enlistment had been a kind of consecration. Like "a fire long smouldering," Winthrop's life "suddenly blazed up into a clear, bright flame, and vanished."[46]

For Hawthorne, the war had done precisely the opposite. It had doused a fervent literary imagination, ended an illustrious career. In

"The Custom-House" introduction to *The Scarlet Letter*, he had recounted the story of the "noble and heroic" General James F. Miller, whose response to a command that he take a British battery had been, "I'll try, Sir!" Later in the introduction, when the ghostly Surveyor Pue begs the narrator from beyond the grave to tell the story of Hester Prynne, the reply is more assertive: "I will!"[47]

Hawthorne had been a writer whose only heroism had been to write, whose valor consisted chiefly in the effort to create sympathetic portraits of various perspectives, multiple points of view. In the fiery incandescence of partisanship and war, his own flame weakened, sputtered, and went out. Three months after abandoning all literary efforts, he died. James T. Fields, substituting the hero's flag with a manuscript, placed *The Dolliver Romance* on the coffin. As it was about to be lowered, however, the editor thought better of it and retrieved Hawthorne's last romance.[48]

CHAPTER 9

In a Gloomy Wood

IT WAS THE first summer of the war and Henry Wadsworth Longfellow was sitting in his spacious, book-lined study when he heard a cry from the room next door. Rising from his desk, he turned to see a nightmare. It was Fanny Longfellow, his beloved wife, standing in the threshold. She was engulfed in flames.

She had been sealing a lock of their daughter's hair in a sheet of paper with a candle. One moment, she was engaged in the kind of cozy domestic scene her husband was famous for transforming into poetry; the next, her summer dress was on fire, a coffin of flame. Frantic, Longfellow threw a small rug over his wife. He wrapped his arms around her, dragged her to the floor, trying to smother the fire and in the process badly burning his face and hands. Fanny died the next day.

Overwhelmed by grief, America's most honored and popular poet immersed himself in a project he had considered for decades: translating Dante's *Divina Commedia*. He had worked intermittently on the fourteenth-century masterpiece for several decades, in part as a way to keep up his Italian, in part because he disliked the recent translations glutting the market. But after Fanny's death, the work took on greater urgency. The poem haunted him with its depth and form, its intricate rhythms and lilting rhymes, and most of all, its strange and strangely hopeful story.

The *Divine Comedy* was written amid civil war, a bloody contest between Guelphs and Ghibellines in early Renaissance Tuscany. The epic begins with a poet named Dante, who finds himself "in the midway of this our mortal life," lost and afraid "in a gloomy wood."[1] There is nothing quite like this forest in Western literature. In a few simple words, Dante transports us to a dark and trackless setting familiar to anyone who has felt spiritually adrift, shattered by grief, beset by the terrifying beasts of doubt and fear. From this doleful opening, Dante's masterpiece then traces his passage into the successive circles of hell's underworld, led by the ancient Roman poet Virgil, who patiently explains the bizarre torments witnessed along the way and then guides the poet through purgatory. The final book describes Dante's ascent to heaven in the company of Beatrice, the beautiful young woman with whom he had fallen in love at first sight, who had died before he could even utter a word to her.

As the war escalated from Shiloh to Antietam, Fredericksburg to Gettysburg, Longfellow worked with increasing intensity on his translation of the *Divine Comedy*. When Hawthorne met him in the office of Ticknor and Fields in 1863, he noticed a profound change in his college friend: "His hair and beard have grown almost entirely white," Hawthorne remarked, "and he looks more picturesque and more like a poet than in his happy and untroubled days." There was, he noted, "a severe and stern expression in his eyes, by which you perceive that his sorrow has thrust him aside from mankind and keeps him aloof from sympathy."[2]

Longfellow completed his translation just as the war was concluding. "To enliven the winter," he wrote in 1865, "I have formed the Dante Club, consisting of Lowell, [Charles Eliot] Norton, and myself, meeting every Wednesday, with a good deal of talk and a little supper."[3] Eventually, the group expanded to include Oliver Wendell Holmes and William Dean Howells, the latter an earnest and promising young novelist who soon assumed the editorship of the *Atlantic*, signaling a new era and a new direction in that publication's history. These conservators of Brahmin culture stayed up well into the evening, discussing the war, sipping port, gossiping about literary figures, and reviewing the proofs of Longfellow's three-volume translation. A strange elation bordering on giddiness characterized the meetings. The nation, these men believed, had sojourned through hell and purgatory during the past four years, enduring horrors and grotesqueries even Dante had never imagined. Surely, it was ascending toward a promised heaven.

The *Divine Comedy* was much on the mind of Herman Melville, as well. He returned to Dante time and again for inspiration, to refresh his sense of poetry's epic grandeur. But where Longfellow's Dante

Club tended to view life as a divine comedy, trending ever upward toward a cosmic resolution, Melville saw it as tragedy.

Of all the antebellum writers we now consider significant, he is the only one to have participated in an actual military operation during the Civil War. In the spring of 1864, as the war entered its fourth year, the author visited his cousin Henry Gansevoort, a lieutenant colonel stationed with the Army of the Potomac near the tiny, rural Virginia settlements of Vienna and Aldie. There, he took part in a minor raid in the Wilderness, a densely vegetated area that had already been the site of numerous skirmishes and battles. Riding on horseback through these rough backwoods, Melville saw the remains of soldiers who had died the year before in the Battle of Chancellorsville. Vines grew through their polished rib cages. Skulls with empty eye sockets seemed to gaze up from the thick undergrowth.

Melville was almost forty-five. Solidly built, tall, and intense, he seemed to fill any room he entered. Gray hairs now grizzled the full, luxuriant beard he was inordinately proud of. He moved somewhat cautiously, having recently suffered a broken collarbone when a wagon overturned. Those who had known him as a young man, when he had burst upon the literary scene with crackling tales of maritime adventures, remarked that he was no longer so buoyant or so excited by life's possibilities. But he was every bit as ambitious. While the war had defeated Hawthorne's imagination, it reinvigorated Melville's. In 1864, he longed to become the nation's next Longfellow, its most honored and popular poet. He longed, in fact, to surpass the estimable Longfellow, to join the hallowed ranks of Dante, Milton, Shakespeare, and Shelley. The book he was now planning and dreaming about would reclaim his former popularity and secure his place among the literary immortals. It would propel him to those august pinnacles of greatness he had glimpsed so many years earlier, enable him at last to engrave his name in history. The trip to Virginia was part of his grand strategy to get there.

It is difficult, 150 years after the fact, to capture the fear and trepidation a civilian felt when leaving a northern city and traveling into the southern war zone. Trains were frequently stopped or derailed. Bands of guerrilla fighters robbed and sometimes killed Union sympathizers. Night travel was unsafe and unwise. Melville took the train from New York, where he had recently moved, to Washington. He then continued via military wagon into Virginia along a series of jolting corduroy roads. The surrounding countryside was raw and abandoned, smelling of loam and wood smoke. Villages were squat and inhospitable. Most of the houses along the way belonged to Confederate sympathizers.

Then, he came upon a city of white canvas tents, the neatly ordered barracks and stables of a Union camp. The place was a hive of activity. Soldiers were busy grooming horses, drilling on a flat stretch of ground, constructing outbuildings. Inside the tents, which were floored with rough pine planks and warmed by inelegant brick fireplaces, they swapped stories and played cards.

After meeting his cousin and taking a tour of the camp, Melville was introduced to Colonel Charles Russell Lowell, who would have a profound impact on him. The young man was a nephew of James Russell Lowell, and to many New Englanders he was the personification of all that was bright and good and promising about Brahmin culture. Charles Lowell was not just handsome; he was golden. His short, fair hair was parted in the middle; his complexion was tawny and leonine. Hawthorne knew and admired the young colonel. Emerson called him one of the "good crop of mystics at Harvard" and had once invited him to his study in Concord, where he read aloud an essay in progress and asked the young man for his opinion. Years later, Edward Emerson wrote a biography of Lowell that portrayed him as an American scholar come to life, "a New England man, a poet, who also fought for his country."[4] (See figure 9.1.)

A year earlier, Lowell had married Josephine "Effie" Shaw, the radiant, high-spirited sister of his good friend Robert Gould Shaw. "Where in the world," wrote Ellen Emerson from Concord, "could a nobler or a handsomer pair be found!" Charles and Effie were deeply in love, their feelings for one another made deeper and stronger by the urgency of war. Years later, William James recalled seeing the couple on the day the Massachusetts Fifty-fourth marched through the streets of Boston. To him, their future seemed intertwined with the glorious cause of emancipation. "I looked back and saw their faces and figures against the evening sky," he wrote, "and they looked so young and victorious, that I, much gnawed by questions as to my own duty of enlisting or not, shrank back."[5]

Despite his glamorous appeal, there was something reckless and impulsive about Lowell. On April 9, 1863, he arrived at a recruiting office at 2 City Hall Avenue and School Street in Boston, where he encountered a squad of conscripted Irish soldiers who were refusing to obey a company sergeant. "Kill the son-of-a-bitch sergeant," they hollered. Lowell attempted to restore order, arresting the ringleader and promising to hear the men's complaints. When the group continued to resist, however, Lowell borrowed a Colt revolver and shot and killed one of the men.[6]

FIGURE 9.1 Charles Russell Lowell.

The School Street Mutiny, as it was called, generated a political firestorm throughout the North. Lowell was exonerated by the military, but Democratic newspapers united in condemning the shooting as a flagrant example of class prejudice. Irishmen, they claimed, had been disproportionately conscripted to serve in the Union army. These poor men were without the means to pay for substitutes to fight in their place. At the same time, they vehemently disagreed with the shift in war goals, which now included the emancipation of the slaves. The mass of contrabands now flooding northward, these newspapers observed, threatened to take away the livelihoods of hardworking day laborers once the war concluded—something Lowell and his high-toned Brahmin ilk had never bothered to consider when lobbying for the freedom of the slaves.

Several months before Melville's trip to Virginia, Lowell had presided over another troubling incident. This one involved a hapless private named William Ormsby, who had grown sick of military life and deserted camp, only to be captured in a Confederate uniform, blindly drunk and taking potshots at Union officers. Lowell immediately convened a drumhead court-martial and sentenced the man to death. Executions for desertion were not uncommon during the Civil War, but it was illegal under army regulations for a subordinate officer like Lowell to order a drumhead court-martial except in cases of emergency. As with the School Street Massacre, fear of mutiny had driven the young colonel to extreme behavior. When the court reached a guilty verdict, he announced, "[F]or such an offence death is the only punishment and the Comdg officer hopes and believes that the Summary execution today will prevent forever the necessity of the repetition in this Command."[7]

Melville heard of this incident on his visit to Virginia. He squirreled it away, reworking the event twenty-five years later in his last work of fiction, *Billy Budd, Sailor*. In that tale, a young man is falsely accused of mutiny by a bitter, aggrieved master-at-arms. Billy Budd, the young man, accidentally kills his accuser and is sentenced to death by a drumhead court-martial. The officer in charge, Captain Vere, feels enormous sympathy for the man he condemns to death, but he also understands that sympathy has no place in the economy of order and duty required for the smooth functioning of the military during wartime. The innocent Billy acknowledges as much when, just before his hanging from the masthead, he proclaims, "God bless Captain Vere."

William Ormsby, the Union deserter, was similarly ennobled by his execution. He helped to unload his casket from a wagon. He smoothed the hand-drawn target pinned to his chest so that his executioners would have a better shot. Then, the condemned man addressed the regiment: "I am guilty and the punishment is just. I want you to know that I did not desert because I didn't believe in our cause. I know it is right." Moved by this display, the regimental chaplain who attended Ormsby wrote, "Whole years of thoughtless wanderings and heedless sin" had been redeemed in those final minutes. The deserter had been altered, the chaplain believed, transformed as if by "marvelous insight."[8]

When Melville arrived at the same camp in which Ormsby was executed, the dogwoods and redbuds were blossoming. In the late afternoon, the surrounding forest glowed gold and green. But as this light faded, the Wilderness grew thick with shadows, impenetrable and forbidding.

The artist Winslow Homer captured some of the area's oppressive density in *Skirmish in the Wilderness*, a large canvas painted the same year as Melville's trip. The work portrays a miniscule group of Union soldiers who are dwarfed by the towering verdure and impassable thickets of nature. In contrast to the period's typical landscape paintings, Homer's work reveals nature's mystery as well as its cruel indifference to human concerns. The painting seems to convey just how fragile are the moral and civic bonds that prevent people from killing one another (see figure 9.2).

Melville shared the impression. The forest of the Wilderness would play a crucial and formative role in *Battle-Pieces and Aspects of the War*, the book of war poems he was just beginning to write. Beautiful and gloomy, these poems often resemble the disorienting forest that begins

FIGURE 9.2 *Skirmish in the Wilderness* (1864), by Winslow Homer. Courtesy New Britain Museum of American Art.

Dante's *Divine Comedy*. The Virginia backwoods become lush, mythical, often ominous. Mentioned in the book's first poem as "green, / Shenandoah!" the woods assume depth and substance as the collection unfolds. "Nature is nobody's ally," Melville declares in another early poem, setting the stage for the "ghastly gloom" that lures McClellan into the fight at Antietam and for the long poem "The Armies of the Wilderness." "None can narrate the strife in the pines," he remarks in this last work, conjuring up Virginia's tangled wilds as a metaphor for the difficulty of interpreting the great conflict: "Obscure as the wood, the entangled rhyme / But hints at the maze of war—."[9] For Melville, the Wilderness had come to represent the moral confusion of the conflict gripping the country. Who could claim to act with pure motives when violence was used to enforce a cause? he asks. Don't aggression and brutality cause even the most enlightened people to "rebound...whole aeons back in nature"? In a moment of Dantean insight, he remarks that in the Virginia backwoods, "Hell made loud hurrah."[10]

The youthful Lowell seemed less concerned by these surroundings. Brisk, cheerful, gregarious, and socially graceful, he was eager to entertain a literary figure. Charles A. Humphreys, the camp chaplain, reported in his journal that the two men hit it off immediately, discussing literature and philosophy over dinner and chatting amiably around the campfire. At some point, Lowell probably introduced Melville to his wife, Effie, who had shrugged off the discomforts of camp life to be with her husband and who bore the mourning of her brother with tranquil dignity. At some point, Melville explained that he "was out now to learn something of the *soldier's* life, and to see a little campaigning with his own eyes, preparatory to the writing of [his] book."[11] Lowell promptly invited him to accompany his troops on a scouting expedition in search of a Confederate guerrilla leader. John Singleton Mosby was the leader of a detached cavalry unit called the Partisan Rangers, and he was known throughout Virginia as the "Gray Ghost" for his quick raids and uncanny ability to elude the enemy. In one of his more notorious exploits, he had kidnapped a brigadier general while the man was guarded by Union troops. More typically, he led ambushes, disrupted supply lines, stole horses, and shot Union stragglers. Like early morning fog, he then faded into the woods.

Erudite as well as violent, Mosby justified his actions by claiming that, once war spread through the South "like fire on a prairie,...the laws became silent in the midst of arms." He was paraphrasing Cicero. In photographs, his eyes are the cold, metallic blue of freshly pumped water. As a Wisconsin veteran recalled, Mosby's tactics were so ruthless that desertion from the Union army soon ceased to be a problem in northern Virginia. A week or so before Melville's visit, Ulysses S. Grant had barely escaped capture by the renegade Confederate. In response, he issued a terse order: "Where any of Mosby's men are caught hang them without trial."[12] Within days, seven men were hanged with notes pinned to their uniforms warning others to cease their insurrectionary activities. Mosby, in retaliation, ordered the execution of seven Union prisoners.

Melville learned of these details from the men in camp. The conversations were in turn dramatized in "The Scout toward Aldie," the long narrative ballad that provides us with the most comprehensive account of his trip south. Melville considered "The Scout" so important that he separated it from the other poems in *Battle-Pieces* with blank pages. The poem's title was printed in a different typeface in the table of contents, and the work itself was positioned at the climax of the book, appearing out of chronological order.

Distilled through Melville's dramatic imagination, "The Scout toward Aldie" recounts the effort to capture John Singleton Mosby and focuses on a young colonel, hungry for glory, who announces to one of his subordinates, "Peril, old lad, is what I seek." The story begins in a war-ravaged landscape, "An outpost in the perilous wilds," and travels into the enchanted and "Eerie" depths of "Mosby's land." Edmund Wilson declared the work "[o]ne of Melville's most ambitious pieces," comparing its thematic concerns with those of *Benito Cereno* and *Billy Budd*. But he believed that Melville's "complicated stanza form, his knotted and jolting style and his elliptical way of telling the story" bogged down the narrative.[13] This form and style were intentional, however, designed to trip up readers. Throughout the poem, Melville's language forces us to slow down, double back, make our way cautiously through a thick confusion of signs. "The Scout toward Aldie" is nothing less than an aesthetic recreation of the Wilderness.

The young colonel, modeled on Lowell, is accompanied by a "grizzled Major," a surrogate for Melville. The two men, "Like sire and son," represent "Hope and Experience sage." Together, they are leagued against the diabolical Mosby. Confident and brash, the colonel is in the midst of deriding this foe when the older man suddenly interrupts:

> "…but what's that dangling there?"
>   "Where?" "From the tree—that gallows bough;

"A bit of frayed bark, is it not?"
  "Ay—or a rope; did *we* hang last?—
Don't like my neckerchief any how;"
  He loosened it: "O ay, we'll stop
  This Mosby—but that vile jerk and drop!"[14]

In addition to hanging, Lowell's men worried about sharpshooters. A year earlier, Winslow Homer had created another iconic Civil War image, *The Sharpshooter on Picket Duty*, which portrayed a Union marksman perched in a tree, pointing his rifle beyond the field of vision. The painting quietly raised an ethical question. The new tactic of sharpshooting targeted those who were not in the act of combat. At the same time, it distanced the killer from the consequences of his assignment. In a letter that included a pencil sketch of an unsuspecting officer as viewed through the scope of a rifle, Homer described how once, when traveling through Virginia to sketch military life, he had asked to peer through a sharpshooter's weapon. "As I was not a soldier," he concluded, "but a camp follower and artist, the above impression struck me as being as near murder as anything I ever could think of in connection with the army."[15] (See figure 9.3.)

FIGURE 9.3 *The Sharpshooter on Picket Duty* (1863), by Winslow Homer. Courtesy Library of Congress, Prints and Photographs Division (LC-USZ62-178).

Despite the propensity of sharpshooters to target those wearing an officer's crimson sash, Lowell kept his on when he led the expedition. He had requested some 500 men, equal numbers of cavalry and infantry. On a Monday morning, the two detachments split up and departed, each man armed and carrying two days' rations. Melville accompanied the cavalry, following Lowell, who sat erect in the saddle.[16] The column proceeded west to a mill situated in a dense wood of scrub oak and sumac.

During the previous autumn, Union cavalry had engaged Mosby here. At Goose Creek, a comrade had been shot and drowned. The event appears in "The Scout toward Aldie" when the cavalry crosses the stream. "We found the body," a soldier recalls,

> (Blake's, you know);
> Such whirlings, gurglings round the face—
> Shot drinking! Well, in war all's fair—
> So Mosby says.[17]

Near Goose Creek, Lowell's cavalry halted and waited for the infantry to rejoin it. Suddenly, from the emerald shadows, they were fired upon. Bullets sliced through leaves and branches. Men crouched down, shouted warnings. Lowell ordered a charge up the Old Carolina Road, and the entire column galloped in pursuit beneath the canopy of trees. No prisoners were captured.

When the light began to give out, the column bivouacked on the road just outside of a small, rough-looking settlement called Leesburg. Campfires were forbidden. "The night was very cold," recalled Humphreys, the camp chaplain,

> too cold to sleep; and besides there were several attacks upon our pickets that brought us to our feet and made us stand to horse till the danger was past. It was about as easy to stand as to lie down that night. If we lay down, it was at our horses' feet with the bridle rein in our hands; and—not to speak of their uneasy stamping with the iron shoes upon the ground which was our bed,—if they got lonesome they would poke us with their noses. . . . It seems a wonder that—crowded together as we were, the horses standing in column four-abreast in a narrow road—none of us were trampled under their feet.[18]

Melville captured the adrenaline-fueled mirth, the dizzy hilarity of men who knew their lives might end at any moment. He experienced the strange intensification of life, the purification of the moment that every soldier feels in combat. "How strong they feel on their horses free," he wrote. "The sun is gold, and the world is green, / Opal the vapors of morning roll." Describing the second day of the expedition, when eleven of Mosby's guerrillas were captured before noon, he remarked on the "saucy mood" of the prisoners, "handsome—well bred; / In wood or town, with sword or pen, / Polite is Mosby, bland his men."[19]

It is at about this point in the poem that we realize that Mosby's name has been mentioned at least once in every stanza. Repeating the name while keeping the man offstage enables Melville to elevate the guerrilla into myth, much as he had done with the monomaniacal Captain Ahab in the early chapters of *Moby-Dick*. "All spake of him," Melville reports, "but few had seen…; / Yet rumor made him everything." The very sound of Mosby's name must have conjured for Melville the malevolent white whale of his novel. "As glides in seas the shark," he writes, "[so] Rides Mosby through green dark." The guerrilla leader is not simply a force of nature but a satanic figure. Melville repeatedly uses the term *brood* to describe Mosby's band of partisans, relying not only on its convenient rhyme with wood but also suggesting a diabolic gathering in the Wilderness that his friend Hawthorne would have instantly recognized as a covenant with evil.[20]

Toward the close of the second day, a small contingent of Lowell's dismounted troopers stole into Leesburg, hoping to surprise Mosby and his men at a wedding party. Melville remained behind with the majority of the column, biding his time and trying to sleep, but around two in the morning he heard the group straggle into camp, breathless, excited, and bloodied. The detachment had arrived in Leesburg too late to surprise Mosby, but in a confused melee outside the church one of Lowell's men had been killed and three others wounded. A spark of panic ran through the column. What if Mosby's men had followed the detachment back and planned to ambush them?

Melville embellished the episode in his narrative ballad. The young colonel, encountering a wagon driven by an old slave and his veiled mistress, demands to see the woman's face in order to make sure Mosby hasn't disguised himself. He discovers a letter protruding from her dress that reveals that one of Mosby's men is to be married that evening. The grizzled major senses a trap, but his young superior orders his men to the wedding. When the federal troops have to stop because of a tree lying in the middle of the road, they are immediately ambushed and the colonel is killed.

"Dead!" the poet exclaims. "But so calm / That death seemed nothing—even death, / The thing we deem every thing heart can think." Melville seems to be recalling the eerie calm on the faces of the dead scattered throughout the Wilderness. With the death of the colonel, a spell is broken. The poem chronicles the end of enchantment:

> The weary troops that wended now—
> Hardly it seemed the same that pricked
> Forth to the forest from the camp:
> Foot-sore horses, jaded men;
> Every backbone felt nicked,
> Each eye dim as a sick-room lamp,
> All faces stamped with Mosby's stamp.

Asking his readers, "What gloomed them?" Melville answers: "'Tis Mosby's homily—*Man must die.*"[21]

Though Lowell was not killed during Melville's trip, the dramatic death had some basis in fact. The young colonel managed to survive the Battle of the Wilderness, a fierce encounter that began in the first week of May 1864 and began the war of attrition between Grant's and Lee's armies that marked the conflict's final year. In the tangled woods, thick with smoke, both sides inflicted heavy casualties. A Union sharpshooter recalled "the rattle of musketry" as "one deafening uproar" that lasted from dawn to dusk. "Men's heads were knocked to atoms by iron, others were riddled through their bodies with lead. Goodly sized trees were cut off, and brush mowed low; altogether, a most bloody carnival." Ulysses S. Grant, a man seldom given to overstatement, reported, "More desperate fighting has not been witnessed on this continent than that of the 5th and 6th of May." The word *desperate* was his way of honoring the thousands of soldiers he sent to certain death.[22]

Lowell was not so lucky at Cedar Creek, the decisive final battle in the Valley Campaigns of 1864. Stubborn about wearing the insignia and crimson sash of his rank, he was knocked off his horse by a sniper's bullet in the middle of action. In the summer, he had written to his young wife with a premonition: "I don't want to be shot till I've had a chance to come home. I have no idea that I shall be hit, but I *want* so much not to now, that it sometimes frightens me." The bullet collapsed his lung, making it almost impossible for him to speak. But an hour and a half later, he insisted on leading his brigade to capture a battery. He ordered his men to strap him back into the saddle. Again, he was shot. This time, the bullet severed his spinal cord.

Melville alluded to Lowell's fatal wound in "The Armies of the Wilderness," a poem that could serve as an epitaph for the entire era:

"Plume and sash are vanities now—/ Let them deck the pall of the dead."[23]

Melville sought to honor the experience of the Wilderness in *Battle-Pieces*. This ambitious work, arranged in roughly chronological order, was technically innovative, philosophically searching, audacious in its reach. It was also filled with competing perspectives, contradictory interpretations, unresolved conclusions—as if the poet were trying to capture the messy totality of a fractious war. In the prose "Supplement" that concluded the volume, Melville described his guiding principle as the "sacred uncertainty which forever impends over men and nations."[24] The Wilderness that permeates *Battle-Pieces* was meant to portray that uncertainty.

The goal of the book was to instruct an America that for too long had regarded itself as morally innocent. Time and again, Melville urged the nation to accept a less arrogant and more tragic vision of life, to wean itself from the intellectual tradition inspired by Emerson. In "The March into Virginia," for instance, he portrayed the Union debacle at Bull Run as a painful but necessary passage into mature knowledge. The poem describes a group of young soldiers blithely marching toward their fate and rushing into combat "In Bacchic glee." Their notions of war are untouched by experience; battle seems but a pastoral spree in a "leafy neighborhood," a "berrying party, pleasure-wooed." (Melville intended the funereal connotations of the word *berrying* when read aloud.) Consumed with visions of glory, excited to prove themselves as men, these naïfs will discover too late the inadequacy of their understanding. A blaze of artillery serves as the instrument of enlightenment:

> But some who this blithe mood present,
>   As on in lightsome files they fare,
> Shall die experienced ere three days are spent—
>   Perish, enlightened by the vollied glare.[25]

Similarly, in "The College Colonel," Melville paid homage to enthusiastic men like Charles Russell Lowell, who had forsaken secure lives and prosperous careers for a cause they believed in. The poem isn't about a march into battle but rather the return of experienced veterans. The college colonel "brings his regiment home—/ Not as they filed two years before, / But a remnant half-tattered, and battered, and worn." None is more battle-worn than the leader. Missing an arm and a leg, "He has lived a thousand years / Compressed in battle's pains and prayers." Returning on horseback to the cheering crowds of his hometown, he has also gained something crucial from his suffering:

> But all through the Seven Days' Fight,
>   And deep in the Wilderness grim,
> And in the field hospital tent,
>   And Petersburg crater, and dim
> Lean brooding in Libby, there came—
>   Ah heaven!—what *truth* to him.[26]

Modern, mechanical warfare had produced new, uncomfortable truths, and Melville believed that new language, new modes of expression were required to convey those truths. Like Whitman and Dickinson, he considered mellifluous language and metrical smoothness to be a kind of lie: a denial of the harsh, jarring rhythms of contemporary life. More than either of those poets, however, he understood that the Civil War marked the passing of an era, the eclipse of a culture that once had been aptly expressed in pleasing meter. He lamented the waning of this poetic tradition in "The Stone Fleet," subtitled "An Old Sailor's Lament," which recounted the scuttling of sixteen antiquated vessels in the port of Charleston to create a blockade against the southerners. One of these vessels was an aged whaling ship, ingloriously sunk after countless adventures around the globe. Here, Melville slyly refers to his own scuttled contribution to an outmoded Romantic literature:

> You'll say I'm doting: do but think
>   I scudded round the Horn in one—
> The Tenedos, a glorious
>   Good old craft as ever run—
>   Sunk (how all unmeet!)
> An India ship of fame was she,
>   Spices and shawls and fans she bore;
> A whaler when her wrinkles came—
>   Turned off! Till, spent and poor,
>   Her bones were sold (escheat)!
> Ah! Stone Fleet.[27]

In a related nautical poem about the epochal fighting between ironclads, "A Utilitarian View of the Monitor's Fight," Melville explicitly addressed the challenge of fashioning poetic language to the new facts of warfare. The clash between steam-powered ships spelled the end of sailing vessels and a once-picturesque form of combat. It also required changes to poetic language and, more important, to the consciousness of the nation:

> Plain be the phrase, yet apt the verse,
>   More ponderous than nimble;
> For since grimed War here laid aside
> His Orient pomp, would ill befit
>   Overmuch to ply
> The rhyme's barbaric cymbal.

Replacing "the shot heard 'round the world" from Emerson's "Concord Hymn," Melville detected in the ironclads "The ringing of those plates on plates" that "Still ringeth round the world." The industrialization of war meant that battle would be "Deadlier, closer" and at the same time emptier of passion. Heroes were no longer required; "warriors / Are now but operatives."[28]

Most of all, Melville insisted in *Battle-Pieces* that the war might have been avoided if both sides had been less rigid and unyielding in their convictions. The terrible conflict had been created by a stubborn refusal to question one's own assumptions, to examine them from other points of view. Many of the poems attempted to break down this certainty, to reject pat answers and easy interpretations. Melville opened the collection with a poem about John Brown. Usually regarded as a martyr to the cause of freedom or as a domestic terrorist (depending upon a person's sectional and political affiliations), Melville's Brown is neither. Hidden behind the hood Brown wore at his hanging "Is the anguish none can draw."[29] The volatile interactions between historical events and individual personalities are simply too complex to be understood in the shrill and simple terms ladled out by self-interested politicians.

Similarly, in "The Conflict of Convictions," Melville claimed that God rejected "YEA AND NAY—" in favor of a "MIDDLE WAY." The ambiguity of war, its welter of good and bad acts and motivations, rendered WISDOM . . . VAIN, AND PROPHESY." To dramatize this ambiguity, Melville juxtaposed poems from northern and southern perspectives, such as those devoted to Stonewall Jackson and to William Tecumseh Sherman's infamous March to the Sea. He crammed disparate voices into individual poems like "Donelson," where the clamorous, grating perspectives of "eager, anxious people" gathered "About the bulletin-board" is alternated with the inflectionless voice of a newspaper reporter and the perspectives of anonymous members of a Union battalion. In "The Armies of the Wilderness," a poem deeply indebted to his trip to Virginia, he placed rival armies within sight of each other and asked: "*Can no final good be wrought? / Over and over, again and again / Must the fight for Right be fought?*"[30]

Competing voices and disparate perspectives were a product of democracy, and many of Melville's poems wondered whether the nation could create institutional structures that both honored democratic practices and minimized violence. The issue is symbolized in a number of poems by "the Dome"—the Capitol dome destroyed by fire during the 1850s and ordered rebuilt by Lincoln in 1860. Melville had seen the partially completed cast-iron construction when he visited Washington in search of a patronage job in 1861. As a writer fascinated by the interplay between appearance and reality, he took note of the plan to paint the structure white so that it would blend in with the marble building beneath. Throughout *Battle-Pieces*, the Dome stands for a reestablishment of the rule of law and, at times, the will to dominate.

The enormous structure towers over people and landscape in mute splendor. McClellan is said to have "propped the Dome" during Antietam. Robert E. Lee can see it, "Looming," from his Arlington porch. In "The Conflict of Convictions," the voice of skepticism sneers at the perennial optimist, saying, "*The last advance of life—/ Ha, ha, the rust of the Iron Dome!*" Behind this last remark is Melville's fear that state power consolidated during war might destroy the Jeffersonian ideal of individual self-determination:

> Power unanointed may come—
> Dominion (unsought by the free)
> And the Iron Dome,
> Stronger for stress and strain,
> Fling her huge shadow athwart the main.[31]

Even in the dark woods of the Wilderness the poet can faintly discern "The Capitol Dome—hazy—sublime / A vision breaking on a dream." The dissipating dream is presumably the one first articulated by the founding fathers, the expectant, optimistic creed of freedom and equality that had funded American self-identity and been compromised by slavery, a historical irony described by Melville in another poem as "the world's fairest hope linked with man's foulest crime."[32]

In "America," Melville portrayed a different kind of dream. "Where the wings of a sunny Dome expand," he wrote, "I saw a Banner in the gladsome air—." Perched high above the capital city and atop the Dome is the bronze statue of Columbia. Serenely gazing at "The Land reposed in peace below," she is soon shocked by "the ambiguous light-ning" of war. "And the lorn Mother speechless stood, / Pale at the fury of her brood." As civil war erupts below, she falls into a deathlike sleep filled with "contortion[s]" and "The terror of the vision there—/ A silent vision unavowed." At last, she awakens to discover a sharply altered world:

> At her feet a shivered yoke,
> And in her aspect turned to heaven
>   No trace of passion or of strife—
> A clear calm look. It spake of pain,
> But such as purifies from stain—
> Sharp pains that never come again—
>   And triumph repressed by knowledge meet,
> Power dedicate, and hope grown wise,
>   And youth matured for age's seat—
> Law on her brow and empire in her eyes.[33]

Four years of civil war had felt to many Americans precisely like a terrifying dream. Near its conclusion, Lincoln admitted, "It seems to me that I have been dreaming a horrid dream for four years, and now the nightmare is gone." Walt Whitman would capture something of the pervasive dread in the postwar poem "Old War-Dreams," which attempted to exorcise the recurrent nightmare of "the dead on their backs with arms extended wide":

> Long have they pass'd, faces and trenches and fields,
> Where through the carnage I moved with a callous composure,
>   or away from the fallen,
> Onward I sped at the time—but now of their forms at night,
> I dream, I dream, I dream.

More poignant is the private dream of a Missouri woman and southern sympathizer named Elvira Ascenith Weir Scott. Upon learning that her favorite brother had volunteered for the federal army, she wrote in her journal, "I waked up this morning feeling certain that I would hear sad news before nigh. I dreamed that I was in a wild, open space, where the ground looked smooth, but wherever I set my foot it stuck in mud, so that I had no escape from it. I was beside a new-made grave, trying to plant violets."[34]

Melville sought to capture these feelings in the fable of "America." He argued that culture and society were fragile, in need of protection from the darker forces of human nature. He was by no means alone.

"I would love to see the civil law enforced once more in our distracted Country," wrote a young man to his father in the winter of 1863. For some who experienced the war up close, however, systematic cruelty and anarchic killing were not violations of law but rather the natural consequences of law during wartime. "Men are shot or hung every few days on the most trivial of pretexts," noted Elvira Scott. "It has become so common that it excites no remark. Freedom of speech & of the press is a thing unheard of now."[35]

Perhaps not surprisingly, the symbol of these anarchic forces was the volcano. As had so many of his contemporaries, including most prominently Emerson, Melville had once looked to Vesuvius as the emblem of his artistic ambition and creative force. Turbulent, combustible, explosive, the volcano mirrored the heated language and intellectual passion of his best novels. In 1857, he had traveled to the dormant volcano and peered into its chasm. "To Vesuvius on horseback," he jotted in his notebook, capturing the sights in a few terse lines: "Old crater of Pompeii. Modern crater like old abandoned quarry—burning slagmass—Red & yellow. Bellowing. Bellows. flare of flame. Went into crater. Frozen liquorice." Trying to imagine what an eruption would look like, Melville later described "Vesuvius' plume of fire" reddening the bay with its explosion, coloring the masts of ships, illuminating awestruck faces. His granddaughter recalled a print of the volcano "in the front hall" of Melville's New York home. The picture, she wrote, was of an eruption high above "The white sails on the Bay of Naples."[36]

In *Battle-Pieces*, this massive geological force was unpredictable, violent, capable of cracking society in two and destroying everything in its path. The image is most palpable in the poem about the Battle of the Crater, which occurred on July 30, 1864. Following the encounter in the Wilderness, Grant's army had proceeded to the Confederate stronghold on the Appomattox River, located some twenty miles south of Richmond, where it found the enemy entrenched and impregnable. Rather than launch a suicidal offensive, the federal general ordered his troops to dig in. In the sweltering heat of high summer, both armies embarked upon a mutual siege.

To break the stalemate, a Union officer named Henry Pleasants proposed what initially seemed like a farfetched plan. Pleasants had been a civil engineer before the war. He had experience cutting railroad passages through the Allegheny Mountains and mining coal in Pennsylvania's Schuylkill County. His unit, the Forty-eighth Pennsylvania, was largely composed of fellow miners. His plan, which was eventually approved and set into motion, was to build a tunnel some 200 yards through the dense marl clay of Petersburg, directly under the Confederate fort. Pleasants calculated that an explosive charge of six tons of powder would be enough to obliterate the enemy.

Working by night and depositing the excavated dirt in the Appomattox, Pleasants's men had completed the tunnel by June 23. A week later, Union soldiers, awaiting orders to attack, heard a "low rumbling," "a tremble not unlike an earthquake." At first, there was "a deep shock and tremor of the earth," and then "a heaving and lifting of the fort and the hill on which it stood." One soldier recalled a "monstrous tongue of flame [that] shot fully two hundred feet into the air, followed by a vast column of white smoke...then a great spout or fountain of red earth rose to a great height, mingled with men and guns, timbers and planks, and every other kind of debris, all ascending, spreading, whirling, scattering and falling with great concussion to the earth once more."[37] (See figure 9.4.)

At first, the operation seemed successful. The explosion had left an enormous crater, according to one major, "filled with dust, great blocks of clay, guns, broken carriages, projecting timbers, and men buried in

FIGURE 9.4 *Before Petersburg at Sunrise. July 30th, 1864*, by Alfred R. Waud. Courtesy Library of Congress, Prints and Photographs Division (LC-USZC4-10794).

various ways—some up to their necks, others to their waists, some with only their feet and legs protruding from the earth." But soon after the explosion, waves of Union soldiers rushed into this hole—only to find themselves trapped in the sloping basin. "Here in the crater was a confused mob of men," reported one participant, "continually increasing by fresh arrivals.... Any attempt to move forward from this crater was absolutely hopeless." The modern tactic of using explosives now gave way to primitive killing. From the crater's rim, Confederate soldiers fired at the trapped men as if at a turkey shoot. When their ammunition ran out, "they would run down in front of the line and jump over and were met with bayonet and clubbed with musket." In the quagmire of mud and blood, men stabbed and battered one another for more than an hour.[38]

Ulysses S. Grant later believed that the inhabitants of Petersburg knew "they were resting upon a slumbering volcano and did not know at what moment they might expect an eruption." It was this very uncertainty that Melville tried to put into words in his poem about the event, "The Apparition":

> Convulsions came; and where the field
> Long slept in pastoral green,
> A goblin-mountain was upheaved
> (Sure the scared sense was all deceived),
> Marl-glen and slag-ravine.[39]

The pastoral field here is reminiscent of the one in Melville's "Shiloh," a vestigial reminder of a past way of life. But "The Apparition" takes us directly to the moment of action. Before "the eye could take it in, / Or mind could comprehend win," Melville writes, the ground itself "sunk!—and at our feet." The conclusion to be drawn from the event is bleak:

> So, then, Solidity's a crust—
> The core of fire below;
> All may go well for many a year,
> But who can think without a fear
> Of horrors that happen so?[40]

By the time *Battle-Pieces* was published in the late summer of 1866, the war had been over for nearly a year. Atlanta had fallen; Abraham Lincoln had won his reelection. Following Grant's order to burn crops and houses, kill livestock, and destroy civilian infrastructure in an effort to bring the Confederacy to its knees, William Tecumseh Sherman had marched from Atlanta to Savannah doing precisely that. The result, ultimately, was a treaty signed at the Appomattox Court House in Virginia. Five days after the signing, a war-weary but jubilant Abraham Lincoln celebrated the Union victory by attending a play at Ford's Theater. The premise of the comedy, *Our American Cousin*, was similar to the romance Hawthorne had abandoned once the war started. Lincoln was laughing at the story of a backwoods rube in English society when an actor from the company crept into his presidential box and shot him in the head. He died the next morning. "Language utterly fails to express my feelings," wrote a stunned Union soldier, still in camp when he heard the news and expressing the sentiments of many.[41]

Mourning their losses, trying to rebuild their lives, Americans no longer wished to think or read about the four years of bitter fighting. For many in the North, Emerson's dream of liberty had triumphed and prevailed. The Union victory, combined with Lincoln's martyrdom on Easter weekend, restored their sense that America was a sacred text unfolding toward a glorious and foreordained conclusion. Sherman had made famous the phrase "War is hell." Much of the nation was ready to abandon that hell, to skip the purgatory of reconciliation, and to enter at once into a bright and future heaven. As Emerson exalted in his journal, the war had at last "extend[ed] New England from Canada to the Gulf, & to the Pacific."[42]

To Melville, the country still seemed lost in the gloomy wood where it had been before the war had begun. In the prose "Supplement" he appended to his book in 1866, he sought to dampen the North's smug triumphalism. Describing himself as "one who never was a blind adherent," he asked his fellow authors to practice more charity and magnanimity than they had before the war. "Northern writer[s]," he declared, "however patriotic,...must revolt from acting on paper a part any way akin to that of the live dog to the dead lion." He agreed with the Union cause and rejoiced "for our triumph," but he also believed "[t]he mourners who this summer bear flowers to the mounds of the Virginian and Georgian dead are, in their domestic bereavement and proud affection [the same] as are those who go with similar offerings of tender grief and love into the cemeteries of our Northern martyrs."[43]

From his audience, Melville asked for "common sense and Christian charity." He reminded them that "those unfraternal denunciations, continued through years, and which at last inflamed deeds that ended in bloodshed, were reciprocal," and he argued that the inheritors of the system of slavery were "less fortun[ate], not less righteous than we." In order to make this argument, Melville scarcely mentioned the freed slaves. While they appealed "to the sympathies of every humane mind," he admitted, the immediate problem confronting the postwar United States was in bringing together two parties who had fought bitterly and desperately for four years.[44]

Reconciliation was particularly important in 1866. "It is more than a year since the memorable surrender," Melville reminded his readers, "but events have not yet rounded themselves into completion." Hostilities, he feared, might resume at any time if the Republican Congress's punitive legislation toward the South was enacted. To prevent this, he asked his compatriots to put themselves in the place of others, to experience the southerners' feelings, and to appreciate their hardships and desires. He begged his audience to think like novelists. "In imagination let us place ourselves in the unprecedented position of the Southerners," he wrote, asserting that even the benevolent impulses of the abolitionists, "after passing a certain point, can not undertake their own fulfillment without incurring the risk of evils beyond those sought to be remedied." And he predicted dire consequences for the nation if it did not shed its self-righteousness.[45]

Asking his readers "to revere the sacred uncertainty which forever impends over men and nations," he noted that "for them who are neither partisans, nor enthusiasts, nor theorists, nor cynics, there are some doubts not readily to be solved. And there are fears." And he posed an admonitory question: "Wherefore in a clear sky do we still turn our eyes toward the South, as the Neapolitan, months after the eruption, turns his toward Vesuvius?"[46]

"The Scout toward Aldie" concluded with an elegy not for the slain Charles Russell Lowell but for his young bride, Effie Shaw Lowell, who had moved into camp with her husband and who, at the end of war, was left to mourn alone. Ellen Emerson considered Lowell's death "the greatest loss perhaps that Massachusetts has sustained during the War." Countless other tributes would follow. But Melville was more interested in the survivors who were now forced to live out the consequences of their highest ideals. "No joy remains for bard to sing," his poem concludes,

> And heaviest dole of all is this,
>   That other hearts shall be as gay

As hers that now no more shall spring:
To Mosby-land the dirges cling.[47]

As a young woman of seventeen, Effie Shaw Lowell had applauded her brother's enlistment in the army and had written in her war journal, "I believe...that if we had no soldiers and all the officers were drunkards, the Cause, by its own force of right, would run without help from anybody.... 'Our cause can't fail,' because it's God's cause as well as ours."[48] Such touching, youthful confidence would not survive the war.

Effie was eight months pregnant when she learned that her husband had been killed in action. After giving birth to a daughter, Carlotta, she sank into a profound depression. Often during the next four years she was too dejected to tend to the infant. She slept too much or slept too little, had no appetite. "Effie says she no longer wants to live," wrote Lowell's mother, Anna. In her grief, the young woman transformed her room at her parents' Staten Island house into a facsimile of the camp in Vienna. Blankets covered the floor. Lowell's bookshelves and pictures were scattered throughout. She slept in the makeshift bedding, becoming a recluse.[49]

Only gradually did she return to life. She would later say that she was drawn to public works because serving the less fortunate enabled her to consecrate the memory of Charles Russell Lowell and Robert Gould Shaw. She became involved with the New York State Charities Aid Association and by the early 1870s was reporting on the city's jails and almshouses. Soon, she produced a statewide study of poverty, on the basis of which she became the first woman appointed to the New York State Board of Charities. An advocate of the working class, Lowell founded the Consumer's League of the City of New York, which organized boycotts to force employers to provide better working conditions for women employees.

This distinguished career had begun in the ashes of war. Desolate with loss, Effie had tried to find the wife of the man Charles Russell Lowell had shot years earlier in the now-forgotten School Street Mutiny. She failed, but the gesture of reconciliation, the desire to enter into a community of suffering, resembled Melville's anxious hopes in the prose "Supplement" of *Battle-Pieces*.

As for Melville's ambitious book, it would sell fewer than 200 copies. Tired of war, Americans were certainly not interested in ambiguity or self-questioning. The book's scarce reviews were mostly negative—some cruelly so. William Dean Howells condemned Melville's abstract tone in a review for the *Atlantic*, using *Battle-Pieces* to promote the new realism he would champion as the replacement for transcendental Romanticism for decades to comes. Was it possible, Howells wondered, "that there has really been a great war, with battles fought by men and bewailed by women? Or is it only that Mr. Melville's inner consciousness has been perturbed, and filled with the phantasms of enlistments, marches, fights in the air, parenthetic bulletin-boards, and tortured humanity shedding, not words and blood, but words alone?"[50] Melville's hopes for a literary resurrection were crushed. Never again would he venture to dream that his writing would be recognized by a contemporaneous audience.

He lived quietly, obscurely, until 1891, when he died at his house on East Twenty-sixth Street. Lizzie Melville, his wife, soon moved to a new apartment, where she re-created her husband's study in a spare room. His library was organized as it had been; his collection of prints was unchanged; an oil portrait hung above the mantel. On Melville's desk, she kept a tin breadbox that contained the unfinished manuscript of *Billy Budd*.

In 1905, when Effie Lowell was dying of cancer, the documentary photographer Jacob Riis came to visit her. By this time, the widow was one of America's premier philanthropists and most admired women. New York's first memorial to a woman, a fountain in Bryant Park, was dedicated to her. The photographer of the city's poorest neighborhoods had stopped by to pay homage and to praise her career in social work.

"Yes, yes; I know," she replied. "But think of my waiting for my husband forty-one long years, forty-one years."[51]

CHAPTER 10

Heaven

THE RUNAWAY BESTSELLER of 1868 was a slim novel written by an unknown twenty-four-year-old woman from Andover, Massachusetts. Elizabeth Stuart Phelps had inherited her literary talent from her mother, Elizabeth, a gifted author of children's stories. From her father, Austin, a theologian, she received a piercing curiosity about all things otherworldly. Her first novel, *The Gates Ajar*, confronted the wasting carnage of the Civil War, but it wasn't about generals or battles or acts of heroism, nor did it address Shiloh or the Wilderness or the hospitals in Washington. It was about heaven.

In four years of war, the nation had lost an entire generation of young men—at least 620,000 soldiers. From Charleston to Manassas, then west to places like Shiloh, Wilson's Creek, and Chickamauga, men had fought one another for principles that had sounded glorious and noble back home. In pristine meadows and verdant peach orchards, in swamps and forests and along the muddy edges of rivers, these same men had twisted bayonets into one another. They had fired Enfield rifles, blown holes in young flesh with minié balls and explosive artillery. Throughout Virginia, South Carolina, Georgia, Alabama, Tennessee, Missouri, and Pennsylvania, homes had been plundered and burned, the countryside pillaged, buildings and bridges destroyed. Springtime fields were scarred with shallow trenches that served as mass graves, and the efforts to exhume and identify and repatriate these hastily buried bodies would take years.

Phelps's novel sold more copies during the nineteenth century than any work of American fiction except *Uncle Tom's Cabin*. If Harriet

Beecher Stowe's novel had helped to start the war, as Lincoln claimed, *The Gates Ajar* helped its audience to cope with the bewildering grief created by so much destruction. The book takes the form of a journal by Mary Cabot, a young woman who, like so many others, has lost someone in the war. Only a few weeks before the peace settlement at Appomattox, Mary's beloved brother Roy was killed. "Those two words—'Shot dead'—shut me up and walled me in," she recalls in her plain, unadorned style, "as I think people must feel shut up and walled in, in Hell." Plunged into inconsolable grief, the young woman shuts out the small-town doctors and ministers who visit to offer consolation, gently reminding her that death is an expression of God's will and that "[e]verybody knows by what a hair a soldier's life is always hanging."[1]

Mary is rescued from despair by the arrival of her aunt Winifred, a doughty widow from Kansas who spends most of the novel offering her grieving niece a comforting vision of heaven. Heaven is ravishingly beautiful, we learn, but it is far from the diaphanous realm of sun-limned clouds and harp-playing angels many Americans pictured. As aunt Winifred describes it, heaven is nothing more or less than an exalted version of life on earth. The dead live in houses, in towns, amid forests of lindens and elms, just as they had while they were alive. In heaven, there is no alteration of personalities, no changes in bodily form, no annihilation of memory. There is, instead, the fulfillment of desires. Aunt Winifred assures a musical but penniless young woman that a beautiful new piano awaits her in the next world. And she reveals just how close and congruent are the two realms when she calmly asserts, "I do not doubt, I cannot doubt that our absent dead are very present with us."[2]

As Mary comes to learn, soldiers like her brother, killed in combat, are not permanently lost, "*only, out of sight.*" Roy watches after his sister, helping her in unseen ways. Most important, he awaits their reunion in heaven. Aunt Winifred explains to Mary, "you will talk with Roy as you talked with him here,—only not as you talked with him here, because there will be no troubles nor sins, no anxieties nor cares, to talk about; no ugly shades of cross words or little quarrels to be made up; no fearful looking-for of separation." Heaven, in other words, is a better version of life on earth, a cozy, familiar place that erases and transcends all the sorrows of war. For this reason, when aunt Winifred is taken mortally ill at the end of the novel, she departs with serene good cheer, looking forward to meeting her beloved husband as well as President Lincoln and Elizabeth Barrett Browning.[3]

There is little plot or action in *The Gates Ajar*, but there is plenty of talk. Phelps sensed that her readers required words of assurance, quiet discussion, conversation instead of conflict. Her novel, however slight in narrative interest, concerned itself with the central problem beset-ting Americans in the wake of monumental loss. What could so much death possibly mean? What did it say about humans that they could kill so profligately? And how could a nation of wounded survivors regain its health and begin once again to live? *The Gates Ajar* answered these thorny questions with a simple promise: the nation would be reunited one day—if not in this world, then certainly in the next. It encouraged hope in a people who had been forced to forsake it.

"I wonder if Roy has seen the President," Mary wonders aloud and is serenely answered by aunt Winifred, who "says she does not doubt it. She thinks that all the soldiers must have crowded up to meet him, and 'O,' she says, 'what a sight to see!' "[4]

For Thomas Wentworth Higginson, life after the war felt less like heaven than like a very long epilogue, or an interminable second act in which all the important characters had long since departed from the stage. Years earlier, in the torrid 1850s when he had smuggled weapons to the free-dom fighters of Kansas and returned home to New England a minor hero, he had confided in his journal, "I finally discharged my revolver and put it away in my trunk." This simple deed produced in him "the most curious reaction from the feeling with which I had first loaded it," and it "fully came home to me that all the tonic life was ended, and thenceforward, if any danger impended, the proper thing would be to look meekly about for a policeman."[5] The unshakable feeling that his best years were behind him only intensified after the war.

Haggard and weak from the wound he had received on the Edisto River, Higginson slowly recovered in a Newport boardinghouse selected by his increasingly invalid wife. Nearby was the Henry James family, Julia Ward Howe, countless other writers, artists, and sundry crackpots. Higginson largely avoided them, sauntering instead along the steep bluffs overlooking the Atlantic where he could watch the breakers crash, or clambering down to the rough stone beach where he picked up pieces of silvery driftwood and reveled in the roar of the surf. "That I was in [the war] myself seems the dreamiest thing of all," he confessed to a friend. "I cannot put my hand upon it in the least, and if someone convinced me, in five minutes, some morning, that I was never there at all, it seems as if it wd. all drop quietly out of my life."[6] Life had become strangely unreal.

OUR MARTYRS AT HEAVEN'S GATE.

FIGURE 10.1 *Our Martyr at Heaven's Gate* (ca. 1881). Courtesy Library of Congress, Prints and Photographs Division (LC-DIG-pga-02234).

Despite its dreamy quality, the war became Higginson's primary literary topic for the next five years. In a two-volume collection of biographical essays commemorating Harvard students martyred to the Union cause, Higginson seemed to forget the horrors he had experienced on the Edisto River. "Those of us whose fortunate lot was to enlist in the army, during that magic epoch of adventure which has just passed by, will never again find in life a day of such strange excitement as that when they first put on uniform and went into camp." On that memorable day, he observed, the "past was annihilated, the future was all." Now, in these less-adventurous times, "that dimly-visioned future has itself become a portion of the past…and, after all that seeming metamorphosis, the survivors still find themselves with their feet upon the familiar earth, and pursue once more the quiet paths they left."[7]

At the insistence of James T. Fields, who had partnered with James R. Osgood after the death of Ticknor to form yet another successful publishing venture, Higginson began to transform the journal he kept at Port Royal into a series of articles for the *Atlantic*. These were eventually collected in 1869 as *Army Life in a Black Regiment*. The book is an elegy to a past life, a Victorian portmanteau bulging with descriptions of the Sea Islands' fauna and slave spirituals, night swims and military expeditions. On a personal level, it is Higginson's effort to achieve catharsis, to fix and pattern an ambiguous period, and to close the door on a tumultuous experience. Mostly, it is a remarkable, heartfelt chronicle of daily life with the first black regiment in the Union army. Higginson's pride in his company illumines his prose throughout. He marvels at the hundreds of anonymous men who had fled from slavery, desperate for freedom and glimpsing an opportunity, and now placing their lives in jeopardy by fighting for the North. Such courage, the book implies, was a perishable commodity, an item from another time. Now that "we seem nearly at the end of those great public wrongs which require a special moral earthquake to end them," he warned readers of the *Atlantic*, "there seems nothing left which need be absolutely fought for; no great influence to keep us from a commonplace and perhaps debasing success." He praised the reformers of previous eras and asked if a national literature untethered to great social causes could ever achieve the glory of Emerson and his contemporaries.[8]

Yet, in other moods, Higginson seemed relieved that the fever of the 1850s and early '60s had passed. The further the war receded in time, the more he had the nagging suspicion that the North had been too self-righteous in its rhetoric. In his youth, he had argued, "There are times and places where Human feeling is fanaticism,—times and places where it seem[s] that a *man* can only escape the charge of fanaticism by being a moral iceberg." Emotions, he now believed, were dangerous, which is why he increasingly came to feel that art and politics shouldn't mix. "Why should we insist," he asked, "on playing all the parts? The proper path of the statesman and the artist may often cross, but will rarely coincide." Gradually, ineluctably, he came to see that there were at least two sides to every historical question.[9]

Increasingly, he devoted himself to art, channeling his infectious enthusiasm into literary efforts. "I do not think that anything except putting on a uniform and going into camp," he confided in his journal in 1869, "has ever given me such a strange fascinating life as the thought that I can actually construct a novel." He was speaking of *Malbone*, a Hawthornesque romance he wrote in a burst of excitement toward the end of the decade. The *Atlantic* ran the novel—Higginson's only one—serially. *Malbone* recounts the story of an artist, an aesthete, who falls passionately in love with the half sister of his fiancée, Hope. This half sister, endowed with "gypsy taste" and "silky hair of darkest chestnut," is made "most irresistible" by "a certain wild, entangled look..., as of some untamed out-door thing, and a kind of pathetic lost sweetness in her voice."[10] Her name is Emilia. Throughout the book, she is called Emily.

The real-life Emily had been on his mind since the war's conclusion, when he and the poet had resumed their remarkable correspondence. The letters began with a simple announcement from Amherst that Dickinson's beloved dog had died. It continued with a series of inquiries about a social visit. Higginson repeatedly invited his mysterious and elusive friend to Boston, only to be rebuffed. "I must omit Boston," Dickinson explained. "Father prefers so. He likes me to travel with him but objects that I visit." She offered to host his stay at the Amherst Inn and, as usual, proceeded to send him poem after poem.[11]

"I think if I could once see you & know that you are real," Higginson wrote in the spring of 1869, "I might fare better." Dickinson's response was uncharacteristically forthcoming. "Of our greatest acts we are ignorant," she wrote. "You were not aware that you saved my Life. To thank you in person has been since then one of my few requests." Writing now as if to meet her in person would save his own life, Higginson replied, "I have the greatest desire to see you, always feeling that perhaps if I could once take you by the hand I might be something to you; but till then you only enshroud yourself in this fiery mist & I cannot reach you, but only rejoice in the rare sparkle of light."[12]

The stalemate would continue until August 1870, when Higginson's older brother died in Deerfield, Massachusetts, not far from Amherst. After attending the funeral, the retired colonel and budding novelist, the one-time radical cut adrift from his past, stood musing on the steps of the Amherst Inn. No longer quite so handsome nor so energetic, he stepped off the porch and into the radiant sunshine, proceeding ner-

vously along Amherst's prim and orderly Main Street toward the forbidding blank face of the Dickinsons' Homestead.

Earlier on that momentous day, Emily Dickinson had neatly and conspicuously placed on the parlor table her copies of Higginson's 1863
collection of nature essays, *Out-Door Papers*, and his novel, *Malbone*.
Then she went upstairs to await the sound of the doorbell.

She was forty, increasingly eccentric. She dressed now only in white
stayed within the confines of the Homestead, tending her garden,
tending her parents, baking bread, answering letters, and in the pri-
vacy of her room still writing poems. Like Higginson, something had
gone out of her after the war. During that tumultuous period, she had
lived with intensity and fury, poetry exploding from her restless mind
in white-hot torrents, words coming as quickly as she could write them.
Having long considered the universe a treacherous place, having
observed life to be a tenuous affair marked by certain death and an
uncertain afterlife, she had felt confirmed in these suspicions by the
war, which amplified her fears and proved just how brutal and senseless
human existence could be. In those days, she had written poetry to
calm herself, to ease her anxiety. "We—tell a Hurt," she observed,
"—to cool it."[13]

Now, five years after the war's conclusion, she was lucky to write a
poem a month. Words no longer came so readily or with such urgency.
Instead of verse, she increasingly wrote letters, continuing the episto-
lary friendship with Higginson as a kind of duty, an homage to someone
who had once meant more than anyone else in her life. She sent him
old poems mixed with the occasional new, promising "never to reject
your knife" and admitting respectfully, "Your opinion gives me a serious
feeling. I would like to be what you deem me."[14]

Now, eight years after she first wrote to him, she waited upstairs,
wearing a blue knit shawl despite the heat, startling when she heard
someone at the door, heart racing at the steps of the servant. After
pausing to gather herself, she descended the dim staircase and proceeded to the tall visitor, whose clean white chin peered from between
enormous side-whiskers. Placing two daylilies in his hand, she breath-
lessly informed him, "These are my introduction," and then began to
talk without pause for the remainder of the visit. "I find ecstasy in
living," she told him, "the mere sense of living is joy enough." She
asked him, "How do most people live without any thoughts?" and thus
hit upon another formulation for her poetry: "Truth is such a *rare* thing
it is delightful to tell it."[15]

Higginson was, understandably, overwhelmed. He was also just a little disappointed. Comparing her to the most talkative person he knew—Bronson Alcott—he later declared to his wife that he had never encountered anyone "who drained my nerve power so much. Without touching her, she drew from me." He had imagined someone more ethereal, more mysterious—someone like Emilia in his novel—and had discovered instead an intense and lonely woman, a human instead of an ideal. It was almost like being wounded all over. "I am glad not to live near her," he remarked to his wife, and later, in a magazine piece about Dickinson for the *Atlantic*, he added: "The impression undoubtedly made on me was that of an excess of tension, and of an abnormal life. Perhaps in time I could have got beyond that somewhat overstrained relation which not my will, but her needs, had forced upon us.... She was much too enigmatical a being for me to solve in an hour's interview."[16]

As for Dickinson, meeting Higginson in person seems to have left a similar impression. If she hadn't realized it before, she now understood that it was *she* who was the "preceptor," the "master," the one who had something interesting and original to teach about poetry. In the spring of 1873, three years after their meeting, Higginson enclosed a poem he had written to commemorate the war dead on Decoration Day, the holiday that would eventually become Memorial Day. The poem was entitled "Decoration," and it began with a speaker bearing lilies in his hand amid "flower-wreath tombs":

> Comrades! In what soldier-grave
> Sleeps the bravest of the brave?
> Is it he who sank to rest
> With his colors round his breast?
> Friendship makes his tomb a shrine;
> Garlands veil it; ask not mine.

The speaker's attention is drawn to a low grave beneath the trees, ungarlanded, bereft of flowers. It is the grave of a woman, a hero of the domestic sphere, whose death has perhaps been prompted by the loss of a loved one on the battlefields of war.

> ... [No] heart more high and warm
> Ever dared the battle-storm,
> Never gleamed a prouder eye
> In front of victory,
> Never foot had firmer tread
> On the field where hope lay dead.

"Turning from my comrades' eyes" and walking beyond the decorated graves of the honored veterans, the speaker instead strews "lilies on the grave / Of the bravest of the brave."[17]

Dickinson referred to Higginson's "beautiful Hymn" the next year when her father died, asking, "Was it not prophetic?" Three years later, in 1877, she again mentioned the poem. "I was rereading your 'Decoration,'" she told him, and attached the first four lines of her own version:

> Lay this Laurel on the one
> Triumphed and remained unknown—
> Laurel—fell your futile Tree—
> Such a Victor could not be—[18]

Higginson later admitted that Dickinson's revision was "the condensed essence" of his own, "& so far finer." He had come at last to value the terse, elliptical style of his pupil, to recognize just how conventional was the language of his own poetry. And he shared with his stalwart correspondent a sense that, when the two of them were gone, verse would be the only monument remaining to commemorate and immortalize the dead.[19]

Early in May 1886—less than two weeks before she died—Dickinson learned from the *Springfield Republican* that Higginson had been prevented by an illness from speaking at a Browning Society meeting in Boston. She dashed off a letter, her last but one, fully aware she had little time left to live. In it, she inquired: "Deity—does he live now? My friend—does he breathe?"[20]

The war didn't make a poet of Walt Whitman. He was already that when the conflict began. It did, however, bring him back to life, and it established his poetic reputation. An unpredictable sequence of events following the end of hostilities ensured his transformation from eccentric and slightly outré misfit to beloved national poet.

The first of these was Lincoln's assassination. Whitman wasn't in Washington on that tragic Good Friday. He was back in Brooklyn, in his mother's teeming home, having taken a two-week furlough from his latest job at the Bureau of Indian Affairs. He had come home to see his brother George, who had enlisted at the start of the war and had now, four years later, been released from a Confederate prison camp, where he had suffered from fever, malnutrition, and exposure to the elements. Back in Brooklyn, George was suffering in other ways. He suffered night terrors, insomnia, survivor's guilt. He jumped at sudden

THE ASSASSINATION OF PRESIDENT LINCOLN.
AT FORD'S THEATRE WASHINGTON D.C. APRIL 14TH 1865.

FIGURE 10.2 *The Assassination of President Lincoln,* by Currier and Ives (1865). Courtesy Library of Congress, Prints and Photographs Division (LC-USZ62-2073).

noises, broke unaccountably into a cold sweat. Unable to sleep at night in his bed upstairs, he came down to the sofa and spent the dark hours alert and watchful.

Whitman would learn the details of what happened at Ford's Theater from his friend and possible paramour Peter Doyle. A compact, red-headed Irishman, Doyle had met Whitman in the winter of 1865 aboard a horse car traveling up and down Pennsylvania Avenue. Soon, the two were inseparable. Doyle had been in attendance at Ford's Theater on the Friday after the cessation of hostilities. He would later tell Whitman how the bantering dialogue of the light comedy had been suddenly interrupted by the sharp report of a pistol, how a man had leaped from the president's box, a man later determined to be John Wilkes Booth, his boot snagging on the patriotic bunting draped there. Booth crashed heavily to the stage and hollered out something Doyle either didn't understand or didn't quite catch—*Sic semper tyrannis!*— before hobbling offstage. The theater erupted in wailing cries and shrieks of panic.

Whitman read about the president's death the next morning in the newspaper as breakfast was being served. No one in the family ate a bite of the warm food; no one said a word. The poet got up and did what he always did in times of excitement, stress, or depression. He took the ferry to Manhattan and walked up and down the broad avenues and teeming streets.

Soon, he was back in Washington, where he watched with delight and sorrow the impressive military parade that filled the streets with returning soldiers. It would take some time for him to absorb the national tragedy of Lincoln's death, but by summer he was composing lines about the assassination that remain among his best-known works. "O Captain! My Captain!" completes the circle he began with "Ship of Libertad!" portraying the fallen president as the captain of a ship successfully piloted through the storm of war.

> O Captain! My Captain! Our fearful trip is done,
> The ship has weather'd every rack, the prize we sought is won
> ...But O heart! heart! heart!
> O the bleeding drops of red,
> Where on the deck my Captain lies,
> Fallen cold and dead.[21]

"When Lilacs Last in the Dooryard Bloom'd" is a more ambitious eulogy that recounts the somber cortege that carried Lincoln's body from Washington to Springfield, Illinois, stopping in numerous cities so that some 11 million Americans could view the casket. At the beginning of the war, the North had been festooned in flags and red, white, and blue bunting; now, it was covered in black crape. A nine-car train draped in mourning cloth steamed through cities and towns also swathed in black. "Coffin that passes through lanes and streets," Whitman wrote,

> Through day and night with the great cloud darkening the land,
> With the pomp of the inloop'd flags with the cities draped in black,
> With the show of the States themselves as of crape-veil'd women standing,
> With procession long and winding and the flambeaus of the night,
> With the countless torches lit, with the silent sea of faces and unbarred heads,
> With the waiting depot, the arriving coffin, the somber faces.[22]

In incantatory rhythms, Whitman sought to weave together the fractured nation, his poem following the funeral train through town and city, forest and swamp, reuniting a grieving and bitterly divided people. To describe a nation saturated with death, he employed a tightly woven trio of images, simple and highly effective. The western star, appropriately enough, is Lincoln; the thrush is the poet; and the sprig of lilac, fragrant and delicate, its bloom lasting only a few days, is the poem offered up to the fallen leader. Through the alchemy of these combined images, "When Lilacs Last in the Dooryard Bloom'd" would become the lachrymose voice of an entire nation, a communal expression of mourning for the slain president and, through association, for the hundreds of thousands killed in the war.

> I saw battle-corpses, myriads of them,
> And the white skeletons of young men, I saw them,
> I saw the debris and debris of all the slain soldiers of the war,
> But I saw they were not as was thought,
> They themselves were fully at rest, they suffer'd not,
> The living remain'd and suffer'd, the mother suffer'd,
> And the wife and the child and the musing comrade suffer'd,
> And the armies that remain'd suffer'd.[23]

"O Captain!" and "Lilacs" appeared in 1865 in a slim collection of fifty-three poems entitled *Drum-Taps*, which further bolstered Whitman's postwar reputation. Whereas *Leaves of Grass* was bound in vibrant green cloth, the new book was issued in funereal black. Most critics at the time failed to appreciate Whitman's unconventional poems, but when reviewing *Drum-Taps* they invariably mentioned his war service as a nurse in the hospitals of Washington, endowing the book with biographical interest and helping it to reach a larger audience than any Whitman had before.

Ultimately, though, it was another book that fixed Whitman's reputation as the nation's poet. *The Good Gray Poet* was a pamphlet written by William Douglas O'Connor, a close friend, soon after Whitman was dismissed from the Bureau of Indian Affairs for his allegedly immoral poetry. Praising Whitman's wartime service and mocking the rigid moralizing of the Republican administration, O'Connor bequeathed to his friend an alliterative sobriquet that would be used to describe him for the rest of his life. A single phrase helped to transform Whitman in the public mind from the depraved advocate of free love and poet of the sewers to the "good gray poet."

Like Dickinson, whom he would never meet, Whitman's poetic productivity decreased sharply after the war. More and more, he found himself tending his fame, revising the ever-expanding *Leaves of Grass*, which would soon include *Drum-Taps*, and railing against the loss of individuality and tolerance that had once defined his America. A natural raconteur, he held forth to an expanding coterie of acolytes who transcribed his every word. Despite the adulation, he never allowed himself to forget the fundamental experience that had made him who and what he was. Reflecting in *Specimen Days* on the guerrilla tactics of John Singleton Mosby, he found the war characterized by "lurid passion, the wolf's, the lion's lapping thirst for blood—the passionate volcanoes of human revenge for comrades, brothers slain." Yet something redemptive lay in this very brutality. According to Horace Traubel, who collected the reminiscences while the great man spoke, Whitman recalled, "There were years in my life—years there in New York—when I wondered if all was not going to the bad with America—the tendency downwards—but the war saved me: what I saw in the war set me up for all time—the days in the hospitals."[24]

Nor did he fail to remember that death, not poetry, had knit the nation together. Death had become a nation of its own, the great harmonizer dissolving boundaries between body and soul. In a sketch entitled "The Million Dead, Too, Summ'd Up," an older, frailer Whitman invoked

> the dead, the dead, the dead—*our* dead—or South or North, ours all, (all, all, all, finally dear to me)—or East or West—Atlantic coast or Mississippi valley—somewhere they crawl'd to die, alone, in bushes, low gullies, or on the sides of hills—(there, in secluded spots, their skeletons, bleach'd bones, tufts of hair, buttons, fragments of clothing, are occasionally found yet)...the single graves left in the woods or by the road-side,...the corpses floated down the rivers,...the infinite dead—(the land entire saturated, perfumed with their impalpable ashes' exhalation in Nature's chemistry distill'd, and shall be so forever, in every future grain of wheat and ear of corn, and every flower that grows, and every breath we draw)—not only Northern dead leavening Southern soil—thousands, aye tens of thousands, of Southerners crumble today in Northern earth.[25]

As usual, the public and the private Emerson were slightly at odds with each other about the end of the fighting. The war's successful outcome had been a victory of principle, proof that right must and would prevail. He declared as much when he described the end of the war as "a joyful day" that glorified the "Allegheny ranges, Northern Lakes, Mississippi rivers and all lands and men between the two Oceans, between morning and evening stars."[26] Privately, however, he found himself dwelling on the immeasurable toll exacted by the previous four years. As Whitman had lamented, American soil was laden with bodies, drenched in blood. The land stank with the remains of those who had given their lives for what Emerson believed was a holy cause. He did not doubt the basic fitness of that cause; he did not question that securing basic human rights was worth any price. But in the stillness of his study, in the sleepless hours of night, he found himself wondering what new growth could possibly emerge from a country befouled, polluted, and wasted by so much violence.

Two weeks into the war, Emerson's friend Henry Wadsworth Longfellow had noted in his journal, "The word *May* is a perfumed word....It means youth, love, song; and all that is beautiful in life. But what a May-day is this! Bleak and cheerless." Five bloody springs had prompted Elizabeth Stuart Phelps to describe the month of May as burdened with a "bitter Peace."[27] Springtime—the season most often celebrated in American writing before the war—had been radically transformed into a killing time, the renewal of violence after the war's winter cessation. It now became a potent emblem for Emerson, a poetic symbol in which to work out the meaning of the past four years.

In his journals, Emerson tried to assure himself that, while the destruction of slavery was worth "ten years of war," it would not "cost so much time to get well again. How many times France has been a warfield," he marveled, adding that "a new year's labor, a new harvest" had created "prodigious wealth & repair[ed] the damage of ten years of war." "We can let the year go round," he elsewhere noted, "if we know that October brings thoughts, & March lustres, & May love, and the tenth year honor for the insults & ribaldry of the nine foregoing winters."[28]

In "May-Day," one of the longest poems he ever wrote, spring is a welcome force capable of healing all the wounds of war. A descriptive celebration of rebirth, a paean to the way in which "the earth renews, / The wealth of forms, the flush of hues," the poem is also a meditation on peace and compromise after the bitter winter of violence and death. Spring is a "Daughter of Heaven and Earth," an idyllic season when the "sudden passion[s]" of winter and summer, of North and South, languish in delightful coexistence, and when "All grating discords melt, / No dissonant note is dealt." When Emerson invoked "the deluge of heat" pouring "Broad northward o'er the land," he was describing not simply the seasonal tilting of the earth's axis, but a process by which the chastened South would "Climb...the northern zones" and join the tattered nation. And within this process, Emerson believed, resided a harbinger for regeneration:

> So deep and large [Nature's] bounties are,
> That one broad, long midsummer day

> Shall to the planet overpay
> The ravage of a year of war.[29]

Yet even as he extolled the spring's ability to "Modulat[e] all extremes," Emerson could not forget the fundamental injustices that had prompted the war in the first place. In a stanza extolling the refreshing mixture of warm and cool weather, he suddenly digressed:

> As Southern wrath to Northern right
> Is but straw to anthracite;
> As in the day of sacrifice,
> When heroes piled the pyre,
> The dismal Massachusetts ice
> Burned more than others' fire.[30]

The stanza points to a basic problem that the poem is incapable of resolving. Spring is a *temporary* state, a brief and transient period of truce between two extremes. The moment one begins to look toward the future with hope, the moment one strives to forgive and forget, the bitter and cyclical past returns, reigniting old grievances.

In many ways, the task of assimilating the war imaginatively—of constructing a coherent narrative about the conflict that would make sense of its bitter costs and enable Americans to adapt to a changed national landscape—would fall less upon Emerson and his contemporaries than upon the next generation of authors. Mark Twain, Stephen Crane, and Ambrose Bierce were just a few of the many writers who participated in an epic reimagining of the war in the last third of the nineteenth century. For them, the war was a tragic farce, a sick joke that belied the lofty rhetoric of writers and politicians from the previous generation. Avatars of a new literary realism that would dominate American letters through the end of the nineteenth century, their attitude toward the killing was also a minority view.

More typical were the nostalgic and nationalistic expressions of the conflict as a heroic event that simultaneously evoked nobler times and unified America. Countless postwar narratives obscured the political and social contexts of the conflict in order to emplot the theme of reunion and reconciliation in writings that often united southern and northern lovers through marriage. An enormously influential series of articles published in the 1880s by *Century* magazine, "Battles and Leaders of the Civil War," presented the reminiscences of white participants in order to bring "about a better understanding between the soldiers who were opposed in that conflict," remarking with approval on "the number of fraternal meetings between Union and Confederate veterans, enforcing the conviction that the nation is restored in spirit as in fact."[31] These recollections were serialized in *Century* precisely during the period in which the magazine introduced such masterworks of realism as *Huckleberry Finn*, *The Portrait of a Lady*, and *The Rise of Silas Lapham*, by Mark Twain, Henry James, and William Dean Howells, respectively. The bullet lodged in Silas Lapham's thigh, the feverish passion that Isabel Archer recalls feeling as a child for the Union cause are touchstones of the war reworked and refigured so as to displace the horrors of national self-mutilation. Huck's adventures with Jim, conversely, present the era before the war as a halcyon period of innocence and interracial harmony. These and many other narratives reflected the nation's selective amnesia, its willingness to gloss over the painful issues that led to the war in the first place in order to begin the agonizing process of healing and reconciliation.

Conspicuously missing from this cultural project of unification were the people for whom the war had been fought. "We Negroes love our country," Frederick Douglass proclaimed in 1893 at the World's Columbian Exposition in Chicago, hoping to remind his audience about the true meaning of the war. He was seventy-five, still strong, still vibrant, but angered and saddened by the lynchings and political apartheid that characterized the triumph of Jim Crow in late nineteenth-century America. "We fought for it. We ask only that we be treated as well as those who fought against it."

More pained in her survey of life after the great conflict was Susie King Taylor, whose *Reminiscences of My Life in Camp with the 33rd United States Colored Troops, Late 1st S.C. Volunteers* was published in 1902. "What a revolution!" she recalled of the historic event that had changed her life as a young woman. "In 1861 the Southern papers were full of advertisements for 'slaves,' but now, despite all the hindrances and 'race problems,' my people are striving to attain the full standard of all other races born in the sight of God." Yet, given the lack of progress in race relations during the intervening four decades, she found it difficult to sustain this hopeful tone. After the war, "we thought our race was forever freed from bondage, and that the two races could live in unity with each other," she recalled. Now, she was no longer so certain. "[W]hen we read almost every day of what is being done to my race by some whites in the South, I sometimes ask, 'Was this war in vain? Has it brought freedom in the full sense of the word, or has it not made our condition more hopeless?'"[32]

Emerson's "May-Day" foretold the difficulty of reconciling one's partisan convictions with the desire for a new beginning. He was left wishing for a season that would one day

> Sweep ruins from the scarped mountains,
> Cleanse the torrent at the fountain,
> Purge alpine air by towns defiled
> Bring to fair mother fairer child.[33]

In 1842, when he had been at the height of his power, Emerson confidently noted in his journal that "the volcano ... from which the conflagration rises toward the zenith an appreciable distance toward the stars—[this is] the most affecting symbol ... of what man should be. A spark of fire is infinitely deep, but a mass of fire reaching from earth upward into heaven, this is the sign of the robust, united, burning, radiant soul."[34] After the war, that spark no longer seemed as bright or radiant. Emerson began to dim and wane, to forget words and people's names. Increasingly, he found himself lost in daydreams, unable to follow a thought to its conclusion.

Sometime in 1866, when Edward Emerson was visiting from Harvard, his father asked him to sit in his study and listen as he read aloud his last great poem, "Terminus." The poem is a salute to conclusions, a valedictory to a life well lived. "It is time to be old," Emerson quietly read. "To take in sail."[35] Prior to the reading, Edward noted, "No thought of his aging had ever come to me, and there he sat, with no apparent abatement of bodily vigor, and young in spirit, recognizing with serene acquiescence his failing forces."[36]

Ironically, it was during precisely this period that his reputation achieved a springtime renewal. The five years immediately following the war provided Emerson with his most active and remunerative years on the lecture circuit. He traveled everywhere, spoke to larger and larger audiences. In 1866 appeared the first of numerous *Complete Works* (although this one was a pirated English edition). His extreme pronouncements and radical past forgotten, Emerson had become by 1872 "an accepted fact" of American culture. "The enthusiasm with which Ralph Waldo Emerson is greeted in every part of the United States," observed an international reporter, "is a phenomenon which cannot escape the attention of those who study the affairs and tendencies of that country." Schools and universities were named after him. On the walls of these institutions, his portrait accompanied those of Washington and Lincoln. He had become a cultural icon, an institution.[37]

FIGURE 10.3 Ralph Waldo Emerson's study (ca.1888). Courtesy Library of Congress, Prints and Photographs Division (LC-USZ62-62248).

Thirty-five years earlier, when he had returned from Europe to Concord to begin his work as author, philosopher, and lecturer, he had carried under his arm a large wrapped package purchased overseas. In the entranceway of his Concord home, he hung the bright, framed picture of Vesuvius spewing molten lava, belching forth clouds of cinders. The print was the first thing visitors saw when they entered the house. It was the last thing they saw before stepping outside.

Often, during the four years of war, when Emerson returned from his frantic lecture schedule, when he stood in the entranceway and put on his coat in order to take a ramble around Walden Pond, or when he returned from town with news of recent casualties or victories to the south, often during that period when his heart had beat triumphantly, or troublingly, he had paused before the print, his eyes fixed on the volcano, distant, lost in reverie. The coming of the millennium had seemed at hand. The times were alive, burning, strangely joyous, a dream come true, a nightmare. Never again would the human soul be dormant.

Notes

ABBREVIATIONS

AL	Thomas Wentworth Higginson, *Army Life in a Black Regiment and Other Writings*, ed. R. D. Madison (New York: Penguin, 1997)
BP	*The Battle-Pieces of Herman Melville*, ed. Hennig Cohen (New York: Yoseloff, 1964)
CE	*The Centenary Edition of the Works of Nathaniel Hawthorne*, 23 vols., ed. William Charvat et al. (Columbus: Ohio State University Press, 1962–1980). Cited by volume and page numbers
"Chiefly"	Nathaniel Hawthorne, "Chiefly about War-Matters," *Atlantic Monthly* 10 (July 1862), 43–61
Complete	*The Complete Civil War Journals and Select Letters of Thomas Wentworth Higginson*, ed. Christopher Looby (Chicago: University of Chicago Press, 2000)
Corr	Walt Whitman, *The Correspondence*, vol. 1: *1842–1867*, ed. Edwin Haviland Miller (New York: New York University Press, 1961)
CP	Ralph Waldo Emerson, *Collected Poems and Translations* (New York: Library of America, 1994)
ED	Emily Dickinson
EL	Ralph Waldo Emerson, *Essays and Lectures*, ed. Joel Porte (New York: Library of America, 1983)
FD	Frederick Douglass
HM	Herman Melville
JMN	*The Journals and Miscellaneous Notebooks of Ralph Waldo Emerson*, 16 vols., ed. William H. Gilman et al. (Cambridge, Mass.: Belknap, 1960–1982). Cited by volume and page numbers
Letters	*The Letters of Emily Dickinson*, ed. Thomas H. Johnson (Cambridge, Mass.: Belknap, 1958). Cited by number

LMA	Louisa May Alcott
NH	Nathaniel Hawthorne
Poems	*The Poems of Emily Dickinson*, 3 vols., ed. R. W. Franklin (Cambridge, Mass.: Belknap, 1998). Cited by poem title and number.
PP	Walt Whitman, *Poetry and Prose* (New York: Library of America, 1982)
RWE	Ralph Waldo Emerson
SL	*The Selected Lectures of Ralph Waldo Emerson*, ed. Ronald A. Bosco and Joel Myerson (Athens: University of Georgia Press, 2005)
TWH	Thomas Wentworth Higginson
Writings	*The Life and Writings of Frederick Douglass*, vol. 3, ed. Philip S. Foner (New York: International, 1952)
WW	Walt Whitman

Introduction: Emerson's Dream

1. RWE, *JMN*, 15:146.

2. Ibid., 146–47.

3. RWE, *Nature, EL*, 7.

4. The contemporary was Oliver Wendell Holmes Sr., and he was speaking of Emerson's essay "The American Scholar." Qtd. in Wilson Sullivan, *New England Men of Letters* (New York: Macmillan, 1972), 235–36.

5. Qtd. in Richard B. Sewall, *The Life of Emily Dickinson* (New York: Farrar, Straus and Giroux, 1974), 1:115n15; Ellen Tucker Emerson, *The Letters of Ellen Tucker Emerson*, ed. Edith E. W. Gregg (Kent, Ohio: Kent State University Press, 1982), 1:248.

6. Abraham Lincoln, "'House Divided' Speech at Springfield Illinois, June 16, 1858," in his *Speeches and Writings, 1832–1858* (New York: Library of America, 1989), 426.

7. *JMN*, 4:143, 148; RWE, *The Letters of Ralph Waldo Emerson*, 6 vols., ed. Ralph Rusk (New York: Columbia University Press, 1939), 1:371.

8. *JMN*, 4:146, 147.

9. Qtd. in *Littell's Living Age*, 20 (January–March 1849), 479.

10. Edmund Burke, *Reflection on the Revolution in France* (1790; New York: Oxford University Press, 1999), 62–63.

11. HM, *Moby-Dick; or, The Whale*, in *The Works of Herman Melville* (New York: Russell and Russell, 1963), 2:220; Thoreau's journal passage and the speculation about its relation to Church's painting appear in Barbara Novak, *Voyages of the Self: Pairs, Parallels, and Patterns in American Art and Literature* (New York: Oxford University Press, 2007), 178n30.

12. "I have never seen 'Volcanoes'—": *Poems* 165; "A still—Volcano—Life—": *Poems* 517; "The reticent volcano keeps": *Poems* 1776; "On my volcano grows the Grass": *Poems* 1743; "Volcanoes be in Sicily": *Poems* 1691; "The Soul has Bandaged moments—": *Poems* 360.

13. Nathaniel Peabody Rogers, *A Collection from the Miscellaneous Writings of Nathaniel Peabody Rogers* (Boston: Benjamin B. Mussey, 1849), 307; Eric Foner, ed.,

The Life and Writings of Frederick Douglass (New York: International, 1950–1975), 5:113; Herman Melville, *The Writings of Herman Melville*, vol. 9: *The Piazza Tales and Other Prose Pieces, 1839–1860*, ed. Harrison Hayford, Alma A. MacDougall, et al. (Evanston, Ill.: Northwestern University Press, 1987), 68.

14. RWE, *JMN*, 15:170.

Chapter 1. Beat! Beat! Drums!

1. WW, "Ship of Libertad," in *Notebooks and Unpublished Prose Manuscripts*, 6 vols., ed. Edward F. Grier (New York: New York University Press, 1984), 1:437.

2. TWH, *Cheerful Yesterdays* (1898; New York: Arno, 1968), 230.

3. ED, *Letters*, no. 261; WW, *PP*, 1326.

4. RWE, "The Poet," *Essays: Second Series* (1844), *EL*, 465, 450, 462, 447.

5. John Townsend Trowbridge, "Reminiscences of Walt Whitman," *Atlantic Monthly* 89 (Feb. 1902), 166; WW, *Leaves of Grass* (1855), *PP*, 5, 6, 13.

6. WW, *Corr* 1:49.

7. Ibid., 1:50.

8. "Where Will It End?" *Atlantic Monthly* 1 (Dec. 1857), 242, 245, 248.

9. James Russell Lowell, "Ode Recited at the Harvard Commemoration," in *The Poetical Works of James Russell Lowell* (Boston: Houghton Mifflin, 1897), 4:21.

10. "Editor's Table," *Southern Literary Messenger* 25 (Dec. 1857), 472; qtd. in Kathleen Diffley, *Where My Heart Is Turning Ever: Civil War Stories and Constitutional Reform, 1861–1876* (Athens: University of Georgia Press, 1992), xxii.

11. WW, *Prose Works, 1892*, ed. Floyd Stovall (New York: New York University Press, 1963–1964), 2:493–94.

12. WW, "For You O Democracy," in *Leaves of Grass* (1891–1892), *PP*, 272.

13. WW, *Corr* 1:49.

14. Henry Wadsworth Longfellow, *The Works of Henry Wadsworth Longfellow*, ed. Samuel Longfellow (Boston: Houghton Mifflin, 1891), 13:416; NH, *CE* 18:379; George William Curtis, "Editor's Easy Chair," *Harper's New Monthly Magazine* 23 (July 1861), 266.

15. For information on Ticknor and Fields's profitability, see Michael Winship, *American Literary Publishing in the Mid-Nineteenth Century: The Business of Ticknor and Fields* (Cambridge: Cambridge University Press, 1995), 170–87. According to Winship, the only twelve-month period in which the firm lost money was April 1861–April 1862. Oliver Wendell Holmes, "Bread and the Newspaper," *Atlantic Monthly* 8 (Sept. 1861), 347.

16. Qtd. in Fahs, *The Imagined War: Popular Literature of the North and South, 1861–1865* (Chapel Hill: University of North Carolina Press, 2002), 21.

17. Edward Everett to Joshua Bates, Boston, May 2, 1861, U.S. Civil War Letters (MS Am 1626), Houghton Library, Harvard University; Henry Wadsworth Longfellow, *The Letters of Henry Wadsworth Longfellow*, ed. Andrew Hilen (Cambridge: Harvard University Press, 1972), 4:236; John Greenleaf Whittier, *The Letters of John Greenleaf Whittier*, ed. John B. Pickard (Cambridge: Harvard University Press, 1975), 3:18.

18. WW, *Specimen Days*, *PP*, 708.

19. Ibid., 706–7.

20. Qtd. in Justin Kaplan, *Walt Whitman: A Life* (New York: Simon and Schuster, 1980), 262.

21. TWH, *Cheerful Yesterdays*, 230–31.

22. Theodore Winthrop, "New York Seventh Regiment: Our March to Washington," *Atlantic Monthly* 7 (June 1861), 745.

23. "Washington as a Camp," *Atlantic Monthly* 7 (July 1861), 109, 113, 116.

24. Elbridge Colby, *Theodore Winthrop* (New Haven, Conn.: Yale University Press, 1965), 76–77.

25. George William Curtis, "Theodore Winthrop," *Atlantic Monthly* 8 (Aug. 1861), 242, 245, 242, 251.

26. WW, *Drum-Taps*, in *Leaves of Grass* (1891–1892), *PP*, 419.

27. J. Newton Breed, "The First Battle of Bull Run as Seen by a Bugler in the Fifth Massachusetts Volunteers," typescript (1896?), U.S. Civil War Letters (MS Am 1626), Houghton Library, Harvard University.

28. WW, *Specimen Days*, *PP*, 711, 708.

29. Julia Ward Howe, "Harvard Student's Song," in *Later Lyrics* (Boston: J. E. Tilton, 1869), 29.

30. WW, *Specimen Days*, *PP*, 710, 708.

31. Ibid., 711, 710.

32. Ibid., 420.

33. WW, *Corr* 1:57.

34. Qtd. in Roy Morris Jr., *The Better Angel: Walt Whitman in the Civil War* (New York: Oxford University Press, 2000), 179; George Whitman to mother, Feb. 9, 1862, in "Civil War Letters of George Washington Whitman from North Carolina," ed. Jerome Loving, *North Carolina Historical Review* 50 (1973), 76.

35. WW, *Memoranda during the War* (1875; Bedford, Mass.: Applewood, 1993), 3.

Chapter 2. Concord

1. This account of Thoreau's death and funeral service, including the statements by Bronson Alcott and Emerson, is from LMA, *The Selected Letters of Louisa May Alcott*, ed. Joel Merson and Daniel Shealy (Boston: Little, Brown, 1987), 74–75.

2. Moncure Daniel Conway, *Life of Nathaniel Hawthorne* (New York: Scribner and Welford, 1890), 204.

3. NH, *CE* 10:31–32.

4. Brown qtd. in RWE, *The Complete Works of Ralph Waldo Emerson*, ed. Edward Emerson (Cambridge, Mass.: Riverside, 1904), 11:268. Important reconsiderations of Brown include David Reynolds, *John Brown, Abolitionist: The Man Who Killed Slavery, Sparked the Civil War, and Seeded Civil Rights* (New York: Vintage, 2005), and Bruce A. Ronda, *Reading the Old Man: John Brown in American Culture* (Knoxville: University of Tennessee Press, 2008).

5. Emerson's precise wording has been the source of some controversy. For a brief recapitulation, see John J. McDonald, "Emerson and John Brown," *New England Magazine* 44 (1971), 386–87.

6. NH, *CE* 18:463.

7. Ibid., 14:381, 18:352.

8. Descriptions of Jim Lowell's death and Holmes's wounding can be found in Carol Bundy, *The Nature of Sacrifice: A Biography of Charles Russell Lowell, Jr., 1835–64* (New York: Farrar, Straus and Giroux, 2005), 208–9, 230. That Hawthorne quit reading newspapers is reported by Edward Hutchinson Davidson, *Hawthorne's Last Phase* (New Haven, Conn.: Yale University Press, 1949), 7; NH, *CE* 18:380.

9. NH, *CE* 18:380, 363.

10. Ibid., 1:9.

11. Ibid., 18:380–81, 387.

12. Ibid., 18:382, 394, 428.

13. Ibid., 18:457.

14. NH, "Chiefly," 43–44.

15. Elijah Rhodes qtd. in Geoffrey C. Ward, *The Civil War: An Illustrated History* (New York: Knopf, 1990), 57; RWE, *JMN*, 15:200.

16. Edward Dicey, "Nathaniel Hawthorne," in *Hawthorne in His Own Time*, ed. Ronald A. Bosco and Jillmarie Murphy (Iowa City: University of Iowa Press, 2007), 118.

17. NH, *CE* 18:441.

18. Ibid., 1:36.

19. NH, "Chiefly," 43, 50.

20. Oliver Wendell Holmes, "Hawthorne," reprinted in Bosco and Murphy, *Hawthorne in His Own Time*, 128.

21. NH, "Chiefly," 54, 55.

22. Ibid., 46, 47.

23. Ibid., 51.

24. Ibid.

25. Ibid., 50.

26. Dicey, "Nathaniel Hawthorne," in Bosco and Murphy, *Hawthorne in His Own Time*, 119; NH, "Chiefly," 50.

27. NH, "Chiefly," 50.

28. Ibid.

29. James M. McPherson, *Ordeal by Fire: The Civil War and Reconstruction* (New York: McGraw-Hill, 1991), 117; John Brown note qtd. in David S. Reynolds, *John Brown, Abolitionist: The Man who Killed Slavery, Sparked the Civil War, and Seeded Civil Rights* (New York: Vintage, 2005), 395; "Second Inaugural Address," in *Abraham Lincoln: Speeches and Writings 1859–1865* (New York: Library of America, 1989), 687.

30. NH, "Chiefly," 50.

31. Ibid., 56.

32. Ibid., 61.

33. NH, *CE* 18:443.

Chapter 3. Shiloh

1. Qtd. in *Voices of the Civil War: Shiloh* (Alexandria, Va.: Time-Life Books, 1996), 101; "Coming Up at Shiloh," *Continental Monthly* 6 (Oct. 1864), 401–2.

2. Grant, *Memoirs and Selected Letters*, eds. Mary D. McFeely and William S. McFeely (New York: Library of America, 1990), 231–32; Grant's letter qtd. in Shelby Foote, *The Civil War: A Narrative* (New York: Random House, 1958), 1:335–36.

3. This incident is recorded in Larry J. Daniel, *Shiloh: The Battle That Changed the Civil War* (New York: Simon and Schuster, 1997), 207.

4. Grant, *Memoirs and Selected Letters*, 246; *Voices of the Civil War*, 121; Grant's reply qtd. in Daniel, *Shiloh*, 249–50.

5. William Tecumseh Sherman, *Memoirs of General W. T. Sherman* (New York: Library of America, 1990), 268.

6. Abraham Lincoln, "Proclamation of a National Fast Day, August 12, 1861," in *Speeches and Writings, 1859–1865* (New York: Library of America, 1989), 264; Abraham Lincoln, "Proclamation of Thanksgiving for Victories, April 10, 1862," in *The Collected Works of Abraham Lincoln*, ed. Roy P. Basler (New Brunswick, N.J.: Rutgers University Press, 1953), 5:185–86.

7. Parker qtd. in "The Moral Arc of the Universe: Bending toward Justice: A Sermon by the Rev. Susan Manker-Seale," Jan. 15, 2006, http://www.uucnwt.org/sermons/TheMoralArcOfTheUniverse%201-15-06.html.

8. "The Great Boston Organ," *Harper's Weekly* (Dec. 12, 1863), 796.

9. RWE, "Self-Reliance," *Essays: First Series* (1841), *EL*, 262.

10. RWE, *JMN*, 5:274.

11. Ibid., 11:412, 197; RWE, *The Letters of Ralph Waldo Emerson*, 10 vols., ed. Ralph L. Rusk and Eleanor M. Tilton (New York: Columbia University Press, 1939), 5:18.

12. RWE, *The Complete Works of Ralph Waldo Emerson*, 12 vols., ed. Edward Waldo Emerson (Boston: Houghton Mifflin, 1903–1904), 11:247, 298–99.

13. RWE, *JMN*, 15:404.

14. Ibid., 15:172; RWE, "Fortune of the Republic," *SL*, 313, 325.

15. RWE, "Fortune of the Republic," *SL*, 321; RWE, *Letters* 5:252–53; RWE, *JMN*, 15:292–93.

16. Both men qtd. in Joseph Allan Frank and George A. Reaves, *"Seeing the Elephant": Raw Recruits at the Battle of Shiloh* (New York: Greenwood, 1989), 67.

17. Abraham Lincoln, *Speeches and Writings, 1859–1865*, 314.

18. RWE, *JMN*, 15:249.

19. Henry David Thoreau, *Walden* (New York: Norton, 1966), 207.

20. RWE, *JMN*, 15:249–50.

21. See the headnote to "Moral Forces" in *The Later Lectures of Ralph Waldo Emerson 1843–1871*, vol. 2: *1855–1871*, ed. Ronald A. Bosco and Joel Myerson (Athens: University of Georgia Press, 2001), 274.

22. Ibid., 274, 275.

23. Ibid., 275, 274.

24. Ibid., 278.

25. Ibid., 279.

26. Ibid., 280, 281–82, 282.

27. Ibid., 276, 280.

28. Ibid., 276, 283.

29. RWE, *JMN*, 15:250, 250–51.

30. HM, *Correspondence*, ed. Harrison Hayford, Hershel Parker, G. Thomas Tanselle, and Lynn Horth, vol. 14 of *The Writings of Herman Melville* (Evanston, Ill.: Northwestern University Press and Newberry Library, 1989), 213, 119, 121.

31. Ibid., 121.

32. Ibid., 191.

33. Lawrence Buell, "Melville as Poet," in *The Cambridge Companion to Herman Melville*, ed. Robert S. Levine (Cambridge: Cambridge University Press, 1998), 139. For more on Melville's career as poet, see Hershel Parker, *Melville: The Making of a Poet* (Evanston, Ill.: Northwestern University Press, 2007); and Edgar Dryden, *Monumental Melville: The Formation of a Literary Career* (Palo Alto, Calif.: Stanford University Press, 2004).

34. RWE, *Nature*, *EL*, 10; "The Poet," *EL*, 459.

35. RWE, "Art," *Essays: First Series*, *EL*, 431.

36. RWE, "The Poet," *EL*, 455.

37. Jay Leyda, *Melville Log* (1951; New York: Gordian, 1969), 2:648–49.

38. RWE, "The Poet," *EL*, 457; Leyda, *Melville Log*, 2:648–49.

39. HM, *BP*, 71–72.

40. Qtd. in Bell Irvin Wiley, *The Life of Billy Yank: The Common Soldier of the Union* (Baton Rouge: Louisiana State University Press, 1971), 80. This correspondent also noted how, in the tumult of battle, "scores of rabbit[s] fled for protection to our men lying down in line on the left, nestling under their coats and creeping under their legs in a state of utter distraction."

41. Luke 12:6–7. Hennig Cohen makes this claim about swallows in Renaissance painting in his introduction to *Battle-Pieces*.

42. John Weiss, "War and Literature," *Atlantic Monthly* 9 (June 1862), 674, 676; Richard Grant White, *Poetry Lyrical, Narrative, and Satirical of the Civil War* (1866; New York: Arno, 1972), iii; "Some Soldier-Poetry," *Atlantic Monthly* 10 (July 1862), 1.

43. "Bridegroom Dick," in *The Poems of Herman Melville*, ed. Douglas Robillard (Kent, Ohio: Kent State University Press, 2000).

44. John Greenleaf Whittier, *The Poetical Works of John Greenleaf Whittier* (Boston: Houghton Mifflin, 1892), 3:223–24.

45. Ibid., 226.

46. Ambrose Bierce, "What I Saw of Shiloh," in *A Sole Survivor: Bits of Autobiography*, ed. S. T. Joshi and David E. Schultz (Knoxville: University of Tennessee Press, 1998), 12.

47. Ibid., 19.

48. Ibid., 21–22.

Chapter 4. Telling It Slant

1. ED, *Letters*, no. 260.

2. Tilden G. Edelstein, *Strange Enthusiasm: A Life of Thomas Wentworth Higginson* (New Haven, Conn.: Yale University Press, 1968), 38, 1, 97.

3. RWE, "The American Scholar," *EL*, 54; TWH remarks in Edelstein, *Strange Enthusiasm*, 140. For an engaging account of this definitive event in the history of antislavery activism, see Albert J. von Frank, *The Trials of Anthony Burns: Freedom and Slavery in Emerson's Boston* (Cambridge, Mass.: Harvard University Press, 1998).

4. Qtd. in Edelstein, *Strange Enthusiasm*, 159.

5. TWH, "A Visit to John Brown's Household in 1859," in *AL*, 240.

6. Qtd. in Richard B. Sewall, *The Lyman Letters: New Light on Emily Dickinson and Her Family* (Amherst: University of Massachusetts Press, 1965), 78.

7. ED, *Letters*, no. 261.

8. Edward Dickinson qtd. in Brenda Wineapple, *White Heat: The Friendship of Emily Dickinson and Thomas Wentworth Higginson* (New York: Knopf, 2008), 49; qtd. in Richard B. Sewall, *The Life of Emily Dickinson* (New York: Farrar, Straus and Giroux, 1974), 1:536. To date, Wineapple's book is the most thorough exploration of the enigmatic relationship between Higginson and Dickinson.

9. Qtd. in Sewall, *Life*, 1:106.

10. "Christian Theism: The Testimony of Reason and Revelation to the Existence and Character of the Supreme Being," *New Englander and Yale Review* 14.56 (Nov. 1856), 628. The remaining statements against Darwin's theory are found in "Darwin and His Reviewers," *Atlantic Monthly* 6 (Oct. 1860), 409, 411.

11. "I had some things that I called mine—": *Poems* 101.

12. Perry Miller and Thomas H. Johnson, eds., *The Puritans: A Sourcebook of Their Writings* (New York: Harper and Row, 1963), 1:198.

13. "Of God we ask one favor, that we may be forgiven—": *Poems* 1675.

14. For more on this conundrum, see Shira Wolofsky, *Emily Dickinson: A Voice of War* (New Haven, Conn.: Yale University Press, 1984).

15. "He put the Belt around my life—": *Poems* 330; ED, *Letters*, no. 459a.

16. "Tell all the truth but tell it slant": *Poems* 1263.

17. Qtd. in James H. Moorhead, *American Apocalypse: Yankee Protestants and the Civil War, 1860–1869* (New Haven, Conn.: Yale University Press), 19, 20, 71. Moorhead's work is an indispensable sourcebook for the militant millennialism informing the war. He does not, however, explore the extent to which this fervor was a compensatory mechanism for dealing with increasing secularization.

18. TWH, "Emily Dickinson's Letters," *Atlantic Monthly* 65 (Oct. 1891), 444.

19. Edelstein, *Strange Enthusiasm*, 82, 49, 243, 236; TWH, *AL*, 147; Edelstein, *Strange Enthusiasm*, 314.

20. Julia Ward Howe, *Reminiscences, 1819–1899* (Boston: Houghton Mifflin, 1899), 274–75.

21. Introduction to TWH, *Complete*, 3; TWH, *John Greenleaf Whittier* (New York: Macmillan, 1902), 150.

22. TWH, "The Ordeal by Battle," *Atlantic Monthly* 8 (July 1861), 94.

23. ED, *Letters*, nos. 268, 261.

24. Ibid., nos. 265, 271.

25. Ibid., no. 245.

26. Ibid., no. 255.

27. Ibid., no. 298.

28. "It feels a shame to be Alive—": *Poems* 524; "They dropped like Flakes—": *Poems* 545; "My Portion is Defeat—today—": *Poems* 704.

29. "It don't sound so terrible—quite—as it did—": *Poems* 384.

30. Ibid.

31. TWH, *Complete*, 225.

32. Qtd. in Edelstein, *Strange Enthusiasm*, 262; Lincoln qtd. in James M. McPherson, *Antietam: Crossroads of Freedom* (New York: Oxford University Press, 2002), 69.

33. McPherson, *Antietam*, 120; George Whitman qtd. in Morris, *The Better Angel*, 46.

34. Karl Marx qtd. in Edelstein, *Strange Enthusiasm*, 280; McPherson, *Antietam*, 8.

35. FD, *Douglass Monthly* (Oct. 1862), 721; RWE, *JMN*, 15:292–93.

36. Edelstein, *Strange Enthusiasm*, 252; Charlotte Forten Grimké, *The Journals of Charlotte Forten Grimké*, ed. Brenda Stevenson (New York: Oxford University Press, 1988), 405.

37. Wineapple, *White Heat*, 121; qtd. in John Weiss, *Life and Correspondence of Theodore Parker* (New York: Appleton, 1864), 2:172.

38. TWH, *Complete*, 226; Grimké, *Journals*, 405.

39. Quotations (in order) are from ED, *Letters*, nos. 261, 268, 261, 265, 268.

40. Ibid., nos. 261, 265, 271.

41. Ibid., no. 274; TWH, "Letter to a Young Contributor," *Atlantic Monthly* 9 (April 1862), 409.

42. "That after Horror—that 'twas us—": *Poems* 243.

43. "Read—Sweet—how others—strove—": *Poems* 323.

44. "Dare you see a Soul at the 'White Heat'?": *Poems* 401. The number of poems stated is from 1863.

Chapter 5. Port Royal

1. TWH, *Complete*, 75–76.

2. Lincoln qtd. in Frederic W. Seward, *Seward at Washington, as Senator and Secretary of State: A Memoir of His Life, with Selections, 1861–1872* (New York: Derby and Miller, 1891), 151.

3. TWH, *Cheerful Yesterdays* (1898; New York: Arno, 1968), 251.

4. Limerick qtd. in Wineapple, *White Heat*, 123; TWH, *AL*, 3.

5. TWH, *AL*, 30–31.

6. Ibid., 31.

7. TWH, *Complete*, 77.

8. FD, *Autobiographies* (New York: Library of America, 1994), 775.

9. Ibid., 790–91.

10. RWE, *CP*, 165.

11. For an account of the circumstances leading to Emerson's poem, see Carl F. Strauch, "The Background for Emerson's 'Boston Hymn,'" *American Literature* 14 (Mar. 1942), 36–47; the quote is ibid., 39.

12. W. E. B. Du Bois, *The Souls of Black Folk* (1903; New York: Dover, 1994), 10.

13. Qtd. in Willie Lee Rose, *Rehearsal for Reconstruction: The Port Royal Experiment* (Athens: University of Georgia Press, 1999), 46.

14. "The Freedmen at Port Royal," *North American Review* 101 (July 1865), 2; "Education of the Freedmen," *North American Review* 101 (Oct. 1865), 547; Rebecca Harding Davis, "Out of the Sea," *Atlantic Monthly* 15 (May 1865), 535; Rev. Joseph P. Thompson, "The Test-Hour of Popular Liberty and Republican Government," *New Englander and Yale Review* 21 (Apr. 1862), 247.

15. John Greenleaf Whittier, "At Port Royal—1861," *Atlantic Monthly* 9 (Feb. 1862), 244.

16. "The Freedmen at Port Royal," *Atlantic Monthly* 12 (Sept. 1863), 291.

17. TWH, *AL*, 2.

18. FD, "How to End the War," *Writings*, 94.

19. FD, "Signs of the Times," *Writings*, 171.

20. FD, "The Union and How to Save It," *Writings*, 63; "The Inaugural Address," *Writings*, 77; "Shall Slavery Survive the War?" *Writings*, 144.

21. FD, *Autobiographies*, 64–65.

22. Ibid.

23. Ibid.

24. FD, "The War and Slavery," *Writings*, 129; "The Decision of the Hour," *Writings*, 123; "The Union and How to Save It," *Writings*, 62; "The Rebels, the Government, and the Difference between Them," *Writings*, 132; "The War and Slavery," *Writings*, 126; "The Duty of the Abolitionists in the Present State of the Country," *Writings*, 165; "The Reasons for Our Troubles," *Writings*, 196.

25. FD, "Shall Slavery Survive the War?" *Writings*, 143; "The Slaveholders' Rebellion," *Writings*, 243.

26. FD, "Notes on the War," *Writings*, 116.

27. FD, "Condition of the Country," *Writings*, 316.

28. Susie King Taylor, *Reminiscences of My Life in Camp with the 33rd United States Colored Troops, Late 1st S.C. Volunteers* (1902; New York: Arno, and New York Times, 1968), 7.

29. Rose, *Rehearsal for Reconstruction*, 145, 265, 267; Grimké, *Journals*, 406.

30. TWH, *Cheerful Yesterdays*, 266–67; Whittier qtd. in R. D. Madson, "Introduction," TWH, *AL*, xiii–xiv.

31. "Two Weeks at Port Royal," *Harper's Monthly Magazine* 27 (June 1863), 112; "Under the Palmetto," *Continental Monthly* 4 (Aug. 1863), 189.

32. TWH, *AL*, 10, 109, 13.

33. TWH, *Complete*, 272, 270; TWH, *AL*, 116.

34. TWH, *AL*, 149.

35. Grimké, *Journals*, 389–90.

36. TWH, *AL*, 173.

37. TWH, *Complete*, 247, 269.

38. TWH, *AL*, 55.

39. Ibid., 66.

40. Ibid., 69–70.

41. Qtd. in James M. McPherson, *Battle Cry of Freedom: The Civil War Era* (New York: Oxford University Press, 1988), 565.

42. Taylor, *Reminiscences*, 22–23.

43. Ibid., 24; TWH, *AL*, 95.

44. Ibid., 96–97.

45. *New York Times*, Apr. 17, 1863, 4.

46. James Branch Cabell and A. J. Hanna, *The St. Johns: A Parade of Diversities* (New York: Farrar and Rinehart, 1943), 209–10.

47. Grimké, *Journals*, 457.

48. WW, *Specimen Days, PP*, 729.

49. TWH, *AL*, 136.

50. Ibid., 120.

51. Ibid., 136; TWH, *Cheerful Yesterdays*, 263.

52. TWH, *AL*, 174.

53. TWH, *Complete*, 297.

Chapter 6. Fathers and Sons

1. Qtd. in Fred Kaplan, *Henry James: The Imagination of Genius* (New York: Morrow, 1992), 55.

2. Ibid., 52.

3. Edward Waldo Emerson, *The Early Years of the Saturday Club, 1855–1870* (Boston: Houghton Mifflin, 1918), 328.

4. Qtd. in Louis Menand, *The Metaphysical Club: A Story of Ideas in America* (New York: Farrar, Straus and Giroux), 85; Henry James Sr., *The Social Significance of Our Institutions: An Oration Delivered by the Request of the Citizens of Newport, R.I., July 4th, 1861* (Boston: Ticknor and Fields, 1861), 27, 33.

5. Kaplan, *Henry James*, 57.

6. Henry James, *Notes of a Son and Brother* (New York: Scribner's, 1914), 467, 473.

7. Ibid., 383.

8. Qtd. in R. W. B. Lewis, *The Jameses: A Family Narrative* (New York: Farrar, Straus and Giroux, 1991), 147–48.

9. RWE, *JMN*, 15:x.

10. Ibid., 211.

11. Qtd. in William Seraile, "The Struggle to Raise Black Regiments in New York, 1861–1864," *New-York Historical Society Quarterly* 58 (Sept. 1974), 224; "The Freedmen at Port Royal," *Atlantic Monthly*, 300.

12. RWE, *JMN*, 15:212.

13. Ibid., 213.

14. Qtd. in Abraham Lincoln, "Seventh and Last Debate with Stephen A. Douglas at Alton, Illinois," Aug. 21, 1858, in *Collected Works*, 3:9.

15. W. E. B. DuBois, *Black Reconstruction in America: An Essay toward a History of the Part Which Black Folk Played in the Attempt to Reconstruct Democracy in America, 1860–1890* (New York: Atheneum, 1935), 110.

16. Qtd. in Menand, *The Metaphysical Club*, 23–24.

17. Qtd. in Carol Bundy, *The Nature of Sacrifice: A Biography of Charles Russell Lowell* (New York: Farrar, Straus and Giroux, 2005), 90.

18. Qtd. in Robert Gould Shaw, *Blue-Eyed Child of Fortune: The Civil War Letters of Robert Gould Shaw*, ed. Russell Duncan (Athens: University of Georgia Press, 1992), 240.

19. Ibid., 24.

20. Ibid., 47.

21. Ibid., 51.

22. Russell Duncan, *Where Death and Glory Meet: Colonel Robert Gould Shaw and the 54th Massachusetts Infantry* (Athens: University of Georgia Press, 1999), 114.

23. Ibid., 123; Elizabeth Gaskell, "Robert Gould Shaw," *Littell's Living Age* 80 (Jan. 9, 1864), 69; Duncan, *Where Death and Glory Meet*, 54.

24. Isabella McFarlane, "The Death of Colonel Shaw," *Continental Monthly* 5 (Apr. 1864), 488.

25. RWE, *JMN*, 15:30, 218.

26. Ibid., 334, 165, 261, 402, 165.

27. Ellen Tucker Emerson, *The Letters of Ellen Tucker Emerson*, ed. Edith E. W. Gregg (Kent, Ohio: Kent State University Press, 1982), 1:219.

28. Ibid., 261.

29. Qtd. in Moncure Daniel Conway, *Emerson at Home and Abroad* (Boston: James R. Osgood, 1882), 141.

30. RWE, "Experience," *Essays: Second Series, EL*, 473.

31. RWE, *JMN*, 11:291–92.

32. Ellen Tucker Emerson, *Letters*, 240, 298.

33. *Selected Letters of Lidian Jackson Emerson*, ed. Delores Bird Carpenter (Columbia: University of Missouri Press, 1987), 219, 216.

34. RWE, *Letters*, 258, 288.

35. RWE, *JMN*, 15: 434, 316, 170.

36. RWE, *Letters*, 332.

37. Ellen Tucker Emerson, *Letters*, 262.

38. Lidian Emerson, *Selected Letters of Lidian Jackson Emerson*, 232.

39. Ellen Tucker Emerson, *The Life of Lidian Jackson Emerson*, ed. Delores Bird Carpenter (Boston: Twayne, 1980), 142.

40. I wish to thank Jessie Bray for calling this letter to my attention at the 2007 conference of the American Literature Association. RWE, Nov. 12, 1863, used with permission of the Joel Myerson Collection of Nineteenth-century Literature and Periodicals, Thomas Cooper Library, University of South Carolina.

41. Lidian Emerson, *Selected Letters*, 221.

42. RWE, *CP*, 168.

43. Ibid., 166.

44. Ibid., 166–67.

45. Abraham Lincoln, "Gettysburg Address," in *Collected Works*, 7:23.

Chapter 7. Phantom Limbs

1. Charles I. Glicksberg, ed., *Walt Whitman and the Civil War: A Collection of Original Articles and Manuscripts* (1933; New York: Barnes, 1963), 81.

2. Qtd. in Justin Kaplan, *Walt Whitman* (New York: Simon and Schuster, 1980), 268; WW, *Corr* 68; Lincoln qtd. in McPherson, *Battle Cry of Freedom*, 574.

3. WW, *Specimen Days*, PP, 712.

4. WW, *Drum-Taps*, in *Leaves of Grass* (1891–1892), PP 441.

5. Ibid., 418.

6. Qtd. in Charles I. Glicksberg, ed., *Walt Whitman and the Civil War: A Collection of Original Articles and Manuscripts* (1933; New York: Barnes, 1963), 69–70.

7. Qtd. in the introduction to LMA, *Hospital Sketches*, in *Alternative Alcott*, ed. Elaine Showalter (New Brunswick, N.J.: Rutgers University Press, 1988), xiii, xviii, 23.

8. LMA, *The Journals of Louisa May Alcott*, ed. Joel Myerson and Daniel Shealy (Boston: Little, Brown, 1989), 109.

9. LMA, *Louisa May Alcott: Her Life, Letters, and Journals*, ed. Ednah D. Cheney (Boston: Roberts Brothers, 1891), 141.

10. LMA, *Hospital Sketches*, 22.

11. LMA, *Journals*, 109.

12. Oliver Wendell Holmes, "The Human Wheel, Its Spokes and Felloes," *Atlantic Monthly* 11 (May 1863), 574.

13. LMA, *Hospital Sketches*, 36, 24, 25.

14. Qtd. in Morris, *The Better Angel*, 95.

15. "The Great Army of the Wounded" is reprinted in Whitman, *The Wound Dresser: Letters Written to His Mother from the Hospitals in Washington during the Civil War*, ed. Richard M. Bucke (1897; New York: Bodley, 1949), 1–10. The notebook entry is reproduced in Glicksberg, *Walt Whitman*, 93.

16. Qtd. in Bell Irwin Wiley, *The Life of Billy Yank: The Common Soldier of the Union* (Baton Rouge: Louisiana State University Press, 1971), 147.

17. This quotation comes from Garry Wills, *Lincoln at Gettysburg: The Words That Remade America* (New York: Simon and Schuster, 1992), 21, which contains an excellent (and horrific) account of the aftermath of Gettysburg.

18. Qtd. in Gaby Wood, "Not a Happy Fraction of a Man," *Cabinet* 22 (Summer 2006), http://www.cabinetmagazine.org/issues/22/wood.php.

19. Qtd. in S. Weir Mitchell's introduction to *Injuries of Nerves and Their Consequences* (1871; New York: Dover, 1965), xiii.

20. Ibid., 348.

21. Ibid., 350.

22. Qtd. in Anna Robeson Burr, *Weir Mitchell: His Life and Letters* (New York: Duffield, 1930), 114.

23. S. Weir Mitchell, "The Case of George Dedlow," *Atlantic Monthly* 18 (July 1866), 2.

24. Ibid., 3–4.

25. Ibid., 5.

26. Ibid.

27. Ibid., 5, 7.

28. Ibid., 7–8.

29. Ibid., 8.

30. Ibid., 9.

31. Ibid., 11.

32. Ibid.

33. WW, *Corr* 170–71. Redpath's comment is in n. 10.

34. Ibid., 159, 81–82.

35. Mary Clemmer Ames qtd. in *The City of Washington: An Illustrated History*, by the *Junior League of Washington* (New York: Knopf, 1977), 206.

36. WW, *Specimen Days, PP*, 718, 733.

37. Ibid., 733.

38. Ibid., 718–19, 720.

39. Ibid., 719.

40. Ibid., 718–19, 734–35; WW, *Corr* 68–69.

41. WW, *Drum-Taps*, in *Leaves of Grass* (1891–1892), *PP*, 444–45.

42. Ibid., 442–43.

43. Ibid., 443–44.

44. Ibid., 439.

45. Ibid., 442; WW, *Corr* 105; WW, *Drum-Taps*, in *Leaves of Grass* (1891–1892), *PP*, 445.

46. WW, *Corr* 111, 115.

47. Ibid., 81.

48. Qtd. in Horace Traubel, *Walt Whitman in Camden* (New York: Rowman and Littlefield, 1961), 3:582.

49. LMA, *Hospital Sketches*, 101.

50. Julian Hawthorne, *The Memoirs of Julian Hawthorne*, ed. Edith Garrigues Hawthorne (New York: Macmillan, 1938), 63.

51. Morris, *The Better Angel*, 93.

52. "I dwell in Possibility—": *Poems* 466.

53. ED, *Letters*, no. 290.

54. Ibid.

55. Ibid.

Chapter 8. The Man without a Country

1. For more on the career and politics of Leutze, see Barbara S. Groseclose, *Emanuel Leutze, 1816–1868: Freedom Is the Only King* (Washington, D.C.: Smithsonian Institution Press, 1975); review qtd. ibid., 40.

2. NH, "Chiefly," 45.

3. NH, *CE* 18:445, 446.

4. Ibid., 444.

5. Moncure Daniel Conway, "Nathaniel and Sophia Hawthorne," in Bosco and Murphy, *Hawthorne in His Own Time*, p. 213.

6. Amos Bronson Alcott, "From *Concord Days*," in Bosco and Murphy, *Hawthorne in His Own Time*, 153.

7. Henry James, *Hawthorne* (1879; New York: Collier-Macmillan, 1966), 151; Dicey, "Nathaniel Hawthorne," in Bosco and Murphy, *Hawthorne in His Own Time*, 120.

8. Rebecca Harding Davis, "Memories of the Hawthornes at the Wayside in 1862," in Bosco and Murphy, *Hawthorne in His Own Time*, 101.

9. Ibid., 103.

10. NH, *CE* 16:568.

11. Ibid., 1:131.

12. Ibid., 18:543, 604.

13. Edwin Haviland Miller qtd. in Randall Fuller, "Hawthorne and War," *New England Quarterly* 80 (Dec. 2007), 679; NH, *CE* 13:369, 351.

14. NH, *CE* 18:619.

15. Ibid., 543.

16. Moncure Daniel Conway, *Life of Nathaniel Hawthorne* (New York: Scribner and Welford, 1890), 206.

17. ED, *Letters*, no. 153.

18. Edward Everett Hale, "The Man without a Country," *Atlantic Monthly* 12 (Dec. 1863), 667.

19. Ibid., 670.

20. Ibid., 669.

21. Ibid., 677, 675, 677.

22. Ibid., 679.

23. NH, *CE* 13:27.

24. Ibid., 285, 235, 302.

25. Ibid., 129.

26. Ibid., 130.

27. Ibid., 131.

28. Ibid., 240, 228, 256.

29. Ibid., 18:446; qtd. in James Mellow, *Nathaniel Hawthorne in His Times* (Boston: Houghton Mifflin, 1980), 561.

30. NH, *CE* 18:605.

31. Stowe and Emerson qtd. in Mellow, *Nathaniel Hawthorne in His Times*, 570.

32. NH, *CE* 5:4.

33. Ibid., 13:400.

34. Ibid., 448.

35. Qtd. in Mellow, *Nathaniel Hawthorne in His Times*, 574.

36. Ibid.

37. Ibid., 573.

38. Qtd. in James T. Fields, *Yesterdays with Authors* (Boston: Houghton Mifflin, 1871), 118.

39. NH, *CE* 13:447.

40. Ibid., 464.

41. Ibid., 5:4.

42. Qtd. in RWE, *JMN*, 15:59–60.

43. Henry Wadsworth Longfellow, "Hawthorne," in *The Complete Poetical Works of Henry Wadsworth Longfellow*, ed. Horace E. Scudder (Boston: Houghton Mifflin, 1893), 289.

44. RWE, *JMN*, 15:59–60.

45. NH, *CE* 18:632, 641.

46. Qtd. in George Fredrickson, *The Inner Civil War: Northern Intellectuals and the Crisis of the Union* (1965; Champaign-Urbana: University of Illinois Press, 1993), 34.

47. NH, *CE* 1:19, 21, 28.

48. James T. Fields, *Hawthorne* (Boston: Osgood, 1876), 127.

Chapter 9. In a Gloomy Wood

1. Dante, *Vision of Dante Alighieri; or, Hell, Purgatory, and Paradise*, trans. H. F. Cary (New York: Dutton, 1923), 1. While Longfellow relied on the original, this is the translation with which Melville was familiar.

2. NH, *CE* 18:545.

3. Qtd. in *Life of Henry Wadsworth Longfellow, with Extracts from His Journals and Correspondence*, ed. Samuel Longfellow (Boston: Houghton Mifflin, 1891), 3:65.

4. Edward Emerson, *Life and Letters of Charles Russell Lowell: Captain Sixth United States Cavalry, Colonel Second Massachusetts Cavalry, Brigadier General United States Volunteers* (Boston: Houghton Mifflin, 1907), 71. Emerson's praise is recorded in Bundy, *The Nature of Sacrifice*, 82.

5. Ellen Tucker Emerson, *Letters*, 325; William James qtd. in Menand, *The Metaphysical Club*, 74.

6. Bundy, *The Nature of Sacrifice*, 270.

7. Edward Emerson, *Life and Letters*, 350; Emerson claimed to be repeating the incident as it was described by Effie Shaw. Lowell's order qtd. in Stanton Garner, *The Civil War World of Herman Melville* (Lawrence: University Press of Kansas, 1993), 308. See also Bundy, *The Nature of Sacrifice*, 270.

8. Qtd. in Bundy, *The Nature of Sacrifice*, 368.

9. HM, *BP*, 51, 77, 101.

10. Ibid., 37, 89, 125.

11. Qtd. in Hershel Parker, *Herman Melville: A Biography*, vol. 2:*1851–1891* (Baltimore, Md.: Johns Hopkins University Press, 2002), 568.

12. John Singleton Mosby, *Mosby's War Reminiscences and Stuart's Cavalry Campaigns* (Boston: Geo. A. Jones, 1887), 5. The Grant anecdote appears in David Blight, *Race and Reunion: The Civil War in American Memory* (Cambridge, Mass.: Belknap, 2001), 199; *The War of the Rebellion: A Compilation of the Official Records of the Union and Confederate Armies* 43, pt. 1, 811.

13. HM, *BP*, 173, 163, 164; Edmund Wilson, *Patriotic Gore: Studies in the Literature of the American Civil War* (New York: Oxford University Press, 1963), 324.

14. HM, *BP*, 169–70.

15. Qtd. in Harry S. Stout, *Upon the Altar of the Nation: A Moral History of the Civil War* (New York: Viking, 2006), 161–62.

16. My account of the expedition is indebted to the meticulous research of Garner, *The Civil War World of Herman Melville*.

17. HM, *BP*, 167.

18. Qtd. in Parker, *Herman Melville*, 570.

19. HM, *BP*, 165, 174.

20. Ibid., 164, 163. Mosby himself would later note, "As for myself, it was for a long time maintained that I was a pure myth, and my personal identity was as stoutly denied as that of Homer or the Devil." See Mosby, *Mosby's War Reminiscences*, 117.

21. HM, *BP*, 182, 183, 184.

22. Qtd. in *Voices of the Civil War: The Wilderness* (Alexandria, Va.: Time-Life Books, 1998), 41; Ulysses S. Grant, *Personal Memoirs of U. S. Grant* (1885–1886), in *Memoirs and Selected Letters*, eds. Mary D. McFeely and William S. McFeely (New York: Library of America, 1990), 534.

23. HM, *BP*, 100.

24. Ibid., 200.

25. Ibid., 44.

26. Ibid., 113–14.

27. Ibid., 49.

28. Ibid., 69, 70, 71.

29. Ibid., 35.

30. Ibid., 41, 95.

31. Ibid., 70, 39, 40.

32. Ibid., 188, 37.

33. Ibid., 144, 146–47.

34. Qtd. in Shelby Foote, *The Civil War: A Narrative* (New York: Random House, 1958), 3:896; WW, *Drum-Taps*, in *Leaves of Grass* (1891–1892), *PP*, 484; Diary of Elvira Ascenith Weir Scott (1821–1910), typescript by Donald W. Riddle entitled "A Diary of the Civil War on the Missouri Border," courtesy Missouri State Historical Society, Western Historical Manuscript Collection, 146.

35. Letter, E. A. Christy, Feb. 24, 1863, courtesy Missouri State Historical Society, Western Historical Manuscript Collection; Diary, Elvira Ascenith Weir Scott, 164.

36. HM, *Journals*, ed. Howard C. Horsford and Lynn Horth (Evanston, Ill.: Northwestern University Press, 1989), 454n.

37. Alan Axelrod, *The Horrid Pit: The Battle of the Crater, the Civil War's Cruelest Mission* (New York: Carroll and Graf, 2007), 119.

38. Ibid., 131, 135, 145.

39. Grant, *Memoirs and Selected Letters*, 613; HM, *BP*, 140.

40. HM, *BP*, 140–41.

41. Diary of Charles Lowell Nightingale, private of 29th Massachusetts, U.S. Civil War Letters (MS Am 1626), Houghton Library, Harvard University.

42. RWE, *JMN*, 15:445.

43. HM, *BP*, 197–98.

44. Ibid., 199.

45. Ibid., 196, 200.

46. Ibid., 196, 200.

47. Ellen Tucker Emerson, *Letters*, 317; HM, *BP*, 185.

48. William Rhinelander Stewart, *The Philanthropic Work of Josephine Shaw Lowell* (New York: Macmillan, 1911), 15.

49. Bundy, *The Nature of Sacrifice*, 483.

50. William Dean Howells, "Herman Melville's *Battle-Pieces and Aspects of the War*," *Atlantic Monthly* 19 (Feb. 1867), 252.

51. Bundy, *The Nature of Sacrifice*, 485.

Chapter 10. Heaven

1. Elizabeth Stuart Phelps, *The Gates Ajar*, ed. Helen Sootin Smith (1868; Cambridge, Mass.: Belknap, 1964), 7, 5.

2. Ibid., 60.

3. Ibid., 56.

4. Ibid., 57.

5. Qtd. in Edelstein, *Strange Enthusiasm*, 195.

6. Qtd. in Wineapple, *White Heat*, 170.

7. Thomas Wentworth Higginson, "Preface," in his *Harvard Memorial Biographies* (Cambridge, Mass.: Welch, Bigelow, 1866), 1:iii.

8. Thomas Wentworth Higginson, "Literature as an Art," *Atlantic Monthly* 20 (Dec. 1867), 745.

9. Qtd. in Edelstein, *Strange Enthusiasm*, 89, 308.

10. Ibid., 311; TWH, *Malbone: An Oldport Romance* (Boston: Fields, Osgood, 1869), 7, 8.

11. ED, *Letters*, no. 453.

12. ED, *Letters*, no. 330; TWH to ED, May 11, 1869, in ED, *Letters*, no. 330a.

13. "The Black Berry—wears a Thorn in his side—": *Poems* 548.

14. ED, *Letters*, nos. 316, 319.

15. Ibid., no. 342a.

16. Ibid., no. 342b; TWH, "Emily Dickinson's Letters," *Atlantic Monthly* 68 (Oct. 1891), 453.

17. TWH, "Decoration," *Scribner's Monthly* 8 (June 1874), 234–35.

18. ED, *Letters*, nos. 418, 503; "Lay this Laurel on the one": *Poems* 1428.

19. TWH qtd. in Millicent Todd Bingham, *Ancestors' Brocades: The Literary Debut of Emily Dickinson* (New York: Harper, 1946), 130.

20. ED, *Letters*, no. 905.

21. WW, *Drum-Taps*, in *Leaves of Grass* (1891–1892), *PP*, 467.

22. Ibid., 460.

23. Ibid., 466.

24. WW, *Specimen Days*, *PP*, 749; Horace Traubel, *With Walt Whitman in Camden*, 9 vols. (New York: Appleton, 1908), 1:332–33.

25. WW, *Specimen Days*, PP, 777.

26. RWE, *Complete Works*, 11:329.

27. Henry Wadsworth Longfellow, *The Works of Henry Wadsworth Longfellow*, ed. Samuel Longfellow (Boston: Houghton Mifflin, 1891), 13:416; Elizabeth Stuart Phelps, *The Gates Ajar* (1868; Cambridge, Mass.: Belknap, 1964), 24.

28. RWE, *JMN*, 15:273–74, 382.

29. RWE, *CP*, 135, 131, 143, 137, 138.

30. Ibid., 144, 133, 137.

31. See Nina Silber, *The Romance of Reunion: Northerners and the South, 1865–1900* (Chapel Hill: University of North Carolina Press, 1993). These pieces were subsequently collected in *Battles and Leaders of the Civil War*, ed. Robert Underwood Johnson and Clarence Clough Buel (New York: Century Company, DeVinne Press, 1887). I quote from 1:ix.

32. Qtd. in Jackson Lears, *Rebirth of a Nation: The Making of Modern America, 1877–1920* (New York: HarperCollins, 2009), 25; Taylor, *Reminiscences*, 75, 61.

33. RWE, *CP*, 148.

34. Qtd. in Robert D. Richardson, *Emerson: The Mind on Fire* (Berkeley: University of California Press, 1995), 572.

35. For a discussion of the problematic dating of "Terminus," see Carl F. Strauch, "A Critical and Variorum Edition of the Poems of Ralph Waldo Emerson" (Ph.D. diss., Yale University, 1946).

36. Qtd. in Richardson, *Emerson*, 554.

37. J.A. Bellows, "Mr. Emerson's New Book," *Liberal Christian*, Jan. 22, 1876; "Mr. Emerson at Harvard," *Every Saturday*, Sept 21, 1867. Both quotations come from Richard E. Teichgraeber III, "'Our National Glory': Emerson in American Culture, 1865–1882," in *Transient and Permanent: The Transcendentalist Movement in Its Contexts*, ed. Charles Caper and Conrad Edick Wright (Boston: Massachusetts Historical Society, 1999), 499–526.

Index

Aaron, Daniel, ix
Agassiz, Louis, 127
Alcott, Anna, 140
Alcott, Bronson, 22, 34, 35, 36, 40, 99, 140, 156–157, 165, 166–167, 214
Alcott, Louisa May, 8, 22, 99, 129, 140–143, 151, 156–157, 158, 173, 176
Alcott, Louisa May, writings:
    Hospital Sketches, 142–143, 150;
    Little Men, 157; *Little Women*, 157
Allen, William, 107
American Theological Review, 82
Andrew, John Albion, 121
Anthony, Aaron, 104–105
Antietam, Battle of, 32, 87, 88, 92, 120, 124, 131, 183, 198
Ashe, Sam, 27
Atlantic Monthly, 18–20, 22, 25, 27, 34, 36, 41, 43, 46, 49, 69, 77, 83, 90, 101, 126, 140, 147, 148, 150, 166, 168, 169, 174, 178, 180, 183, 206, 211, 212, 214

"Battles and Leaders of the Civil War," 221–222
Beauty of Holiness, 95
Bernard, Claude, 146
Bierce, Ambrose, 221
Bierce, Ambrose, writings: "What I Saw of Shiloh," 71–73

Big Bethel, Battle of, 27, 28, 44, 53, 180
Booth, John Wilkes, 216
Boston Commonwealth, 126, 142
Boston Evening Transcript, 5, 28
Boston Music Hall, 55–56
Bowles, Samuel, 77
Brady, Mathew, 161–164, 171, 173
Breed, John Newton, 29–30
Bridge, Horatio, 41, 176
Bright, Henry A., 168–169
Brisbane, William Henry, 94, 95
Brooks, Preston, 57
Brown, Anne, 39
Brown, John, 14, 38–40, 44, 46, 50, 51, 57, 74, 77, 80, 84, 95, 101, 126, 197
Brown, Sarah, 39
Browning, Elizabeth Barrett, 85, 90, 208
Browning, Robert, 90
Bryant, William Cullen, writings: "Our Country's Call," 30
Bull Run, Battle of (Manassas), 28–31, 33, 43, 47, 53, 55, 59, 195
Burke, Edmund, 6
Burns, Anthony, 75
Burnside, Ambrose, 136–137
Butler, Benjamin, 27, 47

Cabell, James Branch, 113
Cabot, James Elliot, 58
Cedar Creek, Battle of, 194
Century, 221, 222
Chancellorsville, Battle of, 111, 184
Channing, William Ellery, 35
Chickamauga, Battle of 148, 207
Child, Lydia Maria, 124, 126
Church, Frederic Edwin, 7
Church, Frederic Edwin, works:
    Cotopaxi, 7
Cicero, 189
Clarke, James Freeman, 83, 179
Coleridge, Samuel Taylor, 56
Continental Monthly, 109, 126
Contrabands, 47–49, 61
Conway, Moncure Daniel, 34, 36,
    123, 165, 169
Crane, Stephen, 221
Crater, Battle of the, (Petersburg),
    200–202
Curtis, George William, 22, 25, 27,
    167, 180

Dana Jr., Richard Henry, 75
Dante, 65, 182–184
Dante, writings: *The Divine
    Comedy*, 182–184, 189
Darwin, Charles, 80
Darwin, Charles, writings: *On the
    Origin of the Species*, 80
Davis, Rebecca Harding, 100,
    166–167
Davis, Rebecca Harding,
    writings: *Life in the Iron
    Mills*, 166, 169
Dawes, John, ix
"The Dead at Antietam," 164–165
Delany, Martin R., 105
Dicey, Edward, 49, 165–166
Dickens, Charles, 142
Dickinson, Austin, 78, 79
Dickinson, Edward, 78, 79
Dickinson, Emily, 3, 7–8, 16, 24, 74,
    77–82, 84, 90–92, 94, 110, 115,
    158–159, 166, 169, 179, 196,
    212–215, 218

Dickinson, Emily, writings: "A
    still—Volcano—Life—" 7; "Dare
    you see a Soul at the 'White
    Heat'?" 92; "He put the Belt
    around my life—" 81; "I dwell in
    Possibility—" 158; "I had some
    things I called mine—" 80; "I
    have never seen 'Volcanoes'—" 7;
    "It don't sound so terrible—
    quite—as it did—" 87; "It feels a
    shame to be Alive—" 86; "Lay
    this Laurel on the one," 215; "My
    Portion is Defeat—today—"
    86–87; "Of God we ask one favor,
    that we may be forgiven—"
    81; "Read—Sweet—how others—
    strove—" 92; "The reticent
    volcano keeps," 7; "The Soul has
    Bandaged moments—" 8; "The
    Soul selects her own Society," 91;
    "Tell all the truth but tell it
    slant," 81; "That after Horror—
    that 'twas us—" 91–92; "They
    dropped like Flakes—" 86;
    "Volcanoes be in Sicily," 7
Dickinson, Emily Norcross, 78
Dickinson, Lavinia, 78
Donelson, Fort, 53, 55
Douglas, Stephen, 122
Douglass, Frederick, 8, 89, 97–98,
    99, 101–106, 222
Douglass, Frederick, writings: *My
    Bondage and My Freedom*, 103;
    *Narrative of the Life of Frederick
    Douglass, an American Slave,
    Written by Himself*, 103–104
Douglass Monthly, 101
Doyle, Peter, 216
Dred Scott, 57, 105
DuBois, W. E. B., 99, 122–123
Duyckinck, Evert A., 63–64

Edwards, Jonathan, 25
Eldridge, Charles, 12, 14, 20
Emancipation Proclamation, 93–94,
    95, 99, 106, 111, 120, 124, 130,
    131, 132, 135

Emerson, Charles, 127
Emerson, Edith, 100
Emerson, Edward, 127
Emerson, Edward Waldo (son), 117, 127–130, 131–133, 185, 223
Emerson, Ellen, 3–4, 127, 128, 129–130, 132, 185, 204
Emerson, Lidian, 129, 130, 132, 133
Emerson, Mary Moody, 127
Emerson, Ralph Waldo, 1–5, 8, 9–10, 16, 17, 18, 20, 22, 33, 34, 35, 37, 38, 39, 40, 41, 43–44, 46, 55–63, 64, 65, 75, 80, 84, 89, 91, 99, 101, 103, 120–124, 126, 128, 129, 130–131, 132–135, 151, 157, 165, 167, 173, 174, 180, 185, 195, 200, 203, 211, 219–221, 223–224
Emerson, Ralph Waldo, writings: "The American Scholar," 75, 94; "Art," 66; "Boston Hymn," 98–99; *Complete Works*, 223; "Concord Hymn," 197; "Courage," 39; *Essays: First Series*, 60; *Essays: Second Series*, 127; "Experience," 129; "Fortune of the Republic," 58; "May-Day," 220–222, 223; "Mind and Manners in the Nineteenth Century," 63–64; "Moral Forces," 55, 60–63, 67, 98; *Nature*, 3, 60, 66; "The Poet," 16, 66–68; "Self-Reliance," 56; "Terminus," 223; "Voluntaries," 126, 133–135
Emerson, Waldo, 129, 133
Emerson, William, 1, 25, 120, 130,
Engels, Friedrich, 88
Everett, Edward, 169

Fahs, Alice, ix
Faulkner, William, writings: *Light in August*, 105
Fields, Annie, 176–178
Fields, James T., 22, 25, 37, 140, 142, 157, 161, 168, 173, 174, 176, 180, 181, 211

Forbes, John Murray, 100, 132
Forbes, William Hathaway, 100
Fort Pillow Massacre, 178
Frank Leslie's Illustrated Weekly, 122
Fredericksburg, Battle of, 32, 136–137, 143, 153 158, 173, 183
Frederickson, George M., ix
French, Mansfield, 95
Fugitive Slave Law, 57
Fuller, Margaret, 165

Gansevoort, Henry, 184
Gardner, Alexander, 161, 164, 173
Garnet, Henry Highland, 105
Garrison, William Lloyd, 61, 103, 110, 124
Gaskell, Elizabeth, 126
Gettysburg, Battle of, 111, 114, 124, 131, 135, 146, 183
Gilman, Charlotte Perkins, writings: "The Yellow Wallpaper," 146
Goethe, Johann Wolfgang von, 6
Grant, Ulysses S., 53, 54, 55, 176, 190, 194, 202
Grant, Ulysses S., writings: *Memoirs*, 54
Greeley, Horace, 126
Grimké, Charlotte Forten, 90, 94, 105, 107, 110, 113–114, 124

Hale, Edward Everett, writings: "The Man without a Country," 169–171
Hallowell, Edward, 133
Hammond, William, 144
Harpers Ferry, 44, 46, 57, 74, 77
Harper's Monthly, 22, 109, 167
Harper's Weekly, 28
Hathorne, John, 42
Hawthorne, Julian, 39, 41, 44, 127, 157, 173
Hawthorne, Nathaniel, 8–9, 22, 25, 36–51, 52, 63, 65, 68, 105, 157, 158, 159–169, 171–181, 183, 184, 185, 193, 203

Hawthorne, Nathaniel, writings:
"Chiefly about War-Matters," 34,
45–51, 160, 169; *The Dolliver
Romance*, 179, 180, 181; *The Elixir
of Life*, 168, 171–175, 178, 179;
The *Marble Faun*, 49, 167; *Mosses
from an Old* Manse, 37; *Our Old
Home*, 174, 179; *The Scarlet
Letter*, 37, 42, 45, 167, 178, 181
Hawthorne, Sophia Peabody,
37, 42, 51, 157, 161, 173, 176,
178, 179
Hawthorne, Una, 44, 127, 173
Herald of Freedom, 8
Higginson, Thomas Wentworth, 12,
24, 74–77, 79, 82–84, 86, 87,
88, 89–90, 91, 93, 96, 99, 101,
103, 106–115, 120, 123, 124,
125, 146, 158–159, 169, 179,
209 215
Higginson, Thomas Wentworth,
writings: *Army Life in a Black
Regiment*, 109, 211;
"Decoration," 214–215; "Letter
to a Young Contributor," 77, 91;
Malbone, 83, 212, 213; *Out-Door
Papers*, 213; "A Visit to John
Brown's Household in 1859," 77
Histories of Specimens, 144
Holmes, Oliver Wendell, 17, 18, 22,
45–46, 57, 142, 179, 183
Holmes, Oliver Wendell, writings:
*The Autocrat of the Breakfast-
Table*, 18; "Old Ironsides," 12;
"The Wide-Awake Man," 30
Holmes, Jr., Oliver Wendell, 41,
123, 124, 131
Homer, Winslow, works: *The
Sharpshooter on Picket Duty*, 191;
Skirmish in the Wilderness, 188
Hooper, Edward W., 94
Howe, Julia Ward, 30, 61, 83, 99,
209
Howe, Julia Ward, writings: "The
Battle Hymn of the Republic,"
30, 83
Howe, Samuel Gridley, 83

Howells, William Dean, 183,
205–206
Howells, William Dean, writings:
The Rise of Silas Lapham, 222
Hugo, Victor, 6
Hugo, Victor, works: *Les
Misérables*, 94, 109, 117, 165
Humphreys, Charles A., 189, 192

Iliad, The, 127, 131

Jackson, Thomas Jonathan
"Stonewall," 166, 197
Jacobs, Harriet, writings: *Incidents in
the Life of a Slave Girl*, 14
James, Alice, 116, 117
James, Garth Wilkinson (Wilky),
116–119, 120, 125, 127
James, Henry, 116, 119, 165
James, Henry, writings: *The Portrait
of a Lady*, 222
James Sr., Henry, 116, 117, 119, 209
James, Robert (Bob), 116–117, 127
James, William, 116, 117, 119, 185

Kafka, Franz, 81
Kansas-Nebraska Bill, 56

Lee, Robert E., 87, 88, 114, 137,
166, 194, 198
Leutze, Emanuel, 160–161, 175
Lincoln, Abraham, 4, 9, 21, 24, 43,
44, 46, 50–51, 55, 57, 59, 60,
87–88, 89, 93, 98, 99, 106, 122,
135, 136, 153, 169, 198, 199, 202,
203, 208, 215–218, 223
Lincoln, Abraham, writings:
"Gettysburg Address," 135, 169;
"House Divided" speech, 4, 57;
Second Inaugural Address, 50
Lincoln, Mary Todd, 153
Lincoln, Willie, 153
Literary World, 160
Longfellow, Fanny, 182
Longfellow, Henry Wadsworth,
17, 18, 21–22, 179–180, 182–183,
184, 220

Longfellow, Henry Wadsworth, writings: *The Divine Comedy* (translation), 182–183; "O Ship of State," 12
Lowell, Anna, 123, 205
Lowell Charles, 123
Lowell, Charles Russell, 123, 124, 144, 185–187, 189, 190, 192, 194–195, 204, 205, 206
Lowell, James Russell, 17, 18–20, 41, 44, 179, 183, 185
Lowell, James Russell, writings: *Biglow Papers*, 18
Lowell, James J. (Jim), 41, 126, 131
Lowell, Josephine "Effie" Shaw, 185, 189, 204–206

Mann, Horace, 39
Mann, Mary, 39
Marx, Karl, 88
Mayflower, 49–50
McClellan, George B., 44, 59, 88, 136, 175, 189, 198
McFarlane, Isabella, 126
McKim, Lucy, writings: *Slave Songs of the United States*, 110
Melville, Herman, 9, 63–70, 123, 183–185, 187–206
Melville, Herman, writings: "America," 198–199; "The Apparition," 202; "The Armies of the Wilderness," 187, 194–195, 197–198; *Battle-Pieces and Aspects of the War*, 188–189; 195–206; *Benito Cereno*, 8, 190; *Billy Budd, Sailor*, 187, 190, 206; "The College Colonel," 195–196; *The Confidence Man*, 65; "The Conflict of Convictions," 197, 198; "Donelson," 197; "Hawthorne and His Mosses," 65, 66; "The March into Virginia," 195; *Moby-Dick*, 7, 65, 193; *Omoo*, 66; "The Scout toward Aldie," 190–194, 204–205; "Shiloh. A Requiem (April, 1865)," 68–70,

202; "The Stone Fleet," 196; "Supplement," 195, 203–204, 205; *Typee*, 66; "A Utilitarian View of the Monitor's Fight," 196–197
Melville, Lizzie, 206
Milton, John, 184
Mitchell, Silas Weir, 145–150
Mitchell, Silas Weir, writings: "The Case of George Dedlow," 148–150, 169; *Gunshot Wounds and Other Injuries of the Nerves*, 147, 151; *Injuries of Nerves and Their Consequences*, 147
Miller, Edwin Haviland, 168
Mosby, John Singleton, 189–190, 192–194, 219

National Preacher, 82
Newton, Benjamin Franklin, 169
New York Daily Tribune, 39
New York Leader, 28
New York Times, 88, 113
Norcross, Frances, 84, 85
Norcross, Louise, 84, 85
North American Review, 178
Norton, Charles Eliot, 183

O'Connor, William Douglas, writings: *The Good Gray Poet*, 218
Ormsby, William, 187–188
Osgood, James R., 211
Our American Cousin, 203

Parker, Theodore, 39, 55, 61, 75, 90
Patton, William, 82
Pfaff's beer cellar, 17, 24
Phelps, Elizabeth Stuart, 207, 220
Phelps, Elizabeth Stuart, writings: *The Gates Ajar*, 207–209
Phillips, Wendell, 75, 99
Pierce, Franklin, 37, 174, 179
Pleasants, Henry, 200–201
Poe, Edgar Allan, writings: "The Fall of the House of Usher," 4
Pompeii, 5, 200
Present, 83

Redpath, James, 150–151
Redpath, James, writings: *Echoes of Harper's Ferry*, 14; *The Public Life of Capt. John Brown*, 14
Rhodes, Elijah, 43
Richter, Johann Paul Friedrich, 10
Riis, Jacob, 206
Rogers, Nathaniel Peabody, 8
Russell, Cabot, 119

Sanborn, Franklin B., 39, 127, 142
Saxton, Rufus, 94, 101, 106, 112
Scott, Elvira Ascenith Weir, 199, 200
Scott, Sir Walter, 166, 167, 170, 171
Secret Six, 39, 74, 77, 83, 99
Seven Days Battles, 41, 87
Seward, William H., 44, 88, 93
Seymour, Horatio, 121
Shakespeare, William, 13, 65, 184
Shakespeare, William, writings: *King Lear*, 12
Shaw, Francis, 25, 123, 126
Shaw, Robert Gould, 88, 115, 118, 120, 123–124, 126, 127, 133, 135, 144, 185, 205
Shaw, Sarah, 124
Shelley, Percy Bysshe, 184
Sherman, William Tecumseh, 55, 176, 197, 203
Shiloh, Battle of, 52–55, 59, 60, 62, 65, 66–67, 70, 71–73, 86, 92, 120, 176, 183, 207
Southern Literary Messenger, 20
Spofford, Harriet Prescott, 90
Springfield Republican, 77, 91, 158, 215
Stearns, Frazar, 84–85, 91
Stearns, George L., 99
Stowe, Harriet Beecher, 140, 174
Stowe, Harriet Beecher, writings: *Uncle Tom's Cabin*, 9, 75, 124, 207–208
Strong, George C., 124
Sumner, Charles, 57
Sumter, Fort, 11, 21, 22, 24, 25, 40, 167

Swedenborg, Emanuel, 117
Sweet, Timothy, ix

Taney, Roger, 105
Taylor, Susie King, 106
Taylor, Susie King, writings: *Reminiscences of My Life in Camp with the 33rd United States Colored Troops, Late 1st S.C. Volunteers*, 112, 222
Thackeray, William Makepeace, 178
Thayer, William, 12, 14, 17, 20
Thompson, Joseph P., 100
Thoreau, Henry David, 7, 18, 34–35, 37, 59–60, 63, 75, 126–127, 165, 167, 173–174
Thoreau, Henry David, writings: "A Plea for John Brown," 39; *Walden*, 60
Ticknor, William D., 21, 37, 41, 43, 175–178, 211
Ticknor and Fields, 21, 178, 183
Traubel, Horace, 219
Turner, J, M. W., works: *Eruption of Vesuvius*, 6
Turner, Nat, 101 122
Twain, Mark, 221
Twain, Mark, writings: *Huckleberry Finn*, 222
Twenty-eighth Congregational Society, 39, 55, 61, 67

Vesey, Denmark, 101
Vesuvius, Mount, 5, 6, 200, 204, 224
Vicksburg, Battle of, 111

Walden Pond, 43, 59–60, 67, 127, 224
Walker, Susan, 106–107
Washington Crossing the Delaware, 160
Washington, George, 14, 170, 223
Weiss, John, 69
Welles, Gideon, 88

Westward the Course of Empire Takes Its Way, 160

White, Richard Grant, 69

Whitman, George Washington, 23, 31–33, 88, 136, 137, 150, 215–216

Whitman, Walt, 8, 11–21, 23–24, 28, 30–33, 66, 69, 79, 114, 123, 136–140, 144, 150 156, 158, 196, 215–219

Whitman, Walt, writings: *The Banner at Day-Break*, 21; "Beat! Beat! Drums!" 28, 31, 139, 154; "Calamus" poems, 21; *Drum-Taps*, 33, 154, 218; "Enfans d'Adam" poems, 20, 21; "For You O Democracy," 21; *Leaves of Grass*, 12, 14, 15–17, 21, 31, 33, 60, 139, 154, 155, 156, 218; *Memoranda during the War*, 33, 153; "The Million Dead, Too, Summ'd Up," 219; "O Captain! My Captain!" 217, 218; "Old War-Dreams," 199; "Ship of Libertad," 12, 217; "A Sight in Camp in the Daybreak Gray and Dim," 137–139; "Song of Myself," 14; *Specimen Days*, 33, 219; "The Wound-Dresser," 154–155; "When Lilacs Last in the Dooryard Bloom'd," 217–218

Whittier, John Greenleaf, 17, 22, 100–101, 107–108

Whittier, John Greenleaf, writings: "At Port Royal," 100–101; *In War Time*, 70; "The Watchers," 70–71

Wilderness, Battle of the, 32, 194, 207

Williams, Henry Willard, 158

Wilson, Edmund, ix, 190

Wilson's Creek, Battle of, 53, 207

Winthrop, John, 24–25, 80

Winthrop, Theodore, 24–28, 44, 45, 70, 88, 123, 124, 126, 180

Winthrop, Theodore, writings: "Our March to Washington," 25; "Washington as a Camp," 25–27

Wordsworth, William, writings: *Lyrical Ballads*, 121

DATE DUE